Note on The Salamander Oasis Trust

This collection of manuscripts, and the selection and editing of this anthology, were carried out by The Salamander Oasis Trust. The Trust, a registered charity (274654), was founded in 1976 from among those who served and wrote in the Middle East in World War Two – and who took part in the original *Oasis* anthology, Cairo 1942/3. The Trust was set up to collect manuscripts of poetry – and prose – from the Second World War and to get them published. The Trust has published four books (including this anthology) from the Middle East, Italy and then from all fronts in *Poems of the Second World War: The Oasis Selection* (Dent), to which this is a companion volume. The Trust has also produced a tape (C–90, The Talking Tape Company, Martin Jarvis and others reading) and sponsored a TV programme *The War Poets of '39*, transmitted on BBC 2 and repeated on BBC 1. VHS video distributed by Pergamon Educational Productions, Exeter. The long-term aim of the Trust is to get the poetry into schools and universities.

In December 1986, four MPs who act as 'Friends of the Trust' in the House, Andrew Bowden, Rt. Hon. Denis Healey, Rt. Hon. Merlyn Rees and Peter Rost, organised an Early Day Motion to be signed by members of all sides of the House that recognised the work of the Trust. The cost of this work to the Trust is considerable and would not be possible without the generous support of Paul Getty Jr, The Dulverton Trust, The Esmée Fairbairn Charitable Trust, The Fitton Trust, The Grocers' Charity and members of the 7th Armoured Division Officers' Association.

The Trust's officers are:

After 1990 the Poetry Society will take over the Trust to ensure the continuity of its work. Members of the Trust and Oasis poets will form a Salamander Oasis group to advise and help.

The Trust continues to seek sponsorship for its projects and support for its day-to-day operation. The Trust collaborates with the Imperial War Museum, to which it hands over mss and material collected.

MORE POEMS OF THE SECOND WORLD WAR

The Oasis Selection

Editor-in-chief
Victor Selwyn

Editors
Erik de Mauny, Ian Fletcher, Robin Ivy

Advisers
Field Marshal Lord Carver, General Sir John Hackett,
Hamish Henderson, John MacInnes,
William E. Morris (NZ)

J.M. Dent & Sons Ltd: London
EVERYMAN'S LIBRARY
in association with
THE SALAMANDER OASIS TRUST

First published in Great Britain 1989.
© Selection, introductory material and notes,
The Salamander Oasis Trust 1989.

This book is set in Linotron Bembo
by Deltatype, Ellesmere Port
Printed in Great Britain by
The Guernsey Press Co. Ltd.,
Guernsey, C.I.

British Library Cataloguing in Publication Data

More poems of the Second World War:
  the Oasis Selection
  1. Poetry in English, 1945. Anthologies
  I. Title   II. Selwyn, Victor
  III. de Mauny, Erik   IV. Fletcher, Ian,
  1920–
  821'.914'08

  ISBN 0–460–13001–3
  ISBN 0–460–15782–5 Pbk

The compilation of this Anthology is the copyright of The
Salamander Oasis Trust. Every endeavour has been made by the
Trust to contact poets, who have been previously published, and their
publishers. Where the Trust has established the holder of copyright of
a specific poem, this has been indicated in Acknowledgements,
together with permission to publish. The Trust retains copyright of
poems first published in its books, RETURN TO OASIS (1980) and
FROM OASIS INTO ITALY (1983) and POEMS OF THE
SECOND WORLD WAR (1985), and the poems not previously
published in this anthology, except where the poet has written
otherwise. This is also indicated in the Acknowledgements.
Contributors have signed a declaration that no TV or Radio
reproduction of their poems can be made without first permission of
The Salamander Oasis Trust. Keith Douglas' poems, as in previous
OASIS anthologies, original version taken from *Alamein to Zem–Zem*,
published by Editions Poetry London (Tambimuttu), rights assigned
to Trust.

Contents

Dedication

From earliest times the poet has been war's reporter. In our anthology we have over one hundred named reporters, some with no names, who took part in war and saw and wrote with a poet's eye. They wrote mainly of people. For war is about people, those who survive and those who do not.

Many who did not return were the poets.

This then is also their memorial, to live on with their fellows, who returned speaking to generations to come of what men and women did, thought and felt in the War of Nineteen Thirty Nine to Forty Five.

Let it be the last!   V.S.

An Historical Record

by Field Marshal Lord Carver

In compiling this fourth volume of poetry written by men and women while serving in the armed forces in the Second World War, the Salamander Oasis Trust has added a major contribution to the social history both of the twentieth century and of war in all centuries. The several volumes it has helped to produce show that, to those who participated, life in wartime has not generally conformed to the pattern in which it has often been represented. At times, for some of the participants, there have been moments of heroism and glory; at others of intense danger, fear and suffering; but for most of the time life was lived in a state between the two.

Poems are not necessarily a true reflection of the experience of all who served. Those who are inclined to write them tend to be the more sensitive and thoughtful, and their output to be the product of especial emotions. Nevertheless, because all the poems in these volumes were written at the time of their authors' experience, they remain a true record of the feelings of a wide and varied cross-section of those who have served in all ranks of all three services.

There is an impression in some literary circles that the Second World War produced few poets from among the fighting forces, in contrast to the First World War, Keith Douglas and a few others being an exception. It is true that most of the well-known poets of that period wrote from the sidelines; but the lie to that idea is given by the previous volume selected by the Trust, *Poems of the Second World War* in the Everyman Library. Of the 201 poets who contributed to that volume, all of whose poems were written while they were serving in the armed forces during the war, eighteen lost their lives in it. Ten of the 110 poets in this volume also lost their lives.

All the contributions to these volumes – over 14,000 poems and letters – have been deposited with the Imperial War Museum, where they constitute an unique record of those caught up in the trammels of twentieth-century war.

In Memory[1]

ALLISON, John Drummond: Lieutenant, East Surrey Regiment *Italy, 2 December 1943*

ALLWOOD, John Brian: Leading Aircraftman, RAFVR *Italy, 30 June 1944*

DOUGLAS, Keith C.: Captain, Derbyshire Yeomanry[2] *Normandy, 9 June 1944*

GOW, Roderick George Alistair: Captain, Royal Artillery *Arnhem, 19 September 1944*

JARMAIN, William John F.: Major, Royal Artillery *Normandy, 26 June 1944*

RICHARDSON, George Sidney: Flight Lieutenant *Far East, 26 January 1942*

ROBINSON, Bernard Charles Paterson: Lance-Corporal, Lancashire Fusiliers *Cassino, Italy, 17 May 1944*

SHARLAND, Malcolm N.: Lieutenant, Royal Engineers *Cassino, Italy, 19 July 1944*

SPENDER, Richard W.O.: Lieutenant, Parachute Regiment *North Africa, 28 March 1943*

THOMPSON, William Frank: Major, Royal Artillery *Bulgaria, 10 June 1944*

[1] Regiments and Units as listed by the War Graves Commission and War Office Records.
[2] Served with Sherwood Rangers

Foreword

by General Sir John Hackett

The once widely-held conviction that while some fine poetry had come out of the First World War nothing of any value had emerged from the Second has taken time to shake. This fourth volume of poems from World War Two, put together by the Salamander Oasis Trust, should do much to help ensure its final demolition. Those responsible for its collection and publication, amongst whom Victor Selwyn chiefly deserves our grateful recognition, little knew what they were starting when some of them brought together verse originating in the wartime Middle East and published it under the title *Return to Oasis*, with an open request for more. These people were pulling out a stopper and if they expected a trickle could not fail to be surprised at what turned instead to be a deluge. The first wave furnished the material for the next collection, published in 1983 under the title *From Oasis into Italy*. The flood continued unabated and by the time *Poems of the Second World War: the Oasis Selection* was published in 1985, some 10,000 manuscripts had come in. The compilers were the victims of their own huge success and the editorial burden was enormous. The BBC put on a presentation of some of this verse, in an *Open Space* programme at 7.30 p.m. on Wednesday 22 July. Spike Milligan and I both contributed, and verse chosen from this collection was then beautifully spoken by young actors in the presence of some of the authors. This was a moving performance and so well received that it was repeated on Remembrance Sunday, 8 November. Four thousand letters came in to the BBC as a result, most of which the Corporation answered though very many were passed on for action by an undermanned and overburdened Trust. Needless to say, the manuscripts continue to come in and there will be a big body of material for eventual deposit in the Imperial War Museum. Finance, it need hardly be added, is a great and growing problem, in spite of generous benefaction by Paul Getty Jr and charitable Trusts, in contrast to the lack of any funding from the Arts Council or any official body. It is hardly possible to foresee an indefinite prolongation of this series and there will certainly be verse of great value which will never be published at all. A good deal will already have been lost. We can only be grateful that so much, by the devoted action of a few enthusiasts, has been saved.

The question of what qualifies for inclusion in a collection such as this, chosen against what criteria, remains a lively one. It must be said at once that if close and direct association with fighting in battle were the dominant criterion much verse of high value would have had to be omitted. On the other hand, what has been chosen must have been written in time of war and offer clear evidence that it would have been written only under wartime pressure and not otherwise. Literary merit must occupy the highest place in our criteria, but not the only one. It is the breathing of the human spirit that we have to hear, in all its many different modes, in anguish, fear, triumph, disgust, boredom, pleasure, friendship, hatred, love and any other of the infinite variety of emotions and states that make up the distinctive life of man. Some of the richer veins of verse explored yield only coarse material and some of the deepest feeling is expressed in terms of doubtful elegance. What has been put together here, however, is a living tapestry of human experience in wartime, a fitting backdrop to the great events played out before it on the stage.

Introduction

The many poems of the Second World War form a unique genre in British and Commonwealth literary history. From a literate and aware generation, they tell more of aspects of war than many factual accounts and histories. They were written by men and women from all services and all ranks, in contrast to the narrow group of First World War poets. Those who wrote in World War Two were active participants. The **In Memory** *page of this anthology and the previous collections testify to dedication, as do the biographies and letters we received. Their poetry thus enjoys an added quality, the observation, thoughts and feelings of those deeply involved. The poets belonged to the community in which they served. They were not apart.*

Their poetry is personal and direct and always has a point to make. The reader is left in no doubt as to what the poet has to say. The poets were in far too important an activity to indulge in an élitist word-play.

This book, fifty years after the Declaration of war in 1939, marks another stage in the work of The Salamander Oasis Trust, to gather in the poetry of the Second World War, study the mss, select and produce four anthologies of poetry written by those serving in the forces and written at the time. The eye-witness! We began in the Middle East[1] moved to Italy[2] and then covered all theatres of war in the predecessor to this volume *Poems of the Second World War: the Oasis Selection* (Dent, Everyman). It has been a difficult assignment. Through appeals in the media over 14,000 poems have come in from those who served and wrote in World War Two – from all services, men and women, from UK and the Commonwealth, all carefully read and assessed.

When we began we knew the poetry was there – true, neglected, stored in desks and drawers, in boxes gathering dust for 40 years. We knew of the poetry because we had all taken part in the *Oasis Anthology in the Middle East* (Cairo, The Salamander Society, 1942/3), as editors or poets. That exercise confirmed our belief that many, many were writing, compelled by the experience of war with little thought of publication. We regarded

[1] *Return to Oasis* (Shepheard-Walwyn) 1980.
[2] *From Oasis into Italy* (Shepheard-Walwyn) 1983.

the Middle East as exceptional in both inspiration and facilities. It enjoyed an air of freedom and detachment. It had writers and publishers.

However, as our appeals for poetry have established, the creative urge extended to all areas of the war, on a scale no-one could have envisaged, as General Sir John Hackett points out in his Foreword. Poems – well over 3,000 – poured in for this fourth collection, countering the fear that after three anthologies we would be scraping the barrel. There are so many good poems we just cannot use. We have the problem not only of space but of balancing the themes to gain the widest range of experience.

With regret, we may have to draw a line. Looking back our reward has lain in the joy of discovery. The poem 'Luck' by Dennis McHarrie that more than any reflects the attitude of participants in war, came to us as twelve untitled lines at the end of a letter – a poem now recorded many times on radio and TV. The poem of genius 'Thermopylae 41' was conceived by John Brookes as he dug in with the Australian Infantry on the same ground where the Spartans resisted over 2 millennia ago and written weeks later in a POW camp at Salonika. The poet had to be persuaded by his wife to send the poem to us – from a shoe-box under the stairs. Today the poem has become the subject of academic theses.

Discovery certainly continues in this anthology, for it differs from its predecessors in having even more previously unpublished poetry.[1]

Thus we have Phillip Whitfield, a doctor of the RAMC, entering Belsen concentration camp on the Day of Liberation. (We rejected poems by those who were not there.) The poet focuses on one man.

> The moving skeleton
> Had crippled hands,
> His skinny palms held secrets:
> When I undid the joints I found
> Five wheat grains huddled there.

---

[1] The anthology naturally includes a selection of the published: Keith Douglas (original version), Bernard Gutteridge, John Jarmain, Richard Spender, Roy Fuller, Gavin Ewart, Frank Thompson and Commonwealth poets referred to later.

The cameo of the prisoner clutching his 'survival' ration tells us of Belsen more than just the count of the dead. For we can relate to the lonely man hanging on to a few grains of wheat. It is harder to take in the tens, even hundreds of thousands gassed or starved.

It has not been an easy task. Earlier anthologies often selected themselves. This time we have had so many experiences, a wealth of observation to choose from – written at varying literary levels, entailing a chain of selection stages. One poet, Victor West, taken POW in Crete covers such a wide range of experiences, from one POW camp to another, to Eastern Europe and encounters with the Russians; his poetry could fill many pages – we must select.

Many of the close-ups in this anthology make grim reading: 'No other animal stinks so in putrefaction' writes Charles McCausland of the dead Japanese. Martin Southall describes the Infantry burying their dead:

> Arms and legs were broken
> Brought closer to the trunk:
> Not from respect
> But simply to lessen
> The burden of digging.
>
> God! how I hate the sound
> A dead branch makes
> When stepped upon.

As harrowing as many First War poems. We make no apologies for our selection. These poems report a facet of war – in dramatic form.

Interestingly it has taken four appeals to draw these eye-witness records from their hiding places. We have not set out to shock. We have even left some disturbing poems on one side. For, as pointed out, an anthology must achieve a balance – the balance of subject and, above all, a basic balance between content and literary level, achieved, we hope, by the two journalist editors, Erik de Mauny and myself, being off-set by Ian Fletcher, war poet, Professor of English and an authority on twentieth-century poetry.

The structure of the book around the Seven Faces of War ensures a range of themes. Jim Hovell on the habits of a man in the barrack room and his wryly-described leave on the changed home front – or the last laugh on the tart going for rank when picking up soldiers in a bar, observed by Harry Beard in Malta:

> But how I laugh behind the lady's back
> Her Sergeant's local, acting and unpaid!

which so contrasts with Edward Venn's description of 'Easter and the Broken Churches' – the aftermath of an air-raid – or a poem on looting by Geoffrey Holloway, a stoup and a German automatic he had acquired:

> I gave each away –
> the stoup to a lame catholic
> the gun to someone
> crossing the Sahara
> Both became enemies.

As with so many of the poems there is acid in the last line.

Past anthologies have been short on poems from the sea and air. A critic berated us for printing mainly poems from the army. We depend on what we receive. This time we can have poems about the Atlantic convoys and Air Force poems – the strain of surviving one's tour of thirty operations – and a poem of an unusual event – a burial service for a bomber pilot. Peter Roberts in 'Frayed End' describes such a rare occasion – rare, because bomber crews were shot down over enemy territory or into the sea.

Michael Thwaites (Australia) contributes his description of the action of the 'Jervis Bay'. There are outspoken Australian and New Zealand poems. Again we include Les Cleveland (NZ) whose vivid description of action compares with any First War poetry as does that of Uys Krige, South Africa's poet of the War. We see action in the Desert through his eyes, feel the cold of the POW camps in Italy.

As before we have many women's poems. Olivia Fitzroy's series on the Royal Naval Air Service in Ceylon. Joy Corfield and Stephanie Batstone look to civilian life after it is all over. Then the poem of conscience from WAAF Mary Harrison. The poet modelled German towns to brief bomber crews, from maps and photographs. After a very heavy raid on Cologne she studied the photographs – before and after – and cried out in pain:

> How many people have died through me
> From the skill in my finger tips?
>
> . . . . . .
>
> Is there a God up above who listens to all
> Does he know why this has to be?

For here is the dilemma. The torture of someone doing her duty. As Dr John Rae observed, the poems of the Second World War came from an unwarlike generation going to war. That war had to be fought. Hitler had to be stopped. But that does not always endear those who took part to the realities. Hence the poetry – from a literate and aware generation, the last generation before TV, who read and wrote. Far more wrote than their forbears in the First War and they came from a far wider range, men and women from so many backgrounds, from all ranks. Even those who left school at fourteen could write fluently – no problems with grammar, spelling or syntax.

Critics may hold that if so much was written its quality must be poor. This is a *non-sequitur*. There is no necessary relation between the two. True, in our anthologies we have varying literary levels. This is to be expected. But then the poems have to be judged not just as poems – but as *war* poetry, a genre on its own – the point made so often by General Sir John Hackett.

At the end can we say our anthology truly paints a picture of a war? Lord Carver in his Historical Note and Introduction to sections of the book rightly points out that those who write tend to be more sensitive and thoughtful, the poetry the product of heightened emotions. The achievements, the success, the positive aspects of service life are missing.

But perhaps there is a simple explanation for this lack. The generation who fought in this Second World War had been brought up in the shadow of 1914–18. They had no illusions as to what a second world conflict would mean. They felt no compulsion to glorify it and if, in the struggle for survival, they found unsuspecting strength in comradeship and a sense of common purpose and achievement – these were uncovenanted blessings. Above all, this generation of World War Two were a modest lot and took success in their stride.

The RAF 'few' who frustrated the German invasion in the Battle of Britain gained only one Victoria Cross, and after shooting down the Luftwaffe pilots did not go on television to talk about it – there was no TV to go onto. In any case it would have been out of character. The cardinal sin was to boast – not only for the RAF, but for all those on land or sea. There was a job to be done. People went about it quietly and when they met later, the talk would be of cock-ups, of near-misses and luck, spoken of with humour. Would an outsider have guessed that they had actually defeated a highly professional and often better equipped army? That they did this is now a matter of record in the history books.

But the record cannot tell all – certainly not the experiences, the thoughts and feelings of so many who took part.

The poems do.

In retrospect, in face of what is happening in the world today, the poems tell of an age of innocence.*

Arrangement of the Poems

We have structured this anthology around the SEVEN FACES OF WAR:

> *Enlisting/Training*
> *Support*
> *Action on Land*
> *Action Sea/Air*
> *Leave*
> *Behind the Wire*
> *Reflection/Aftermath*

The poems came from all services and theatres of war but whereas our previous anthology *Poems of the Second World War: the Oasis Selection* listed poems by the areas of conflict, we have tried a different approach, to group the poetry under subject. True, certain poems could fall into different categories – a poem in

---

* Of interest, those who came out were not subject on release to the trauma and claims of later conflicts. They were aware, dedicated and did not expect any great reward – did not get any! Sufficient to stop Hitler, Germany and Japan and go back into civilian life with least fuss. They had achieved what they set out to do. It was their war.

Action on land could also be *Reflection*, but in the main, the scheme works. There is also a chronological sequence. We begin with *Enlisting/Training* and have *Aftermath*, preparation for civilian life with *Reflection* at the end.

1. Enlisting/Training

Even before the outset of War members of the Territorial Army and Royal Navy and Royal Air Force volunteer reserves were recalled to join regular sevice units. Volunteers enlisted for all three services. The RAF attracted volunteers from many countries. However, the bulk of the armed forces were to come from the call-up of young able-bodied men, age group by age group, to be trained by the professionals. Later women would also be drafted – for the services or industry.

2. Support

For every man at the front there could be up to ten in support – at base or in lines of communication from base to those in action. An army has not only to be trained and equipped but has to be fed, clothed, transported and paid. There are specialist units, Engineers and Signallers, Royal Army Medical Corps, Intelligence, Education. Many specialists will also be in action, including Padres, who pick up the pieces.

3. Action on Land

We have set-piece battles as at Alamein or prolonged actions at Cassino, Anzio or the Gothic Line, or from the Normandy beaches to Caen to the Low Countries, to Germany, Burma and the Pacific Islands – New Guinea (Australian and New Zealand forces) with river crossings, capture of bases and towns, patrols, skirmishes and artillery exchanges, or the dropping of airborne troops.

4. Action Sea/Air

As well as ferrying troops to landings in Africa, Italy, Normandy, the Navy had to guard the supply route from USA to Britain – the

Atlantic Convoys – or to Murmansk to support the Russian armies. The Navy escorted troop convoys around the Cape to the Middle East or India and the Pacific. The Air Force had a dual function, organised as Fighter Command and Bomber Command, the former frustrating invasion in the Battle of Britain. The Air Force would drop paratroops at Arnhem, support ground units (the Desert Air Force particularly effective here) or drop supplies as in Burma.

Since most units were operational all poems relating to the Navy or Air Force are listed under *Action* – including the women's services, WRNS and WAAFS, Signals, Cyphers and Transport – even though in some cases certain poems could well be classified under *Support* or even *Reflection*.

5. *Leave*

Leave before embarkation, between actions, at regular intervals, 48 hours or 7 days, was particularly important. Leave to get a bath, sleep between sheets, eat and drink in comfort and see the sights, visit arts clubs in Cairo or opera in Italy, find female company – leave in all aspects played a vital role.

6. *Behind the Wire*

Under this heading come both military prisoners of war – Italy, Germany, Poland and in South East Asia –and the victims of concentration camps as at Belsen, about whom we have only included poems of those who went in and saw. This is our approach throughout the anthology. It is the poet's own experience we seek.

7. *Reflection/Aftermath*

So much could be grouped under this heading. The essential quality is a deeper perception, not always related to a specific event, a wry comment perhaps, the observation of people caught up in war. A questioning – why?

We have also included poems looking beyond the end of war, to the preparation for civilian life. They round off the anthology that began six years before.

We have used a poem by Frank Thompson to make a fitting end to the book – 'Polliciti Meloria':

> Write on the stone no words of sadness –
> Only the gladness due
> That we, who asked most of living,
> Knew how to give it too.

Did the poet forsee his own end in Bulgaria, 1944?

The Poems
The Seven Faces of War

The Contents

1. Enlisting/Training

2. *Support*

3. Action on Land

4. *Action: Sea/Air*

5. *Leave*

6. *Behind the Wire*

7. *Reflection/Aftermath*

Introduction

by Field Marshal Lord Carver

1. *Enlisting/Training*
2. *Support*
3. *Action on Land*
4. *Action: Sea/Air*

So many of these poems, whether related to action or to the long and often tedious periods between, are concerned with the contrast between wartime and peacetime life. Some are nostalgic, recalling the joys or quiet contentment of life before the war and hoping for a return to them.

Aircrew, and in a rather different degree, sailors were subject to a greater intensity of contrast, which is reflected in a number of poems. The former, if based in Britain, went directly into action from an almost peacetime environment and returned to it equally sharply, if they were lucky enough to return. The intensity of emotion which this caused, in the aircrew themselves and in those awaiting their return, is made clear. The same sort of feeling was experienced by sailors, although their entry into action and return from it was more gradual, and the interval between the two longer. For the sailor action was less certain than for the airman. Long periods of watch, when the sea itself and the elements provided a more certain hazard, were the norm. For both airman and sailor, the surrounding element itself affected the emotions and the enemy was less personal than he was for the soldier, except in the aerial combat of fighters.

The soldier usually lived more or less permanently in a different sort of world, far removed from peacetime life. It was often the conditions of life, whether in the front line or behind it, which provided the subject for the contemplative thought which he expressed in poetry. The approach to action was generally less of a contrast to the life he had been living just before, although seaborne and airborne landings were an exception. Fear in anticipation of action, the death or wounding of comrades and effects of war on the unfortunate inhabitants of the battlefield area provide the principal themes of poems from the combat zone. Some inevitably reflect the tragedy of the death of youth in battle, a theme for poems down the ages from the earliest times. The tone varies according to the theatre of war. Jungle and desert provided different, and very contrasting backgrounds, regarded by most of those who wrote about them as hostile, but by others as friendly, compared to battlefields in populated regions, like Italy, where death and destruction were not limited to the opposing forces and war was seen in all its horrific aspects, accentuated by rough terrain and harsh winter weather.

Poems from behind the front lines – the *Support* and the *Enlist/ Training* sections – accentuate the ironies of war and the common feeling of being a nameless cog on the wheel of a large machine. The emotions which that aroused were either introspective – to ask oneself who one was and what it was all about – or the opposite: to emphasise the importance of one's immediate friends, with whom one could gang up as defence against an apparently soulless, and perhaps alien machine. An ironic or comic pricking of the bubble of pomposity or authority formed part of this, and the general sentiment was common among Australians and New Zealanders.

War poems have inevitably emphasised the dark side of war. They were written to exorcize emotions which the author wished to release. Few of them reflect the other, more positive emotions which, whether one likes it or not, have formed part of the experience of war and have made it bearable to the participants: the excitement and exhilaration of action in danger; the feeling of being close to nature, living in the open, awake and active at dawn or at dead of night; the bonds of companionship and dedication to a common cause, which one believed was for the good of one's fellow human beings; the satisfaction of challenging tasks successfully accomplished; and even, unfashionable as it may now be, the pursuit of heroism and glory, the desire to stand well, as a full man, in the eyes of one's comrades. All were part of war, but not all soldiers, sailors and airmen were inclined to express their emotions in poetry: indeed it was part of their code of life not to express emotion at all.

These poems therefore reflect aspects of life, in action and out of it, in the Second World War; but not all of them.

John Jarmain

These Poems

You who in evenings by the fire
May read these words of mine,
How let you see the desert bare
In the print-smooth line?

Listen! These poems were not made in rooms,
But out in the empty sand,
Where only the homeless Arab roams
In a sterile land;

They were not at tables written
With placid curtains drawn,
But by candlelight begotten
Of the dusk and dawn.

They had no peace at their creation,
No twilight hush of wings;
Only the tremble of bombs, the guns' commotion,
And destructive things.

Mareth, Tunisia. March, 1943.

1. Enlisting/Training

Herbert Corby

Armament Instructor

Drysouled, he mumbles names of working parts,
   watching the clock and book, scared lest he vary
system laid down. Never gay or merry,
   his words, like cherries, each have solid hearts,
and he spits them to the airmen, deft by habit,
   circumscribed by fear of losing tapes.
If any fidgets, or if another gapes,
   he pops with frightened temper like a rabbit.
Museumpiece himself, he grabs and snatches
   at information twisted, vague, uncommon,
and doles it at the men like mud, in patches.
   Sometimes, despite his fear, he's almost human,
and leaving guns, to human things he looks,
   and natters of glory and honour, both from books.

Lisbeth David

Portsmouth Cypher School

i think this is hell
i'll say it again
   and make my point well
i think this is hell
no doubt you can tell
not prone to complain
i think this is hell
i'll say it again.

Kings Cross to Liverpool

Clinging to small essentials, cup and comb,
We have entrained, half-knowing what we did;
Now we have slept our last long night at home,
Stuck 'CABIN' on our lives and closed the lid.
How many months before we savour rightly
This gentle land that now we leave so lightly?

David Gascoyne

Zero

September, 1939

Who can by now not hear
The hollow and annihilating roar
Of final disillusion; or not know
How our condition is uncertain and obscure
And difficult to bear? Yet through
The blackness of his dungeon there still peer
Man's eyes, unmoving, lit by their desire
To see *the worst*, and yet not die
Of their lucid despair
But in such vision persevere
Through time into Eternity.
For this is Zero-hour
When the most penetrating gaze can see
Only the Void, the emptier than air,
The incoherent *Nada* of the seer:
Who blind is yet not blind, being aware
Of the Negation's double mystery!

Tomb of what was, womb of what is to be.

Stephen Haggard

The Mantle

Recruits are issued with dead soldiers' stock;
Field-muddied webbing, brasswork that must mock
Our novice hopes to get it clean.
No tragedy in that: what of the shock
At this first splash of blood I've seen –
This ground-sheet that has warmed some dying Jock?
'Royal Scots: Dunkirk'! so reads the rune.
– Blood and a name where heroism has been.

This hero's shroud must be my living hide
To shield and warm: Pity is in this pride:
My warmth will never quicken him.
And yet by this he shall be sanctified,
Through blood, and through a bullet's whim;
And the far, uncherished agony he died,
Kindling new life as life grew dim,
Shall lift a new vision above my vision's rim.

Devon, June 1940

Jim Hovell

Taffy

When he walks, Taffy walks just like everybody else,
left arm moving forward with right leg,
right arm with left leg.

But, on the square, marching, it's quite a different matter!
Taffy swings his left arm forward with his left leg,
right arm with right leg,
becoming an ungainly robot from Karel Kapek's play

or a lumbering, life-sized doll,
equipped with a clockwork mechanism
ineptly assembled by a fuddled craftsman.

Ordered out of the squad, Taffy marches away shamefacedly
in his bizarre fashion to the edge of the square
to be individually trained by a Corporal
who shouts, threatens, finally, patience gone,
rushes wild-eyed at Taffy,
grabs his arms, pumps them backwards and forwards,
screams 'Left. Right. Left. Right.
Like this, you Welsh cunt! Like this!'

Later, with the pale evening sun gently illumining
the somnolent barrack-room,
Taffy, plimsole-shod, paces endlessly between the bunks,
solemnly practices the art of marching and day-dreams
of neat terraces of small featureless houses
threading through quiet valleys
between barren and desecrated hills.

Barrackroom Nights

Guy Lester is an Old Harrovian.
I simply mention this as a matter of interest.
I am not in any way implying
that attendance at that respected seat of learning
has anything at all to do with his practice, most nights,
of masturbating so violently, frantically and dedicatedly
that his wooden bunk shakes and shudders and creaks
like some old galleon buffetted by angry winds and waves
during a raging storm of unimaginable ferocity
and threatens to collapse at any moment
into a useless pile of shattered slats and splintered cross-pieces.

For Tom, a meek little South London shop assistant,
who is unlikely to have experienced a storm at sea
or be capable of imagining one,
occupying the bunk above Guy's

must seem like riding on the top deck
of a wildly swaying and speeding tramcar
with some demented or drunken driver at the controls.

Furthermore, his hands being fully occupied
in tightly clutching the sides of the violently rocking bunk
to save himself from being pitched out
and sent crashing down onto the polished and shining floorboards
    below,
the luckless Tom can never himself
enjoy the thrills of a good night-time wank
but can only participate vicariously in the lubricious exertions
of his sweating, straining and single-minded bunkmate below.

John S. Ingram

Selection Board

Three days of testing, observation and strain,
Why do we have it, what do we gain?
Interviewed here, cross-questioned there –
Did you answer correctly that questionnaire?
You think you did and yet daren't swear
That you're doing all right.
No – we're not quite
As bright
As we thought.
Matrices, curving with squiggles and dots,
Lecturettes, slides and group discussion.
'What's the difference 'twixt Nazi and Prussian?'
'What shall be done with the haves and have nots?'
That obstacle course to test our wits,
Should we wear denims or PT kits.
We jump from heights to show we've guts,
Unditch a car that's bogged in ruts.
Sergeants and Corporals, Gunners, too,
Mere numbers here,

trying to get through
And make the grade
Without the aid
Of an old school tie,
Strings pulled on the sly.
Who? Where? When? Why?
That's how it is, there's no omission
When the goal in view is the King's Commission.

December, 1942

Second Subaltern, ATS
A Tribute

Second Subaltern Gwen, of the ATS,
Your hazel green eyes
Should be shaded by Bond Street hats,
Not khaki peaked caps,
Quite jaunty perhaps
Though they are.

Second Subaltern Gwen and your ilk,
Your shapely young legs
Should be gossamer clad in silk,
Not the war-time drab,
Utility tab,
Type of hose.

Second Subaltern Gwen and your girls
Your chestnutty hair
Should be masses of tumbling curls,
Not 'Victory' rolled,
Neat, hard and cold
As it is.

Second Subaltern Gwen and the rest,
The day will soon break
When you'll be entrancingly dressed
In a Lanvin gown
With your old Sam Browne[1]
Cast aside.

But though Alchymist Peace has wrought lead into gold
We'll sigh and remember you as of old,
Second Subaltern Gwen, of the ATS,
God Bless!

July 1943

[1] Leather belt and cross–over.

Audrey Lee

Entry 118, Flight Mechanic (E) RAF Hednesford, Staffs.

I sit here,
Gazing around at the faces
Which unmistakably bear the traces
Of utter boredom.
To my right,
Two WAAFs struggle with the timing
Which they are obviously finding
Far beyond their comprehension.
Cpl. Adams,
The best instructor ever,
Is reaching the end of his tether
At our blatant stupidity.
Whilst Ray,
Best brains of the entry,
Deep in thought, studies intently,

Fits and clearances,
My mistake,
Ray confesses, with a guilty look,
Displaying the incriminating book,
She too writes verse.

Geoffrey Matthews

War has become Official, old Friend

Sealed in at night behind our black windows
We listened to the storm in the suburbs and the trees,
And peered outside at the houses veiled like widows
While gusts of wind like desperate refugees
Tore at the pane . . .
                           . . . and know that all restraint
Is lost for another year. Limeleaves are lying
Sprinkled under the trees like yellow paint,
And the misty avenues yawn for the dead or dying,
And sure enough September is here and Clifton
Suddenly jolts and blinks at the terrible newsboys.

So it is war: through Bootham the twelve-ton
Lorries go south all night with guns and a shrill noise
Like mounting sirens, and from dusk to midnight
The searchlights lean their wigwam patterns over
A minster peeled of glass. No tactless light
Breaks through the muffled streets, kind for the lovers
The County Council and the thief. The stars are wise,
And there have been no faggots falling yet
To spark our heaped, instinctive secrecies;
A city like a burnt-out cigarette.

Today I am sick of sandbags, news, announcements,
And cycle in calm September sunshine across
The plain at Ampleforth where rents
Are paid in heather and the daily profit and loss

Measured at milking-time by the shadows of larches
(And John, if you remember, once taught Greek)
But find no freedom.
                    Under the somnolent arches
Of chestnut where the pigeons used to speak
Their sugared lines, wagons marked WD
Lurch by for France, and over the ripe wheat where
The rooks went lolloping home from field to tree
A bomber's drone fills every crevice of air.
The garden of No Escape . . .
                    Sheffield and Hull,
Bradford and Leeds have billetted children in
These chequered villages; happy and pale they pull
The unripe apples down, and what a sin
It is, I think, to carry a gas-mask through
Cornfields like these. Two kittens box and play
Under a sunny black-out sign, but there are few
Walking in Poland's windy corn today.

Time's come at last to stop and rope in all my
Friends and memory and say goodbye
To you – for one – assailable as moth or moonlight
And ample-minded after my own heart,
Whom I remember in detachment on the low
Tennis-courts, composed and stalking in white,
Or conducting intently at the wide-open window,
Or stormy-eyed or damning Dorothy or alone against
A line of hills, watching a friend pull turnips,
Whose head holds maps of gay water and a chart
Of lilac tears like sand.
                    And here's the strait-laced
Postman brushing aside the fuschia with his hips.

September 1939

Colin McIntyre

Parachute Jump

One recalls not the moment, but the decision –
The push from a comfort of known limitations
Into the hazardous openness of a whole world.
Whipcord cold wind bangs you across fierce air,
To fall helpless, midst a blur of intensity
Till that sudden final umbilical snap.

After that it is easy, to drift, drift, drift,
Revel in the clean joy of a cloudy embrace,
Look down upon tarmac Lilliputian scramblings,
And walk sunlight through a silken limb creation
Made by many women working in dark hangers.
Cruelly those superiorities must then dissolve,
In time to brace, meet that first hard earth-shock.

Colin Sheard

BEF[1] Rookies

Dunkirk was yet to come.
Not that we knew of that.
Of anything!

Greener than grass,
We did arms-drill on the beach:
With broom-sticks!

No less innocent of such things
Than were the lasses, left behind.
And with 'regulars' to teach us

Warfare!
They scorned us. Dared us answer back.
Knowing that, at least, *their* lack

Matched ours.
Other than in theory.
Whilst back home, Churchill pontificated

On his claim that no untrained
British soldier was in France.
Bullshit!

That we knew.
Stuck there. Hit by the effects
Of TT and TAB.[2]

With swollen glands in the oxter
Making even makeshift arms seem heavy.
Yes, Winston should have been

Having qualms about us:
We, his veteran soldiers of
Three days. Three weeks at most!

Who stood no ghost of a chance
In France at that time.
'Fred Karno's army' was our tag,

And Brian Rix would have gagged
In such a fix.
Farce?

It was all my arse.

Until Dunkirk.
There was nothing funny
About that.

[1] British Expeditionary Force, 1940, France.
[2] Injections against Tetanus and Typhoid.

Richard Spender

Before the first Parachute Descent

All my world has suddenly gone quiet
Like a railway carriage as it draws into a station;
Conversation fails, laughter dies,
And the turning of pages and the striking of matches cease.
All life is lapsed into nervous consciousness,
Frozen, like blades of grass in blocks of ice,
Except where one small persistent voice in the corner
Compares with the questioning silence –
With the situation of an electric present –
My self-opinions, pride and confidence of an untried past.

The Officer Cadet

My life darts
Like a worried cocking handle
From bored hotel lounges
Where angular and 'modern' officers' wives
Sit, and sip, and stitch nervously,
Talking confidential nothings
To their loudly precocious sons
In long grey flannel shorts
And to their so grown-up plain daughters
With big-buttocked tartan skirts.

My life jerks,
Like an unwanted casing
Pushed in the back by an ungrateful ejector,
To a pile of stale blankets and damp kit-bags,
Where everything smells of metal and of metal polish,
And where one's world,
Suddenly so remote from anything rational,
Revolves round boot polish and a brighter shine.

I cannot understand why
To fight for a few simple things
Necessitates polishing the toes of one's boots
'Until you can see your face in them.'
I have no wish to see my face;
And there are mirrors.
Neither do I see the cause nor wisdom
Of teaching supple bodies to behave like crank-shafts
And walk about like the most stupid
And self-opinioned wood pigeon in that little spinney
Where I once fell off the old white pony.
But that was in the days when
A bright wit and a clean neck
Were more important than polished buttons and shiny badges.

I have learnt wisdom here.
One can learn to love through opposites.
Sometimes I have unquenchable longings to lie
On the warm grass, perhaps by Binton Woods,
And watch the timid primrose smiling from her bed.

I love most the primrose
When I am surrounded by her opposites;
I can find nothing more unlike
A primrose
Than a Coldstream Guard Sergeant-Major.

Douglas Street

A Musing Upon Being Embodied[1]

Before the end of August
I officered in TA,
A sort of half-civilian
In an especial way;
But now that I'm embodied,

I'm a different sort of bloke,
I'm now a sort of regular –
Believe me that's no joke!

I've newly been embodied; –
Is my brand new body's form,
A comely one and manly? –
Or just my shoddy norm?
When I am disembodied –
I hope one Victory Day –
Will I become civilian
And be an ex-TA?

Or when disembodied
In God's especial way,
Been killed, and sent to 'transit camp',
Till I am re-embodied
On Judgement Day?

TA Drill Hall 1939

---

[1] A special term used to describe the *total* mobilisation of the Territorial Army, August/September, 1939. Some members had to sign a form.
(a) To serve outside UK.
(b) To serve outside the unit in which they enlisted.

Michael Thwaites

Epitaph on a New Army

No drums they wished, whose thoughts were tied
To girls and jobs and mother,
Who rose and drilled and killed and died
Because they saw no other,

Who died without the hero's throb,
And if they trembled, hid it,
Who did not fancy much their job
But thought it best, and did it.

November 1939

Victor West

'Sign Here'

Here, at The Depot, we've got the Lot!
Brass cannons, shouting sergeants,
smart drill squads on the Square . . .
Traditions, Museums, all the Panoply of War,
but In the Stores,
the famous Quartermaster's Stores
they all sing about
there's nothing . . . of any use.
No rifles, no boots, no uniforms . . .
not even Haldane's 1908 Service Dress
with brass buttons, unregimental for the Rifles.
They've loads of paper gadgetry
for detecting mustard gas: Armlets and suchlike . . .
Nasty! and Oh, The Disappointment of beholding
a Soldier's 'Housewife'![1]
                          And then, 'Sign Here!'
For all their warlike talk
one wonders why the Enemy is granting us
this training period unmolested.
Only rain-mist sweeps over the Hampshire hills
across Oliver's Battery, storming neolithic earthworks
whilst the silhouette of sacred grove on St Catharine's
weeps silently for departed, warlike Druids.
The empty military road looks blankly
towards Southampton and the docks, devoid of camions

or the chariots of wrath. Immobilised, we wait
– for the next 'Equipment' Parade. But, of the War, no sign here.

[1] A hold-all with mending materials.

Anonymous

The Romantic Charter

I am not fighting for the Poles or Czechs,
And only indirectly for the Rex.
I do not greatly love the Slav or Greek,
I cannot bear the way Colonials speak.

I loathe efficiency – and Nissen huts,
And as for bonhomie – I hate its guts.
I am not fighting Germans just to get
My democratic share of blood and sweat.

Dear Sir! I feel that you may get the gist
Of all my War Aims from the following list;–

Georgian Houses – red replicas of heaven;
Split pediments; breakfast at eleven;
Large white peonies in big glass bowls,
Asparagus au beurre; whitebait in shoals.

Close-cropped grass, huge trees with cawing rooks,
A sunny breakfast room, a library of books.
Clean white housemaids in new print frocks,
Coachman turned chauffeur-footman on the box.

Dinner parties – all in evening dress,
Glamorous women drenched in 'Mary Chess'.
Charades and paper games – hot houses with the heat on;
Superficiality – and Cecil Beaton.

Shrimps from Moreton Bay; Port that is tawny;
Gin and Dubonnet; soles that are Mornay;
Hot scones for tea, thick cream, the smell of logs,
Long country walks, thick shoes and spaniel dogs.

Ducks in the evening, swishing swans in flight;
Fires in bedrooms flickering at night.
And of this 'autre-fois' all the 'moeurs'

Which are epitomised in 'Valse des Fleurs'.
Fresh shiny chintzes – an herbaceous border.
DEATH AND DESTRUCTION to this damned New Order.

1944

2. *Support*

Brian Allwood

Save your Bones

Bring out your bones, carefully separated they should
   be placed at the back door in an airtight tin.
Your bones will make us fertilizer, fat or aircraft glue.
It is the least, the least you can do.
BRING OUT YOUR BONES.
(Bring out your dead)
An old love letter will make a cartridge wad;
   just think what your bones will do.
YOUR COUNTRY NEEDS YOUR BONES.
Bring out old letters, old iron, red bones, old copies,
Don't be selfish with your bones
(YOUR COUNTRY NEEDS YOUR SORT, MY BOY)
Bring out your bones
YOUR COUNTRY NEEDS YOUR BONES.

North African Occasions

The soldiers are in the middle of tea
in the civilian hangar with asbestos roof
with more holes than have leaves in an ambush
forest. Tarts at this hour, in the hennaed
burnished silences of bed – who knows?
French under the clustered lights that had
almost gone out, discuss allegiances.
Out of the promenade (where the saddle-tank
engines puff splendidly away to miles),
the afternoon thunderbolt sea has ripped
a great hole of obviously inadequate concrete,
and out of the torpedoed poor end of the flotsam
new ship, four American bodies floated.
The sniping from the zoo across the road is
now confined to nights. And the sea has gone

down and the wind and the rain and the sun and
the night. And time comes up to what is wanted.

We are in the middle of what some call tea,
feet wet and not a light all round.
The rotten bombers have arrived. The guns tell
Here they come, wandering in, for all I know it.
If they have a system then it's not obvious
to a million odd people thinking upwards.
Here they come wandering in. They want to come
and be away as silently as miracles.
They ride in under the first drawn skin
of the night, black Valkyries
from an early tea. We know of their noise:
those feet above us now they are speaking
damn foreign noises in a Woolworth box
of foreign tongues. They speak to their land.

Alleyne Anderson

Sand

I am the sand. No;
I will not let you go.
Let the wind come – let the dry squalls blow,
And I arise,
Blinding your eyes,
A smothering cloud.
Try to lift
Your feet from my drift;
Feel: I enfold you:
Stay with me, stay:
I will not let you go away.
Feel my soft fingers hold you,
Soft, as a bride
Reluctant that her man should leave her side
Holds him, gently restraining.
Stay, and remaining

Be one with me in the cold white
Glare of the desert moonlight.
See – your feet slip;
They cannot grip.
Why try?
Lie down with me – and die.
And I will dry you – bleach your bones bare;
White and dry.
In a few months Arabs will stare
At your skull among the stones
And your lovely white bones;
But by then my work will be done;
Helped by wind, drought and sun,
We two shall be one.
Stay with me; stay.
No: you shall not ever get away.

Ma'ater Bagush, Cyrenaica, 1941.

B.H. Appleyard

Highball

The ice clinks against the glass
and the sliced orange and the lime
float idly in the rich amber of the rye.
We hold them before our eyes
feeling the coldness strike our hands,
and our thoughts crowd
swift as photo-montage on a screen . . .
. . . there was no ice there,
only thirst, and the haze which used to rise
quivering and dazzling above the plain:
dust came in clouds to choke and clog our throats
along Axis By-Pass and Bir Hacheim track,
and yet in March, after the winter rain
we once saw poppies growing in the stagnant mud

beside the Derna Road:
the water was always tepid
and salt,
remember the milk and how it curdled in the tea?
dust came in clouds to choke and clog our throats
as we lay flat with stukas overhead:
we were always thirsty then
and our dreams rioted
green fields and trees and streams:
we were never clean,
our clothes and bodies stank,
sweat caked our skins with sand
and fleas held holiday each night . . .
. . . we remembered this and drank.

'Jean, deux encore, s'il vous plait.'

To-morrow we go back.

A.H. Bailey

The Colonel sees the Light

The Colonel looked out on Christmas night
    And saw in a bivvie'[1] a tiny light,
He called to his batman, 'Do my eyes deceive?'
    A light in a bivvie seems hard to believe.
Then said the batman, 'It is quite clear
The sappers have got some Almaza beer,
And seeing tonight is a special Date
    Methinks they mean to celebrate.'
The Colonel said 'Hum.' The Colonel said 'Ho!'
    We must tell them it's wrong a light to show,
Get me that crate at the back of my jeep,
    At this Christmas Party we'll take a peep.'
Across the sand went Colonel and Bat
    Till they reached the tent that the party was at.

The sappers looked up with awful surprise
  But when they saw the crate they wiped their eyes.
Then up and spake young Sapper Jones
  'Come, have some Benghasi chicken bones,'
The Colonel accepted with greatest of zest
  Opened a bottle and said 'All the best!'
Said Sapper Smith 'What about a song?
  I'm glad you brought old Snuffy along.'
The batman, so called, then took the hint,
  And gave his version of 'Sayida Bint.'[2]
They sang of 'Loch Lomond' and 'Rose of Tralee'
  The Colonel obliged with 'Sussex by Sea',
And ever anon they reached to the crate,
  Till each had consumed beer bottles eight.
The songs they sang gay, the singing was high,
  When a night-flying plane of the Luftwaffe went by,
And informed by Rommel, the Colonel's tent,
  A nasty big bomb for a Christmas box sent.
It arrived with a crash. It arrived with a roar.
  The Colonel's bivvie and jeep were no more,
But the Colonel looked out from the Sappers' tent
  And said 'It's the best bloody Christmas I've spent.'
So here is a motto for Colonels and others,
  Always treat your Sappers like brothers.
And if you see a light in their bivvies
  Remember, one day we shall be back in civvies.

Christmas, Western Desert 1941

[1] bivouac.
[2] colloquial Arabic greeting to a 'girl'.

Harry Beard

The Troopship

Through the tropics once again,
with a stinking cargo of two thousand men,
each one sweating in his hammock; –

hip to buttock . . . .
Bear us quickly to our journey's end,
we have our freedom to defend.

She carried prisoners before
to the Antipodes; we go to war:
But here they pack us as they packed the foe,
eighty in this foul-aired space below.
Bear us quickly to our journey's end,
we have our freedom to defend.

At sea, December 1940

Ted Birt

Delirium (or prejudice?)

From daffy DEOLALI to crazy KALYAN,
one wonders now, bemuséd, where Eastern tales began.
A silver night of beauty . . . wond'rous moon above
But deeds were dark and dirty, not sweet and tender love.

All new-chums we . . . we'd all been told
   of fakirs, thugs, and dacoits bold
'The thing you MUSTN'T do,' they said
   'is let them steal your pistol from your bed!'

After khana, what d'you think? . . .
We'd gather in the Mess to drink
Slewing Cyprus brandy . . . so powerful, so strong
No Scotch, so NASIK whisky . . . 'simply CAN'T go wrong!'

Rope-woven charpoy's calling me . . . will rubber-legs still
   wobble back?
Oh, that bamboo basha, palm-thatch and all, . . . it's just a shack!
Wide-open doors and windows, just gaping holes to show
the way of staggering entry . . . candles still aglow!

So, lying there frustrated, all mossie-net enwrapt,
To some, it's real protection . . . but me, I JUST FEEL
    TRAPPED!
Awaken, startled, do not move . . . frozen arms and legs.
Is that a mortal figure? Or just too many pegs?

In moonlight's gleam, a spirit just released
breathes musky, foetid fumes on me, its body so well greased
the skinny claw exploring . . . right in my trembling bed –
crafty, crawling fingers beneath my very head!

'He mustn't get that Smith Three-Eight,'[1] (to wrist with lanyard
    tied)
'and NOW I'm all entangled,' . . . my God, I could have CRIED!
Despairingly, a single shot at gleaming shade so fleet . . .
Just a gentle, fading drumming . . . of swift, elusive feet!

Next morning, bearer, smiling, 'SAHIB SHOOTING IN THE
    NIGHT?'
'Nothing much,' I said, bravado, 'JUST GAVE YOUR MATE
    A FRIGHT!'
'Oh, Sahib, no Sahib, me not making mates – NOT ME –
it was that RIGHT BLACK BASTARD, who live DOWN
    THERE, you see!'

                                                    August 1945

[1] ·38 revolver.

Angela Bolton

Bengal Summer

Egrets haunt the memory,
    Large snow-white birds with green stick legs
Whose delicate feathered crests
    Rise and fall like Geishas' fans.
Cormorants too abound,

Black as night, advertising their presence
With a powerful odour of fish
And a carpet of ivory bones.

The frangipani trees
Swoon in the heat, shedding waxen petals,
Fragrant as the silken saris
The high-caste women wear.
Sharp against the sky
A gibbet tree hangs with strange blossom,
The ragged frames of fruit-bats
Awaiting the coming of night.

May 1942

John Brookes

Officers and Gentlemen Down Under

We had as our platoon commander one
Lieutenant Teague. Nobody knew for sure,
but someone spread the rumour he had done
a bit of wrestling as an amateur.
In fact he was a funny sort of bloke
we had not rumbled yet. When he read out
the leave arrangements no-one put their spoke
in straight away until this bit about
the red light district being out of bounds
to other ranks till further notice. Then
from all three sections came the muttered sounds
of unmistakable frustration. When,
to ease the situation, 'Sarge' stepped in
and like all bloody NCO's rebuffed
the whole platoon concerning discipline
etcetera, some joker said 'Get stuffed!'
The sergeant yelled 'That man is on a charge!'
(not being certain who the bastard was)
and when somebody said 'Good on yer, Sarge!'

this Teague bloke took command again because
the matter looked like getting out of hand.
He brought us to attention 'Shun!', ordered
the corporals to shoulder arms and stand
behind the sergeant which no doubt deferred
to principles wherein to undermine
the NCO's in front of other ranks
was infra-dig, walked up and down each line
like on inspection, then came round the flanks
and took up a position facing us.
You could have heard a pin drop. First he took
his bush hat off and with punctilious
exactitude according to the book,
he placed it carefully upon the ground,
removed his fancy jacket and Sam Browne
and folded them, and then with a profound
deliberation bent and put them down
beside the hat, stood up erect and faced
the lot of us, and anyone could see
that he was lean and muscular. He paced
once forward then with calm authority
he said 'Forget the regulations for
the moment, where if any soldier strikes
an officer he'll get three years or more;
if any one of you brave bastards likes
to put his courage where his mouth is, just
step forward now and try it on. No names,
no pack-drill either. Nothing. Shit or bust!'
An opportunity for fun and games?
My bloody oath! But silence. No-one moved.
So HE had rumbled US! There was no need
for further comment. Mr Teague had proved
his point. And afterwards we all agreed
he was the sort of bloke a man could fight
the war with AND call sir. Too bloody right!

Louis Challoner

Tripoli in Spring

Over her wounds Winter was weeping yet
When first we saw the city of the Trees,
The tumbled roofs gaped to the weeping skies
And shattered walls with rain and blood were wet;
Blinded the windows stared on sullen seas
Grim as the fear in little children's eyes.
Scenes too intense for sorrow or regret
Cling to the passing soldier's memories –

The bells that rang at Zavia for the dead,
The Stukas[1] and the shelling at Kournine,
Bambinos by the wayside begging bread –
The hundred nameless horrors we have seen
Would darken victory, except for these
Gay wreaths of welcome in the flowering trees.

[1] German dive-bomber.

William Clarke

Looters

It seems they'd left the shop in such a hurry
The stock was still arranged upon the shelves,
So when the fellows got down from the lorry
The sergeant simply said to help ourselves

To cigarettes and matches, which we did,
Except that one guy with a conscience still
Took from his tattered wallet half a quid
And rang the change up on the battered till.

We bore with him, of course. We even joked
About his scruples being sadly wasted:
But it was quite some time before we smoked
And then how bitter the tobacco tasted.

African Soldiers

Surprised to see his order
Smartly carried out,
The NCO, still conscious
Of uniform and rank,
Began to realise
What Empires were about
And how the white man's gold
Got in the white man's bank.
All one needed was
The temerity to shout,
Back up, as it were,
By aeroplane and tank.

The Barracks

Once I wept, being a new recruit
In the old barracks on the edge of town,
Because I could not learn to drill and shoot;
But now I weep to see it half pulled down.

I would much rather they had cleared the space
Or finished building the new office block
Or Supermarket that will take its place;
It might have proved a salutary shock.

But I would have been spared this walking round
Looking at doors and windows gaping wide
And letting fancy shape for me the sound
Of all the life that dwindled here and died.

I would have quickly passed and quite forgot
Nor ever resurrected for re-trial
The old regret that roots me to this spot:
Half-truths are worse than a bare-faced denial.

Les Cleveland

Spring

Demolition: Liri Valley

The Allied Military Government
will pay damages, I said
and swung the axe.
It was good swinging that axe;
the six-foot lengths of oak
split clean at every smack.
Stop! yelled the priest,
barbarians make war on churches!
'The flock are cold
and your bloody old church is kaput'.
Antichrist! moaned the priest.
'*Scapare via*', I said,
'no priest tells us what to do'.
Bandits! he shouted
and went to look for the CO.
But first he cursed us
in medieval Latin doggerel
that crackled like dry bones
around our arrogant ears.

Before we left for the line
we chopped up every stick
in the mortuary, coffins first
then beams from the roof.
Pregnant Maria and family
had warm fires and food
while we caroused in their kitchen.
It was a good spring.

Lyn Cooper

Station Scene

'The two-fifteen is running late
and will arrive at three'
chants the announcer
tonelessly.

Thick railway teacups
gathering grime,
watery dishwash
for threepence a time,
but the whisky at two-and-six
is sublime.

Worried bowler-hatted men
on business bent,
war or no war,
cost plus ten-per-cent.
If there were no profits,
how could we pay the rent?

Khaki splashes all over the platform,
kit piled high,
sergeant-pilots brown of face,
keen of eye,
and a curly-headed sailor
kissing his girl goodbye.

'The two-fifteen is running late
and will arrive at three'
repeats the announcer
monotonously.

Joy Corfield

Soldiers' Pets

Those dogs
Scavenging the ruined shells of former homes,
Abandoned by dead or scattered families,
Bewildered and frightened.
Soldiers, grieved by their suffering,
Coax them out,
Smuggle them on advancing trucks,
Sharing their rations
And, maybe their affection.

But soldiers die, are wounded, posted away.
A lucky dog is adopted by a friend,
Then another, and another.
Most of them, like most of the women,
Fail to find a permanent home.

Lisbeth David

Sonnet before D-Day

What can we lay before thy mailed feet
Waiting wing-ready for the streaks of dawn?
What hymns, grey-mantled goddess of the fleet,
Sing we to swell the brazen battle horn?
Stern blades of steel that sightless Vulcan wrought
And arrows swifter than the swallow's wing,
Such gifts as these alas we would have brought
But well thou knowest they are not ours to bring.
And so we come, BELLONA; in our hands
These secret petals from the war-thorned rose,[1]
With hidden truths for him who understands
And all our hearts and happiness for those

Who if unskilled in cyphers still can read
Between each rosy line the words God Speed.

[1] Secret signals were typed on pink paper.

Erik de Mauny

Cairo: The Mokattam Hills

It was in mid-summer we started walking
Over the shale and flint of the Mokattam Hills,
The line of the escarpment flickered like a migraine
But the river was a cool and lovely dancer
Sleeping in the valley bed below.
We chose the agony and the field of stones.

A flight to the field of stones, the red-rimmed hills
Out from the choking boredom of the camp.
Fly-blown mess-rooms, roads like mad equations,
A history of half-thoughts and siestas
The endless solitude of men and tents
And jokes and cruel desires and mugs of tea.

Our eyes were pricked by sweat, our shoulders groaned
Under the red-hot burden of the sky.
The sky was endless, and the deceitful earth
Tore at our feet with dry, innumerable teeth.
A tower Napoleon built was our objective,
Our minds were haunted by the glaze of history.

But history was the valley and the people
And all the patient movements of the river,
History was the stuff that broke our efforts,
The sorrow of the city on the faces
Of girls, and beggars selling birds in cafés,
Eternally meaningful yet whose sense escaped.

We had the chaste, lone weapons of the young:
A sense of the irrelevance of death
And in the eye of love a world made whole.
The hills revealed no answer. I remember
Only the search, the blinding heat, not knowing
Which was more real, the dream, the sharpened dust.

Egypt 1942

Brian Dooley

Diego Suarez

I came here,
to this broken bench
by the whitened bones of a bandstand
in Diego Suarez,
to make a poem.
To make a poem about the stenches
twanging at the nostrils
as one walks with diminishing purpose
through the streets;
About the corrugated iron huts,
pinkly rusty,
The wooden never-quite finished
whitewashed shacks,
The rain-stained cream plaster
Of the Banque de Madagascar,
the cacti in the courtyard
and the bougainvillaea pouring from the wall;
The shuttered droning indifference
Of government buildings.

I came here
to this broken bench,
under the insect-dripping trees,
to make a poem

that would gather the heat of the sun
from the pavements,
the mosquitos whining,
and the cockerels crowing all the morning;
The pattern made by voices
speaking different languages;
And the largeness of small sounds
in empty streets.

But now that I am sitting here,
on this broken bench
in Diego Suarez,
I watch the sea
through this theatrical prop-room balustrade,
and listen to the waves,
no larger than ripples,
washing memories onto the beaches
of my mind.

Diego Suarez, July 1943

Keith Douglas

Egyptian Sentry, Corniche, Alexandria

Sweat lines the statue of a face
he has; he looks at the sea
and does not smell its animal smell
does not suspect the heaven or hell
in the mind of a passer-by,
sees the moon shining on a place

in the sea, leans on the railing, rests
a hot hand on the eared rifle muzzle
nodding to the monotone of his song
his tarbush with its khaki cover on.
There is no pain, no pleasure, life's no puzzle
but a standing, a leaning, a sleep between the coasts

of birth and dying. From Mother's shoulder
to crawling in the rich gutter, millionaire of smells
standing, leaning, at last with seizing limbs
into the gutter again, while the world swims
on stinks and noises past the filthy wall
and death lifts him to the bearer's shoulder.

The moon shines on the modern flats
where sentient lovers or rich couples
lie loving or sleeping after eating.
In the town the cafés and cabarets seating
gossipers, soldiers, drunkards, supple
women of the town, shut out the moon with slats.

Everywhere is a real or artificial race
of life, a struggle of everyone to be
master or mistress of some hour.
But of this no scent or sound reaches him there.
He leans and looks at the sea:
Sweat lines the statue of a face.

Olivia Fitzroy

The End of the Monsoon

I thought I should get used to all these things
But I am not, I am only getting tired of them.
Tired of the monotonous plain wood furniture
And the cane chairs
And the cane mats that trip you up
Oh and the dangling mosquito net
Like a twisted ghost or some monstrous cream cheese.
The rain goes on dripping, dripping,
The palms hang wet untidy heads
And look miserable.
Something has gone wrong somewhere.
This place is all wrong,

It is mad
Fantastic,
People were never meant to take life seriously among the palm
trees
Nor work to a routine,
Not these sort of people,
Not with me.
Nor were these aircraft ever meant to fly
And certainly not here.
Do not leave me.
Do not leave me alone.
Surround me with chatter and bright laughter,
Let me share it.
How otherwise could I keep sane?
It is only by never being left alone,
By never thinking or resting
That one can survive this madness
That has made an air station out of the jungle
And put me in it
Alone.
Do not leave me
you others.
If I want to scream
I shall not,
If I want to run
I shall not,
There is nowhere to run to
No one to scream at.
I will remain amongst you
And you shall not know.

En Route to Ceylon 1944: Seventh Day in Sickbay

I have lain here for so long now,
I am tired of watching cockroaches crawl on the green walls,
Of the barren hideosity of the room,
Redeemed, perhaps, by no pretence to be anything but what it is,
A ship's sickbay.
Oh but I am tired of the bare bunks,

Of the stripped grey mattresses,
Of the piled bamboo stretchers.
And it is so desperately hot.
Through the porthole is a disc of breathless Red Sea,
Ice melts in the water before you can drink it,
My mattress is on fire.
But if I shut my eyes, I can at least dream.
I can dream that I am back in an apple orchard.
It is Spring, warm but cool,
And I lie on my back in the long grass
Watching,
Through buds and pale leaves,
Far effortless vapour trails
And the nearer aerobatics of Seafires.[1]
There are birds everywhere,
Chaffinches, wrens, warblers
And an ugly black crow in the elm tree.
Nice people are round me,
Talking shop in low voices
And laughing,
And you are asleep on your back,
A half-eaten roll spread with bramble jelly in your hand.
Flying is over for the day
And there is all of the long evening . . .
I am brought back from such nonsense by a thermometer,
And, however hard I try,
I cannot help big tears which roll down my face
And drop with the sweat onto my pillow.

[1] Naval plane.

Roy Fuller

Troopship

Now the fish fly, the multiple skies display
Still more astounding patterns, the colours are
More brilliant than fluid paint, the grey more grey.

At dawn I saw a solitary star
Making a wake across the broken sea,
Against the heavens swayed a sable spar.

The hissing of the deep is silence, the
Only noise is our memories.

        O far
From our desires, at every torrid port,
Between the gem-hung velvet of the waves,
Our sires and grandsires in their green flesh start,
Bend skinny elbows, warn: 'We have no graves.
We passed this way, with good defended ill.
Our virtue perished, evil is prince there still.'

War Letters

The letters are shockingly real,
Like the personal belongings
Of someone recently dead.

The letters are permanent,
And written with our hands,
Which crease into their lines

And breathe, but are not so
Living as these letters
Our hands are seas apart;

A pair might cease to live
While the indestructible letter
Turned lies, flew to the other.

The letters express a love
We cannot realize:
Like a poignant glove

Surviving a well-known hand
They can outlast our bodies
And our love transcend.

Spring 1943

The skies contain still groves of silver clouds,
The land is low and level, and the buzzards
Rise from a dead and stiff hyena. Hazards
Of war and seas divide me from the crowds
Whose actions alone give numbers to the years;
But all my emotions in this savage place
This moment have a pale and hungry face:
The vision metropolitan appears.
And as I leave the crawling carcase, turning
Into the scrub, I think of rain upon
Factories and banks, the shoulders of a meeting:
And thoughts that always crouch in wait come burning –
Slim naked legs of fabulous and fleeting
Dancers, and rooms where everyone has gone.

Bernard Gutteridge

Mandalay

Jumping like shrimps, clusters of thin brown children
Quarter the road, chucking bully tins of water
At every giggling, shrieking son and daughter.
It is the Water Festival. But the older people
Lack laughter and energy to crush these crippling years;
Lassitude more expressive now than tears.

The main road has been cleared but no one
Can hide the houses. For each roof is disaster,
The gimcrack walls grey-scarred in coloured plaster.

Pantheons of whitewashed Buddhas gleam in sunshine,
Stolid among the weeds of a stonemason's garden
Touched brown on thighs where swaying seed-pods harden.

Half of a smashed temple contains the crumbling
Remains of another Buddha. Splintered gewgaws
Of gods and devils among which young whores
Ruled by a sharp dark pimp in a brown trilby
Wait the same custom Japs had provided there,
Too tired to coax to life, drabs with greasy hair.

Sometimes the river or trees break through the streets;
Fleshy dollops of mangoes, light green jade,
Hang among dark laurel-like leaves. In shade,
A yellow pi dog scuttles among the bones
Of a dead bullock, looks out timid and mean
Through a cage of ribs the sun burned clean.

The tinsel petalled waves of Bougainvillæa
Lunge purple and scarlet their abandoned heaviness
Over frail bamboo huts. A mincing dancer dances
Bizarre in asters, his face a godlike white,
Blessing the peace of water and the rain's pity
Among the dark cowed people of a ruined city.

Norman J. Higgerty

A Railway Siding in Italy

'Chuck us a fag Lofty' . . . I shouted . . .
across the railway goods truck
in which we had taken refuge.
   'I have to buy these fags' . . . he pouted. . . .
   Which he NEVER did . . . with luck.
It had RAINED now for TWO weeks. . . .
'Sod this country' . . . Lofty swore . . .
as water dripped . . . dripped . . . DRIPPED . . .

and a widening puddle creeps
towards him on the floor.
I drew once more on my cigarette . . .
but the glow made feeble cheer.
Lofty hugged himself . . . and shivered. . . .
    Then cursed the country . . . and the wet.
    but the WEATHER didn't HEAR.
I peered through a crack in the door
to a bomb-blast rubble.
God!! . . . I felt so miserable.
    And then Lofty began to snore . . .
    as he lay in a puddle.
How the hell can he sleep? . . . I wondered
Then MY eyes began to close . . .
and I joined him in oblivion.
    My hours of sleep were numbered . . .
    I startled from my doze.
'The trains MOVING Lofty' . . . I cried.
HE RE-CROSSED HIS FEET.
'I hope it goes on for EVER . . .
    SOD THE WAR' . . . he replied.
    I LAY DOWN . . . AND WENT BACK TO SLEEP.

                               1943

Sabotage

The Jeep hit another RUT . . .
I bounced high on my seat
and, somehow, remained
in contact with the bren gun straps.
    The shell-scarred road cut
    through a field of 'wheat' . . .
    flattened and battle stained
by the truck wheels and armoured tracks.

We bumped over a rise . . .
into a sea of mud.
Home of the 75th Medium,
whose guns we had come to inspect.

Barrels thrusting to the skies
like 'Pointers' smelling blood.
And as if to arrest the tedium
firing a ROUND of respect.

'Those guns should be "muzzled"' . . .
said A.S.M. Wall.
'How can I measure the wear
with all the barrels "red hot"?.'
   The Sergeant looked puzzled . . .
   'We ARE at war . . . I recall . . .
   but TWO guns over there . . .
have TODAY . . . NOT fired a shot'.

We crossed open terrain . . .
and behind a farmhouse ruin
stood . . . Two 25 pounder wrecks.
Massed produced by FACTORY BOSSES . . .
   UNABLE to take the strain
   they'd sent 'chunks' of metal spewing
   into BODIES . . . arms and necks.
NEAR-BY WERE BRITISH CROSSES.

Peter Hopkinson

Crash Dive

Shortly before D Day, our Part Two orders read,
'Get used to the Assault Boats or you're gonna wind up dead'
You know, those six man doughnut things; they're known as
   Spin or Sink
So we had to get familiar or we'd wind up in the drink.

They took us to a river just about a mile away
The Colonel called 'Battalion swimming team here. No delay.
Strip off and if some twit falls in, it's certain he can't swim.
Dive in and save his rifle and if possible, save him.'

Since I was in the swimming team, I said to my mate Dai,
'I could do with a dip, eh Taff?' and Taffy murmurs 'Aye.'
'You topple out the War Canoe and I'll dive in to save.
We'll have a dip and p'r'haps I'll get a gong for being brave.'

Halfway across, dramatic like, Dai gives a mighty yell.
Which of us hit the water first was difficult to tell
But like most other rivers this was only deep in flood
And half a foot of water covered two foot six of mud.

The pack that Dai was wearing saved him much of the distaste
But I hit water headfirst and went in down to my waist
And as I gained my feet and had a monumental swear,
The Colonel asked, 'What's happening? Speak up you. That ma[n]
there!'

I said, 'I'm up to there in shit. I'm covered in this goo!'
Then heard the bastard Adjutant say, 'Tell us something new.'
While Taffy cried, 'There goes your chance to get yourself [a]
gong.
The King would not come near you when you're covered wit[h]
that pong.'

I didn't get a medal, nor I didn't get a swim
But all praise to our Colonel and I must say this for him,
He gave me a huge tot of rum and said, 'Well done my friend!'
And then gave Taff a bollocking, which cheered me up no end[.]

Frederick Horn

Firewatching – Tank Sheds

A chill blue brilliance falls on blanket-buried men
Sleep-severed. Friendly reds have died
In this cold, killing light; faces of comrades gleam
Putrescent in the glare; a yellow rag
Lying with ration remnants on a broken box
Burns vivid as a flame. And I wake only.

This section of the museum harbours homicidal deities,
Haunch-squatting,
In carefully patterned perspectives of pussy-cat peace,
Grey, plump, and slumberous, claws withdrawn;
Models of domesticated feline rectitude,
Latent murderers, sunning themselves in this peculiar glare.
Rank after rank, affectionately named –
Matilda, Valentine, Churchill, General Grant –
Tank after Tank, diminishing in blue haze,
Dreaming of concrete-clangoured moan and roar
With which they split the day.

And all is stillness, silence,
Save for a far, faint snatch of turret-muffled song,
And high-pitched chink of metal
Hammer-struck, and friendly breathing sounds
And I wake only.

1943

Christmas Poem, Indicative of the Power of True Love to Overcome Intellectual Stultification due to Military Causes

The Gods that take aesthetic guys
And stand them in the rain,
Numbered and dressed in Khaki –
Oh, they atrophy the brain!

For to concentrate on Corot
Is impossible, I find,
When you've picquet on the morrow,
And his trees bemoan the wind.

You may contemplate Picasso
In the quietude of a room,
But equipment caked with Brasso
Is a still-life full of gloom.

And though Van Gogh's windswept cornfield
Gave one joy in days gone by,
When you're crawling through the fawn yield
It's but mud that's in your eye.

Though poets may have a music
Underneath a reading lamp,
T.S. Eliot is powerless
'Gainst the Waste Land of the camp.

Oh, cry out annihilation,
Cry the death of deathless prose!
For the safety of the nation
Means the freezing of my toes;

Banish pigment, song, and rhyme,
Banish beauty and the rose!
Forward, cold primaeval slime,
And a running of the nose.

So the masters of each art
Play at treachery, and slip
From the wheel-house of the mind,
Leaving woe to steer the ship.

Well then, Shakespeare, Milton, Donne,
Rembrandt, Whistler, John, – begone!
Base deserters, I'll endure
With my love to think upon!

1944

The writer was an artist.

Conscript

'Of course, it's done him worlds of good', they said,
'He's twice the man he was – a puny chap
he used to be, if you remember – always at books and that,

but since he joined
he's broadened out. They've made a man of him;
You wouldn't know him now'.

Deep-sunk in rain-soaked ditch, with weeds and filth
stopping his mouth, the soldier lies;
swollen and black, his face turns to the skies
in blank, unquestioning stare, his body, tight
and big as flood-drowned pig, lurches and sways,
to wind and water. Yes, he's broadened out –
he's twice the man he was; a pity, though,
his life should run, like bright oil down a gutter,
to implement some politician's brag.

His world went out
through that neat hole in temple, quickly and easily
as words from windy mouths. And loves unknown,
and skies unseen, and books unread,
forever lost, he's dead.

You wouldn't know him now.

December 1940

Robin Ivy

Near Monte Grande

Warm in the straw for the night!
After the ice of the mountain,
After the mule train, the river,
And positions the new troops took over.

Safe in the straw for the night!
Here in the home of the moment,
The sheltering home of the peasant.
Glad to be here for the night!

You sit there in the shadows
Watching us, strangers, soldiers:
You with your tender smiles
After the mud of the night.

You with your eyes shining!
Snow flies
Round the peak of the mountain
Where the new troops took over.
One dies
Huddled up in the snow
And a barrage flares up in the valley.

John Jarmain

Embarkation, 1942

In undetected trains we left our land
At evening secretly, from wayside stations.
None knew our place of parting; no pale hand
Waved as we went, not one friend said farewell.
But grouped on weed-grown platforms
Only a few officials holding watches
Noted the stealthy hour of our departing,
And, as we went, turned back to their hotel.

With blinds drawn down we left the things we know,
The simple fields, the homely ricks and yards;
Passed willows greyly bunching to the moon
And English towns. But in our blindfold train
Already those were far and long ago,
Stored quiet pictures which the mind must keep:
We saw them not. Instead we played at cards,
Or strangely dropped asleep.

Then in a callow dawn we stood in lines
Like foreigners on bare and unknown quays,
Till someone bravely into the hollow of waiting

Cast a timid wisp of song;
It moved along the lines of patient soldiers
Like a secret passed from mouth to mouth
And slowly gave us ease;
In our whispered singing courage was set free,
We were banded once more and strong.
So we sang as our ship set sail,
Sang our own songs, and leaning on the rail
Waved to the workmen on the slipping quay
And they again to us for fellowship.

Uys Krige

The Soldier

In this desolation
of an ashen world
that slowly becomes more fluid,
losing gradually its vague outlines
in a yet more ashen sky,
a single soldier
trudges alone
along the dusty desert track.

And Wajir Fort lies far, lies far
underneath the first pale star.

One soldier
alone
in this immensity
of sand, scrub and stone,
in this limitless dusk
draining the last light,
trudging, trudging out of sight
into the gathering gloom, the Ethiopian night.

And Wajir Fort
– only oasis in this nothingness, this lack
of human life, to which goes wandering each camel track;
where through the thorn-tree leaves at noon at times there is the
rustle of a breeze,
the throb of heat recedes a step, there comes a little coolness and a
little ease;
where there are palms that dipping to the moon glint with the
sheen of shells
and water, sweet clear water, at the bottom of cool shafts, deep in
the ancient wells:
sole outpost in this waste
where a man may find warm voices, lamplight, wine and bread to
taste –
lies far, lies far
underneath the first pale star.

He trudges through the dust
a single grey speck
against the greyer grey
of the domed heavens,
the level earth,
this limbo
where the day meets,
mingles with the night.

And Wajir Fort lies far, lies far
underneath the first pale star.

But while the soldier trudges
trudges on
his shadow, slowly, stretches out,
has slid over a broad lava patch, slipped
in among the thorn-trees.

The soldier's shadow
falls over the desert.

The soldier's shadow
falls over Africa.

Rigid and firm, black, stark in its threat
the soldier's shadow falls
wide over the world.

And Wajir Fort lies far, lies far
underneath the first pale star.

Louis Lawler

A Brown Bay Gelding called Hatrack, in 1940

There's comfort in thinking he had satisfactions –
Good oats gone to cream in his mouth,
And the cool water at dusk in the hard land,
The night and no flies on the horse lines,
No bitter hot wind from the South.

But Remounts for once got no sort of a bargain:
He'd no shine though you'd curry and comb
The day long; and he'd scars you could get fingers into,
Lop ears and ewe neck, a hogged tail –
We ought to have left him at home.

Requisitioned in England but somewhere unlikely,
At Christmas we took him to France –
Marseilles – and then Haifa with two thousand others,
To lines at Affuleh; from then
He never had much of a chance.

He'd no business, sure-footed, clambering rocks
Where dry hills look over to Hermon,
No call to break wind with such hopeless abandon
That Sunday the Padre was preaching
A decently open-air sermon.

When cavalry, mechanised, moved down to Egypt
From Sarafand, Hatrack was sold
To Levantines willing to work him in quarries
Until, just a bagful of bones,
He died long before he was old.

Was there that in his eye from the first time we saw him
Reproached us – the notion's absurd?
He was honest and ugly and very unlucky;
What happened was no one man's doing –
Maybe betrayal is not the word.

Military Hospital

The Matron, red-caped, terrible,
Inspects the ward; incredible
How tall she is – six foot – how stare
Those brown, protruberant eyes – beware,
Beware lest looming by your bed
It enter into her great head –
So huge she is, so weak you are –
To order you an enema.

Barrack Conversation

. . . And talk, traditional, moves on
To knocking shops in Paddington:
How, unbeknown to the parishioners
These all are owned by Church Commissioners;
How every Royal's a Freemason;
And then, in solemn diapason –
Each man the Royals' knowing critic –
How some of them were syphilitic;
How fucking Lady Astor said
In Parliament, all girls should dread
The men who had a sunburnt V

Below the throat, for venery
Had poxed the soldier oversea,
And girls at home must always be
Particularly careful not
To get the dose the soldier got . . .

John Manifold

Camouflage

Because the paint is not the spread of branches
But dies like a fish on the concrete in the sun's glare,
Leaving the mechanical outline bare
To fool only the plane's mechanical glances.

Because this bonhomie is a skinny false
Mask on the iron skeleton of constraint
And freedom in newsprint only a smear of paint
Across the ancient menace, 'Believe, or else . . .'

Therefore if I must choose I prefer to sing
The tommy-gun, the clean, functional thing,
The single-hander, deadly to the rigid line,
Good at a job it doesn't attempt to conceal.

Give me time only to teach this hate of mine
The patience and integrity of the steel.

Derek Martin

Petrol

Petrol for Shopping, Petrol for Fun
Petrol to Drive up the Street.
But when needing a car for a short Duty Run,

The Pilot relies on his feet.
For tho' to the Airman the honour is due
For bringing the Convoys to Port,
The gallons of Juice are for those chosen few
Whose standard of honour is fraught.

They wangle the coupons, misuse the forms
With details of journeys not done.
In their smart limousines with the loud Klaxon horns
They drive for the sake of the run.

Why not cut off the petrol, lay up the cars
Of the people who drive just for fun
And give to the Airmen who fly by the Stars
The Petrol that they've bravely won.

The Shirkers' Brigade

In trouble free towns set well in the West
Away from the rigours of war
Live a small class of people – a positive pest
Who idle and slack as before.
The men of the Shirkers' Brigade.

A select little army of well-to-do folks
With money to spend as they will
In similar patterns of black evening cloaks
They gorge and guzzle their fill.
For theirs is a life of laughter and fun
The peace and contentment it brings
Away from the dangers of airplane or gun
Away from the struggle – away from the Hun
The men of the Shirkers' Brigade.

Though battles be lost and countries laid low
For want of the weapons of war
The Shirkers' Brigade to their pleasures still go
The order is 'play – as before'
Not theirs is the toil of a good fighting man

In factory or airplane or tank
When the fighting began they scuttled and ran
Now they're lounging and scrounging as hard as they can
The men of the Shirkers' Brigade.

                              By what mystic right
The 'Shirkers' Brigade' is allowed.
'To each is accorded only his worth'
Should be our maxim today.

1941, Palace Hotel, Torquay

Geoffrey Matthews

Aubade 1940

Low behind Battersea power-station the dawn sags,
Dipping shafts of madder in a pearl pool.
Across the roofs a dogtail of smoke scampers and wags.

A sentry at the barracks renovates his nail
With bayonet-point, stamps hard to thaw his legs,
Wanting relief, and breakfast, and the mail.

Up from the shelters a new day returns.
Past crestfallen houses and bomb-shuffled slates
Workers kick shrapnel off the paving-stones.

And the whole city opens with a shout.
Hatred's more fierce the fiercer London burns.
The fires their last night's bombing lit are out.

In Bermondsey and Bow the fires are out; the water
That hissed with melted sugar, has been calmed.
And Peace sits spinning like Pohjola's daughter

Virginal on a rainbow. Suspended above doom
On stalks of hope, the barrage-balloons shine bright
Like a hundred shuttles waiting in the loom.

Names

The train stopped without reason half-a-mile from Greenock
After a haggard night,
And we threw open a window to stare out over the docks
Fringing the Forth of Clyde,

And sponged our faces with light and the new northern air,
Like fish opening our gills
To the lank flat smell of open water, and the careering
Racketing gulls.

Children in the town had soiled knees and torn jerseys,
And clamoured with bright eyes
For pence and badges from Dunkirk or Thermopylae.
For hard-hit factories

Too were ragged and blackened, windowless and livid,
Weakened as a child by war,
Sucked to the sinews by the incendiaries' vivid
Vampires of fire.

Bombs had broken the mains in the converted transit-camp,
And drinking in semi-darkness
Grimed and sweaty faces ringed the mess-room lamps,
Lit orange like stokers'.

But words sprang to life while the rim still shone
Undried on the mug:
Who are you, mate? Royal Armoured. *And you?* We're Marines.
Jesus. A mixed bag.

Where are we for? Iceland? Dakar? The Marshalls?
Well, mate, it won't be home.

Had any leave? Have we, luck. And we'll get the next spell
Likely, in kingdom come.

Up from the South, aren't you? Thought so, where from?
Eyes grew devout and blind.
Someone spoke a name, and learned to watch the same
Name on the tongue of his friend.

Sweet as a nut in the mouth the husk of Bermondsey,
And the prom at Scarborough
Spicy with strollers, and Minehead's blackberry-coloured sea,
Sheffield smoking like an altar

In the nave of the North, apple-cheeked Hereford
Where the stone-feathered
Cathedral squats like a broody hen over her orchards,
The starved and withered

Derricks of Jarrow, fattening to health on war,
The pubs in Birmingham
(Those nights with the boys!), coal pits on Tyne and Wear
With wheels turning and turning.

We were obsessed, tireless and fixed as stones,
Dizzy with the dozen letters
Spelling a birthplace, dead set against the German clowns
Who lived nowhere, or in unpronounceable towns,
Who crossed country after country, would just as soon write
letters.

May 1941

Modern Deceit

The farm where I work has ivy at the windows
And filaments of smoke climbing like convolvulus,
But there are no sties nor ploughhands there, the cattle are sham,
The nesting-boxes are a guard against gas.

Wire measures our distance like the ring on a girl's finger
That ropes off the flesh from the intractable spirit;

Frost whitens it with honey, rusty tins are pinned to it
With pebbles in, to sound gongs for an attack.

The huts are camouflaged to imitate labourers'
Cottages, new haycocks, barns, and one is a hothouse
Painted floury like steamed glass, with long blurred
Bines of tomato, and on the dome a slash of sun.

Sometimes at dawn the stilted fur-foot Lysanders.[1]
Stiff dragonflies, whirr down to plummet a message
Into the dew (gay rags flying like a shot mallard
Or a shuttlecock), and the resonant fighters drum

White in the blue, or an enormous bomber lugs its belly
Monstrously overhead, showing the charcoal underside
Borrowed from a butterfly, and the wee guns like cats' whiskers
Pricking the crystal tail. Busy in snow and thunder,

Soldiers cross hurrying the pleasant brick-dust courtyard;
Through visages the colour of canteen tea, city-white
They store their hopes, coddle a doom or a covenant;
None of us are quite what we seem.

In modern deceit it is fruitless even to guess
Which traitor among the blank troops and nippled officers
Will mob the enemy at the last moment, or refuse to shoot,
Or cap his bayonet with a bell of fuchsia.

May 1941

---

[1] RAF support plane used for dropping agents behind German lines.

Colin McIntyre

Linesman

The Bedouin cut the wire to tie his sheep
Closer to his father's tent, for lambing;
Stopped the smooth flow from Brigade HQ,

Hullo Able Baker Charlie Dog, Able Baker
Charlie?

Rude centuries had not stopped for War,
The seasonal birth knew no signal procedure,
And the historical lamb had nulled a calling
Stopgap chrystalline contact made by man,
Hating?

Desert-drift of sand obscured the ends
Of time, deliberately chronometred to Zero,
Only Private Green of the Hammersmith Palais
Came dustily along to establish communication,
Loving?

Eric A. Oxley

Morobe

The sandflies they attack you
And the mossies they ack-ack you,
And sing a little ditty in your ear.
They chuckle with elation
And attack you in formation,
Till you curse and swear and wipe away your tear.

With the comin' of the mornin',
Just another day is dawnin',
The same routine is on again once more,
The 'dengues'[1] buzz around you
And scream 'Ha-Ha' we've found you,
Then dive bomb you from twenty feet or more.

Then you think of dough you've wasted,
And beer that you have tasted,
With steak and eggs and schooners by the score.

When you think of fun you're missin'
Or some sheila you'd be kissin',
Boy, you wish they up and end this bloody war.

Morobe, New Guinea, 1943

---

[1] Mosquitoes that carry dengue fever.

George S. Richardson

Malayan Malady

Oh! how I hate this tropic land,
Its burning sun, its baking sand,
Its heavy, humid, sticky heat,
With odorous decay replete.
I hate the feathery coconut trees
Languidly drowsing in the breeze,
The frangipani's cloying smell
And all the other smells as well.

The tropic moonlight leaves me cold,
And all the myriad stars untold;
The rubber trees – unlovely whores
With obscene scars and running sores –
The black sumatra's sudden rain;
The tom-tom's maddening refrain;
In none of these, for me at least,
Appears the glamour of the East.

I hate the morning's blinding light,
I hate the suffocating night,
I hate the listless afternoons,
I hate the dark that comes too soon.
The amorous cheechak's[1] plaintive trill,
The cricket's serenading shrill,
The whining mossies round my net
Have failed to fascinate me yet.

I hate the khaki tunic drab,
The stupid spurs, the scarlet tab,
The portly blokes in naval rig
Who execute a stately jig,
The army subs. with weak moustache,
The RAF so short of cash,
The colonels' and the captains' wives,
The smug intrigue, the double lives.

The ceaseless quest for quick romance,
The shuffling mob at a Raffles' dance,
The curry tiffins, evening pahits,[2]
The blaring bands and shaded lights,
The futile trek from flick to hop,
The floorshows at the Cathay Top,
The shrivelled dames, the men obese,
From all of these I crave release . . .

Yes! how I hate this sunny clime,
The wanton waste of precious time,
The unmarked flight of heedless days,
Faces that vanish in a haze
Of half-forgotten memories dim,
The apathetic boredom grim,
In all its aspects, fair and bland,
By God! I hate this goddam land.

Lizard.
Drinks.

Singapore Soliloquies
The Service Man

no pubs.
only clubs
Tiger Beer
very queer
no dames
no fun and games
pay day
far away
knees brown
head down
can't think
have a drink
damned hot
'Mespot'[1]
VD
ROTB[2]
What a bore
Singapore

The Business Man

humid air
aching glare
tired feet
prickly heat
monsoon rains
smelly drains
errant wife
what a life!
memory going
paunch growing
lagi stengah[3]
oblivion bringer
hell's door
Singapore!

The Wife

amah lazy
husband crazy
children tiring
boy needs firing
supper date
God! I'm late
lover pressing
keep him guessing
spare tyre
hell's fire
girdle tight
have a pahit[4]
can't deny it
must diet
where's that syce?[5]
I've yelled twice
Lekas![6]
you silly ass!
Tidapore[7]
Singapore!

[1] A 'Dear John' letter.
[2] Roll on the boat.
[3] Another drink.
[4] Drink.
[5] Chauffeur.
[6] Quick!
[7] Tid 'apa – doesn't matter.

Epilogue

blue skies
time flies
heat haze
whisky daze
mossie stings
gin slings

velvet night
devil's delight
gin soaked
sin cloaked
sun drowned
hell bound
misbegotten
dead to the core
Singapore!

Peter Russell

Indian Soldiers Singing

I

On a narrow jungle path
in single file they march.
Not a word disturbs
the people of sun.
The silence of noonday doldrums seems death to me
where snake or the enemy lurks, where thirst tugs
and sweat drips smarting in the eyes without a pause.
I look not for a sign beyond the heat of day

but a thin strain quivers and rises in the sky
and fills all heaven in a mocking melody;
    sound falls loud and profound
    on tangled trees and steaming ground –
Lord Krishna, your soldiers in the jungle sing!

A soldier's voice climbs like a lark to sing,
    stays as a hawk hovering,
filling the whole world a moment with song,
    then falling, his earthly measure filled,
        his voice is still;
but the round sound of the rhythmic marching band

rolls through the mid-day miles –
Lord Krishna, singing
  all Brahmanda's praise.

II

O spirit of love and longing for my day
these sudden voices in the jungle raise
all my hope in to a height of joy
and utter understanding of their song;
these singing soldiers on this jungle path
are one in the world with me now.

Yet all endeavour has an end, and song
like momentary vision dies; it leaves me now
all in a soundless muse and wondering.

III

  Lord Krishna, soldiers die
    and singing has to cease!
  Lord Krishna, shall we sing again?
    O dying song is sorrowful!
    O stay the singing in our hearts!

You came, Lord Krishna, from the silent hills
  and followed us among the jungle trees;
    and shall you be, Lord Krishna,
      in the stone streets of London
        and on the lonely seas?

Lower Burma, July, 1945

F.G.H. Salusbury

(*Daily Herald* War Correspondent)

Epigram

The proprietor of a brothel in Benghazi was decorated by the Germans and the Italians, during the summer of 1942, for devotion to duty.

Benghazi, to its worthy pimp's delight,
Becomes the City of the Dreadful Knight:
And Axis chivalry records his name
Forever in its bawdy house of fame:
As for the ladies, it must be deplored
That lack of virtue is its own reward.

George Shepperson

Askari Song: Airdrop[1]

Amai,[2]
Amai,
The great Brown Bird on high:
Amai,
Amai,
Amai watu.[3]

Cruel the Zungus[4] and weird their ways –
But for their Brown Bird we have only praise,
Dropping white flowers of food from high,
A trail of stars along an empty sky.

We have known hunger, starvation in peace, till
Now, in war, near death, our bellies fill

Amai, let the Bird be very close at hand
When we are back in our Nyasaland.

Amai,
Amai,
The great Brown Bird on high:
Amai,
Amai,
Amai watu.

[1] Nyasaland African soldiers sang about everything – even about Dakotas supplying the forces in Burma with food.
[2] Mother (Nyanja language).
[3] Our mother.
[4] White men.

John Street

Junior Staff Officer

I write letters
    for my betters
to sign.

They decline
    to accept
the inept
    but retract
from the exact.

The result
    is occult
for those who chose
    to enquire
from the higher.

Frank Thompson

Hospital

Long corridor, white beds, red crosses,
Repair-shop for men: half-hearted light
From bosses in the ceiling fails to reach
The tedious tiled floor: without much feeling
They group in dressing-gowns around the doors
Eat pomegranates in a messy way,
Compare their gifts – 'Look at this camel, Bill –
Cost me three-hundred mils – real cedar-wood –
Bought it for Sue – wiv 'Nazareth' on its back' –
Swop thumb-smudged photographs – 'A Russian girl
–Met her in Tel Aviv – very nice too!' –
Mingle approval with sound criticism.
The boy who has lost a hand hangs on the wireless,
Shuffles his feet to music, gropes for rhythm.

Two interruptions – when a sister passes,
Her smooth gray calves like magnets quickly covered
With hungry glances and when laughter breaks
Light and uncertain from that room,
Where the officer with a bullet in his skull
Has lain for months, and is said to have recovered.

October 8 1941

Roger Venables

(Extract from) Bari

As cooling nights succeeded quiet days,
Fear with the dying fires began to sink,
Thinning away like smoke to evening haze.
Closed shops re-opened; laughing children ran
Once more about the street; men ceased to shrink
At unexpected sounds; and the slow stream
Of fugitives flowed back. The past began
To wear the semblance of an evil dream.

And then one night we heard the sirens sound
Their prelude to the guns, and make once more
Shoulders to hunch, jaw tremble, pulses bound
And searchlight beams to sweep, across the sky,
Converging where the tracer bullets tore
Through cloud in which we heard an engine's hum.
This died away; but horror did not die:
We longed for dawn through many nights to come.

But other engines, different blades now beat
Not air but water – ulcerous water strewn
With the decaying debris of defeat,
Which broke the surface as black blisters break;
Till the smooth lilac of late afternoon
Cloaked them, and evening dyed hulls rosy red,
Foam amethyst in the propellor's wake,
At whose dull beat the sea gave up its dead.

Down the worn sea steps, on a wet sea-slab
A naked half-man, gone from the waist up,
Lay stiff and cold and colourless and drab
– A grimy plaster cast on a damp floor.
But, in the flesh, round craters, each a cup,
As though the blood had all been drunk away.
A film of oil, too late to salve the sore,
Besmeared the surface of that lifeless clay.

This fragment which its own unfeeling kind
Had jettisoned, and the compassionate sea
Cast back for burial – and for me to find –
Had been itself a man one week ago.

Jo Westren

Brief Sanctuary

You from the guns
and I from tending
made love at an inn;
deep–dusked
in a narrow room
were freed from war,
from fear of our fear,
made of our smooth limbs
our sweet love
sanctuary
each for the other.

In the empty saloon
drank then cool wine
and sang as you
strummed the piano.
When time moved from us
and we must go,
we drew our glasses close
on the bare table,
their shadows one.
Look, we said,
they will stand here
together
when we have gone,
images of ourselves,
witnesses to our love.
As we left
you smiled at me
lifting the latch,
then the bombs came . . .

Behind the Screens

Meticulously
I dress your wound
knowing you cannot live.
In ten swift rivers
from my finger-tips
compassion runs
into your pale body
that is so hurt
it is no more
than the keeper
of your being.
Behind these screens,
soldier,
we two are steeped
in a peace deeper
than life gives,
you with closed eyes
and I moving quietly
as though you could wake,
all my senses aware
that your other self
is here,
waiting to begin
life without end.

Harold Withington

Nocturne (1943)

Have you ever seen a troop-deck, just before dawn break?
Well, if you've not be glad you've not –
There are hammocks slung haphazard in every sort of place,
And stepping out of one, stand on some squaddie's face!

The language that is common there would intimidate a shark,
And it flows out more copiously with the coming of the dark
As men well for'ard of the deck climb up in to their beds,
Then chaps right up the other end fall out and bang their heads.

Just listen to the music there as you step inside the doors,
'Tis nature's own cacaphony, gentle symphony of snores,
And what of the effluvium that no adjective can tell –
If you stand there long enough you will almost hear the smell!

'Arise, shine, oh slumbering ones!' hear the duty sergeant's cry
May the gods' curse fall upon him; in Glycol may he fry!
So every night before you sleep when you pray 'Forgive our sins
Just think of us who rest below – sardines without the tins'.

Anonymous

Sticking it out at the Cecil

Fighting the Nazis from Simla;
Fighting the Japs from Kashmir;
Exiled from England, we feel you should know
The way that we're taking it here.

Sticking it out at the Cecil,
Doing our bit for the war;
Going through hell at Maiden's Hotel,
Where they stop serving lunch after four.

Sticking it out at the Cecil
For the sake of the land we adore –
But pray do not worry, though continents shake,
Whatever may happen our morale won't break
(Provided that Wenger's don't run out of steak)
Doing our bit for the war.

Tightening our belts at Nirula's;
Taking it all on the chin:
For the sake of the nation we suffer privation –
Just look at the shortage of gin!
We frequently feel that in England, you don't know the straits
that we're in.

The way that we've cried at the newsreels we've seen!
They bring it so near, if you know what we mean –
And only eight bearers instead of sixteen!
Taking it all on the chin.

Roughing it at the Imperial;
Proving we're sound to the core –
We take BOR's for rides in our cars,
Which is (secretly) rather a bore.

Our women – God bless 'em – *their* pluck never fails,
Serving out Horlick's to combatant males,
Though the rust on the teaspoons has ruined their nails,
Doing their bit for the war.

Fighting for freedom in Simla, democracy's cause we defend,
With people to tea from SEAC – what curious people they send.

Fighting for freedom in Simla?
Yes, doing our share and much more.
We'd like to be back in our country so dear –
One day we'll return there, of that never fear –
When the Germans are not so exceedingly near
We'll be doing our bit for the war.

Anonymous: 'G.B.' [Crown Film Unit]

Secret Mission

I'm off on a secret Mission
   To somewhere I mustn't disclose;
I'm going with one electrician
   Whose identity nobody knows.

I've hidden my secret instructions
   Which someone who's nameless has sealed –
I'm working for Hush-Hush Productions
   On something which can't be revealed.

I've a mass of mysterious passes
   For places which aren't on the map;
The painters have blacked out my glasses
   And done something queer to my cap.

I've got an allowance from Fenner
   For standing the Xs a drink
And Miss Mason has added a tenner
   That's stamped in invisible ink.

I'm being collected by Wally
   But he'll find that I'm tricky to see
For I'm covered with camouflage holly
   And look like a tatty old tree.

I wish I could find what my trip is,
   I'm still very much in the dark,
But *the Studio knows* – from the chippies
   To the youngest Mole Richardson[1] spark!

July 1943

---

[1] Electricians hired from the firm Mole Richardson; in the know chippies/carpenters. BBC still uses MR.

3. Action on Land

Michael Armstrong

Monte Ceco (October 1944)

The frost strangles the earth
till it loses its sound-track
buried under the snow,
muffled in its efforts
where the soil is like steel
and the trees are but symbols of trees
rigid and hopeless.
The stars spatter the sky
with spurts of broken light;
all things are waiting
moonless and barren.

We are waiting
gripping the sleeping Bren
under the petrified hedgerow,
waiting apprehensive
but reassured by the Bren
as we peer down the white
shadowed slope of imagination.

Then a thunderclap in our ears,
Reality snaps imagination
and a German whisper deafens,
cold fingers grip the trigger
as boots crunch in the snow.

A report – a sobbing scream
(They have entered our minefield.)
For a moment I stand
in a field at home
startled by the terror
of a snared rabbit.

The moaning dies,
the tension slackens

and the Bren relaxes
on its bipod.
Someone laughs then mutters
'That'll teach em'.
And we echo
'Yes, that'll teach em.'

The mines lie silent
in the pale starlight
and the warm blood
sinks in the blotter of snow.

A man possessed, I dug
suspended on the edge
of that bare and heartless peak
wrapped in the ghastly dark
with bitter rain that spat
into my stinging face.
My numbed and battered hands
held the frantic pick
that struck the clanging rock
and splintered vicious sparks.
I clung to the pick shaft
as a stumbling child clings
to its mother's safe arms;
it was my hope that fought
against the stealthy dawn and death.

So I dug in a chaos
of mad and hideous sound
with a blind energy
driving my fevered brain.
Dug, dug, dug and still dug
a speck of straining life
on the vast and trampled slope.

The dawn came,
slinking at first amid
the misted spears of mountains
then showing in the open
lighting the dripping trees

and the deep scarred valleys,
revealing the swollen river,
shining on the vital road,
picking out crumpled houses
huddled like old women.

The guns screamed out once more.
That moment's peace was smashed
and I crouched in my trench
like a flat-eared rabbit
pressing close upon the grass.
Thick smears of aimless mist
slow-drifting like great ships
split the sunlit browns and golds
and thronged the brightest hills
a thankful heart had ever seen.

Sven Berlin

Burial Squad

Squad of soldiers
Under the tree
Come with your shovels
Bury these three.

Each in his trench
He himself made
Each in his gas-cape
Let him be laid.

Grave young men
Say no prayer –
Lift them up gently –
Bury them there.

Cheux, 1944

Jack Bevan

Italy. Evening on the Gun Position

The time is slack, the evening cocoa's up;
Cordite and cookhouse charge the evening air.
A mess-tin chinks. I take my metal cup
And pause from plotting on the gridded square.
A squeeze-box wheezes down on Number One,
And Sergeant Harris mutters to his crew
Of Alex. Florence, hot from her feast of sun,
Arno and Fiesole curtained from our view.
On Number Four they stagger up with shells
And stack each hundred pounds inside the pit
(Tonight's ten rounds an hour is theirs). The bells
Faintly intone for vespers and bats flit.
Sudden, with terrible bang and flash they start
Loosing them off at us from a forward slope,
Terrific the muzzle velocity, then depart
Over the ridge's rim. I emerge and hope
For 'Prepare to move'. I'd rather like to see
Florence before I join old Gunner Lea.

Allen Birks

The Strategic Retreat

Cursing the sodden clay beneath our feet,
We slip and stumble through the fields
Our fathers knew so many years ago.
Beyond that ridge the same old enemy still waits.
Slumped now in eerie silence, we stare
Into a shapeless night, where every whisper jars
On nerves, now stretched to breaking point.
Men, tense to each false alarm, clutch at their guns,
A quickening pulse betraying hidden fears,
As earth, convulsed, retches and writhes,

And angry flames consume the shadows.
Surprise complete, Confusion adds to disarray,
'Retire,' they whisper down the line,
'Retire and re-deploy. But don't re-treat.'
Those futile days! Relentlessly pursued by planes,
Spewing inevitable death along the roads,
The slaughtered refugees hampering our flight.
Hedgerows, bathed in a setting sun, drip red,
Hiding the earth that's stained a deeper hue
By all the dead.
Outpaced! Outmanned! Outgunned!
We struggle back towards the sea.
Once there perhaps we'll stand and fight.
It's not to be.
The little ships whisk us away into the night.

Bruce Castle

Midday Pause

There was a still, sad place in Italy,
where the sun shone and the dust rolled underfoot.
    Here we gathered like feckless tribesmen
and ate, laughed and talked of loot.

Beside us was a farmhouse, roofless and rank,
and beyond, a wrecked vineyard with young vines
    coming to life like small worms, trying
to grow to their accustomed long, neat lines.

We drank and cursed the sun's unnerving glare
and the stench of death around us. All we knew
    was then no one lived here, no one cared.
Give us our daily death and ration tin of stew.

We could have said 'Amen!' for the dead, God knows,
and saluted with respect the passing peasant glories.

But our prayers were laughs, our tears were oaths
and hope expressed in dirty stories.

Poor padre who would preach to us a text
fit only to echo in a suburban nave.
We had lost faith with the end of a friend,
bundled in a blanket into a shallow grave.

San Donato, July 1944

The Sentry

In the cool counter-point silence of the night
    I am a sentry, stupid and afraid.
Behind me, the wall and a small shrouded light,
    and I lean and think, and strain my sight
to see how life beyond is made.

If I leave my silly body and, in spirit, try
    to look at myself accoutred by the wall,
God, what a caricature of a man am I!
    Half boy, half armed, half wet, half dry –
This is the crummiest soldier of them all.

All for the noble art of sheer defence,
    we're in foreign lands, forlorn.
Minor heroes, with common bloody sense
    to keep our staid but stupid eminence.
For this we live on: for this we're born.

You soldier, with specs and weakling chin,
    trussed up in crude khaki, blanco and brass,
and a solid Tommy-gun to put your trust in –
    You wear the sad travesty of a willing grin
with the cold sweat of fear around your arse.

1945

Sounds

In the darkness there's terror in silence.
All sounds are friendly, familiar.
I have heard the muttering,
the monotonous muttering of men in their sleep.
Yes, and the watch-dog bark of the guns
and the tinkle of the discarded cartridge;
Then, always active, behind me, around me,
the ceaseless chattering of radio phones.

In the darkness ahead the deep silence
is chopped by the sounds of things known:
the door-knock drum-beat of Bren guns,
the raw rasp bitterness of Spandaus.[1]
From ahead come the shells – one, two – more?
the wail, wail of the shells which crash
crumbling on the crossroads,
and the bumble-bee anger of the splinter
that passed me as I lay there.

In the darkness there must be no silence;
all sounds are more friendly than none.
The mud subtly sucking at our boots,
we wait for the shrill protesting whine
of the ammo trucks, tired and heavy,
creeping and rolling in low gear,
the splutter of the D. R's[2] bike
and low pitched voices cursing splendidly.

In the darkness let noises gather.
Anything – everything, keep silence back!
I must hear the toy-shop ring of the D-five phone,
the 'sobbing sisters' sighing and dying
with the infantry, poor buggers, in front –
the splash of thick tea into my mug,
the helpless beating of my heart,
and someone singing badly, but gaily.

Villanuova, River Lamone, 1945

[1] German machine guns
[2] Despatch rider.

Les Cleveland

Italy 1945

Celebration! With champagne
Looted from smashed vineyards,
Truckloads, everything large-scale:
German prisoners, Italian refugees,
And remnants of uneasy battalions
Drink and dance with Europe.
All screech the Millenium!
Exultant, haunted, maimed.

A hungry girl prowling the lines
Snatches at casual hands granting
Scraps of bread and meat, and the
Bitter wine of her bare country:
She undresses, displays the lean,
Frail, brave body and stretches
Limply along the furrow
Where each in turn may enter.

Her pillowed dress receives her pay;
Note by note the girl drudges
At her sentence; the celebrants pant
Quick release into drunken darkness
Till screams, curses, howls of grief
Burst from her half-starved body
With scourging, frantic amplitude.
A thief stole what she earned.

Other darkness smoulders with other thefts,
Other threats from present-devoured past:
Screams came from the shattered mass of
A bombed frontline village,
Flamethrowers followed, then we attacked
To find no enemy, only bodies
And stinking, burning rags
Of women and children's lives.

The wounded strung on surgical wires
In wards like winter-bleached landscapes
Are racked on loving engines of repair
While pus drains daintily from deep wounds
And bone-scraping nightmare meticulously
Mangles them with blunt knives.
Some die after months
Cursing life.

Desperate rafts of communion
Follow shipwreck, but what illusions
Save from quagmires of care
Or frozen mountains of memory?
No ditch hides responsibility
And blame: no clotted earth cleans
Grovelling bodies of
Fear, sorrow, shame.

Autumn 1945
Sparagmos: Riccione

Soldiers sprawled in plough furrows
Beneath untended, crucified vines
Speculate, restless, wary:
Will more infantry reinforce Asian fronts?
Islands eat men,
Airlifts can whirl divisions like dust
Ten thousand miles to face
Death by furnace.

But timely Moloch reprieves pale
Fear of ordeal by tank, rocket,
Minefield and flame: the furnace explodes
To obliterate dread Japanese beach-heads,
But what price and purpose
Does our furtive salvation claim?
Chalky skeletons cram
New ash pits with guilt.

Bert Cole

Patrol

In the hour before sundown
Jokingly we blacked our faces.
'Gurkhas were out last night'.
The major says we look a fearsome bunch,
And are we happy in our task.
Our response gives the lie to our fears.
The spoonful of rum in our tea,
Just enough to drug the fly within.

Hearing encouraging words we leave,
Feeling apart from these
Who wish us luck – godspeed.

Grenade, rifle, bayonet, belt.

Though dark and a mile from them,
We bend double, hugging the dead ground,
As we move through a silence
Broken sporadically by chattering Spandaus.[1]
We halt, and though cold –
Soaked through with sweat, or is it rain.

Then, flares, sudden chandeliers
Lighting the moonscape dunes.
We reach the wire.
Once it's breached we are committed.
This is madness!
Then reality zooms in
Dotting the I's of our futility.
A squaddie tripped a mine,
The explosion took away his feet.
By noon that day he died.
Ill-fitted for battle,
The Burton's suit so lately discarded
For the semblance of soldiery.

[1] German machine guns.

John Cromer

Beyond the Wire

Beyond the wire
An awkward shadow dims the sand,
A twisted body,
Fallen with outstretched hand.

The last patrol
Returned, churning the night's quiet dust,
Leaving on the wire
A stain of blood to rust.

Six men went out
In search of new enemy mines;
Only five returned;
The sixth had found new lines.

As he crouched,
Dark in the pale light of the moon,
A sentry saw him,
Ready, alas, too soon.

The silent night
Leapt with the shock of rifle fire –
Now his body lies
Alone, beyond the wire.

D.E. Curtis

(Extract from) Death's Harvest

I am sitting by the tank, with the gunner named Frank
Corned beef and biscuits in our hands.
Sticking in my back, is the sharp edge of the trace
And our berets soaking wet to the bands.

Our bodies tired and numb, are wreathed in mud and scum
As we fill our gaping stomachs up with food . . . no time for tea

There's a sudden screaming sound, we flatten to the ground
Some lips begin to move in silent prayer.
More shells pass overhead, as we lay there in our dread
Almost too wet and miserable to care.
The shelling stops again, once more we curse the rain
That comes seeping into every niche and groove.
Oh God if it was fine! a shout comes up the line
'Pack up and get prepared to move'.
The start line reached at last, the infantry we've passed
This is it again there isn't any doubt.
A hidden eighty eight, spits out its flame of hate
The leading tank is hit, it stops, it's out.
The flames roar to the sky, and all that crew will die
No, one man's out and jumping to the ground.
Snipers' rifles crack, one hits him in the back
Whilst others chip the earth up all around.

The battle starts in earnest, like a roaring blazing furnace
As we meet the Jerry armour in the clash.
Deaths harvest reaped from mud, swamped in human blood

Crews bale out and roll, into a ditch, a trench, a hole
Cheating death which outstares them in the face.
With shattered flesh and limb, scorched and burning skin.
The padre crouching low, in order to bestow
The last rites on a man about to die.
How often has he cried, in a silent prayer inside
Dear Lord, oh God, Oh why.

A sudden silence, still, then again the lust to kill.

Around these green fields torn, death lies in every form
Broken mangled bodies that once were men.
A shapeless crumpled heap, some as though in sleep
Groups of four and five and sometimes ten.
We push on through the din, though our line is wearing thin
Then halt to hold more firm our hard won gains.

Quick, every red rimmed eye, is turned towards the sky
To catch the tell tale glint of hidden planes.

They come in one by one, with cannon bomb and gun
We dive beneath the tanks to dodge their fire.
The men on Ack Ack guns, fling off empty drums
They work like hell, too scared to seem to tire.
The planes come screaming down, and sometimes even drown
The remainder of the battle's din and roar.
When their devil's work is done, they climb up to the sun
And we feel a ghostly silence reign once more.

Where the battle rolled its tread, we gather up the dead
And lay them in the ground near where they fell.
Hat or helmet give the name, an officer his cane
We lay across the grave as well.
Whatever be its name, these forever will remain
Just Britain and the price men had to pay.

L.D. Deal

Refugees
(Road to La Rochelle, 1940)

The aspens shiver as the Summer breeze
Drifts softly through the avenue of trees.
It ruffles plodding peasant womens' skirts,
Plays over chests, and under open shirts,
And tousles bobbing curls that frame the child,
Who lolls at ease among the chattels piled.
The creaking farm cart trundles through the dust,
Wheels raising clouds, that settle like a crust
On sweating brow, and horse's steaming flank.
None see on high, the glint, the sudden bank,
Or hear the roar, the rattling coughing spit. –
Shocked silence; – then, as fiends from the Pit,
The wailing screams of souls, doomed, damned and lost,

Where crumpled dolls lie sprawling, careless tossed,
With skirts awry, and shirts mere bloody rags;
Yet still the horse plods on, the cart still drags,
The sun still shines; dust hangs still in the air,
And still, among the chattels, I see where
The curly head still lolls, with eyes that gaze
Unseeing at the aspen-filtered rays.

Erik de Mauny

Christmas in Italy, 1944

History will tell that here the battle swayed
Through pastel towns into beleaguered Lombardy,
How for a week and a day they held the river
And patrols went out while the shells flocked and sighed
Like express trains through the frightened air:
When resistance broke, they gave us up a town
Of ghosts and stones, and the blankly heartbreak stare
Of the voiceless houses there. History will tell
This tale of liberation, but be mute
Concerning the private dream, and the small despair,
All kindness gone, the near known faces fading
And courage, the loneliest virtue, for only friend
(Whose voice is silence). History will transmute
Into a cipher the General's brilliant raiding
Party that lies so quietly under the snow.

And in this desert of tanks and guns and men
Christmas has left its faint-as-feather print:
A small irony of yesterday's fairy lights.
Of tinselled trees, and children, and glowing fires
Pierces a moment's sombreness. And then
We forget again – it was such a long time ago.
Behind the iron and passionate headline years
And the national, sovereign grief (too deep for tears!):
The dupe of time at the iron frontier
Leaves his world of regret with a passport of grinning bone.

. . . within the holy silence of the snow.
'to sleep, perchance to dream!' as the Prince said.
But, waiting, I am not frightened of the silence.

Do not think then that I seek to assert:
These are impressions of a festive season
Conceived in a better time. No word of mine
Can change the mystery. So many have seen
The teacher dumbfounded, the lesson gone awry.
In dogma is danger: that I know, having been
Last night in the garden, under the darkened trees
When the bombs came; with the wounded child in my arms.

Keith Douglas

Enfidaville

In the church, fallen like dancers
lie the Virgin and Saint Thérèse
on little pillows of dust.
The detonations of the last few days
tore down the ornamental plasters,
shivered the hands of Christ.

The men and women who moved like candles
in and out of the houses and the streets
are all gone. The white houses are bare
black cages; no one is left to greet
the ghosts tugging at doorhandles,
opening doors that are not there.

Now the daylight coming in from the fields
like a labourer, tired and sad,
is peering among the wreckage, goes
past some corners as though with averted head,
not looking at the pain this town holds
Seeing no one move behind the windows.

But they are coming back; they begin to search
like ants among their débris, finding in it
a bed or a piano, and carrying it out.
Who would not love them at this minute?
I seem again to meet
the blue eyes of the images in the church.

Tunisia, 1943

'I Think I am Becoming a God'

The noble horse with courage in his eye
clean in the bone, looks up at a shellburst.
Away fly the images of the shires
but he puts the pipe back in his mouth.

Peter was unfortunately killed by an 88:
it took his leg away – he died in the ambulance.
When I saw him crawling he said:
'It's most unfair – they've shot my foot off.'

How can I live among this gentle
obsolescent breed of heroes, and not weep?
Unicorns, almost,
for they are fading into two legends
in which their stupidity and chivalry
are celebrated. Each, fool and hero, will be an immortal.

These plains were their cricket pitch
and in the mountains the tremendous drop fences
brought down some of the runners. Here
under the stones and earth they dispose themselves
in famous attitudes of unconcern.

Enfidaville, Tunisia, 1943

I.G. Fletcher

Morte d'Arthur

'So all day long the noise of battle roll'd
Among the mountains by the winter sea . . .'
And Arthur's forward section, man by man,
Had fallen in Tunisia about their Bren;
Smudged shadows lengthened out ahead of night
Emerging from behind the smoking crests;
And tired 'D' Company had lost its count
Of casualties. So, slowly, darkness came
And gave the heights to flames and tracer's sparks.
Alert patrols, wary of night-time's harms,
Crept out to kill the desperate, personal way.
Guns muttered distantly, guns unappeased.
Then grumbled Arthur as they tended him,
'These bastard legs have let me down at last!'
The gunfire answered him. And where his legs
Strong muscled, well reflexed, had been, a mash
Of splintered bone and blood-glued flesh was spread.
He spoke no more but took his time to die.
And Bill, his friend, picked up the photographs,
Threw two away, trampled and stained, and said
'I'll send these 'ome. Our Else'll want 'em back.'
Then orders came to make one more attack.

Bernard Gutteridge

The Puppets at the Winter Palace, Mongmit

The puppets that the children always left sprawling
With pink, branchlike legs and golden sneering faces –
Their dresses touched with fire – have bright, elaborate sequins.
One grows a cock's green head out of a man's body;
One screams in fear as he sees the black skies falling.

Under the charred nursery floor are: a splintered leg
With blue and silver foot; a hand; a thigh; torn trousers.
Before they left the children had set them brawling.

Now we with parachute cords get their thin legs dangling
Once more. After the time the enemy from the Monglong ranges
Had sent the children away, they lay and were bombed and
   burned.
Only five puppets entire among twisted and shattered bodies.
They hint with their crooked jumps at the string's wangling –
As they once more jerk into a mockery of the fascinating evenings
Before the nursery burned – when often the man with muscular
   fingers
Set them to dance for the children, who laughed at their foolish
   jangling.

Geoffrey Holloway

Rhine Jump, 1944

They dropped us on the guns, left us in a flaring
lurch of slipstream kicking like sprayed flies, –
till canopies shook sudden heads, inhaled, held
   a breath, –
alive again we slanted down,
too many, into their doomed sights.

One scrambled moment it was red, green,
dragging to the door of the Douglas then
falling through a monstrous aviary roof
on Guy Fawkes Night (only this was day)
into shrill scarifying glory . . .

then Germany, the Fatherland, a zooming field –
banged down on it, stood up among the chaos,
   with
fingers flopped like rubber gloves trying
to slap one's box, slough the afterbirth of chute,
make somehow that snatch of wood.

There were chutes already in those trees, caught:
battalion boys who'd dropped too late or
     drifted . . .
harness-ravelled, cocooned there –
like silkworms, moveless, wet . . .
so easy, against all that white.

But not so many resistive earthworms –
the early birds had seen to that.
Soon, it was rendezvous: a stodgy farm.
The war was folding: fight-thin.
Prisoners happened; columned, toneless.

Next day it was hearing tales again,
having a kip in a pigsty, scouting the dropping-
     zone
to get silk (knickers for sweethearts, wives);
maybe a green envelope, speculation
about leave, Japan.

Oh and a gun-pit by the way, an 88:
bodiless, nothing special, –
only the pro's interest in other's kit:
grey slacks for the use of, old, ersatz;
with a brown inside stripe: non-ersatz.

Refugees: Belgium, 1940

That month the weather launched into brilliance,
a blitz of sun, it was ridiculous.
We were waiting for final orders
when they started to leak down the road,
a bizarre May Day Procession:
kids in scooters, tethered goats,
carts so jerrybuilt with chattels they lurched.
Fur coated girls gnawed lumps of spud,
a woman dabbed her gutted eye with a hankie.

Two poilus[1] sat on a car roof.
And nuns came (maybe paratroops disguised).

Stukas[2] had been their nearest neighbours,
a machine-gunning, banshee sound-track
sealing off the impossible past.
Now all they could do was move;
anywhere, so it was further off.
But quite a few spoke: some good English,
some pidgin – like the whores we'd known in Lille.
And more than one wished us luck.

Later, in an empty house,
we found a blackbird, caged.
Left as a talisman perhaps, to say
this wasn't really happening.
Or, with the backhanded cruelty of the oppressed,
just left?
And we, did we let it go –
to fly with shrapnel, sing for worms?

Whatever, it would soon be phut.
Like Belgium, France.

[1] French soldiers.
[2] Dive-bombers.

The Vandals

Once more we had the wood surrounded. Where blue
house-smoke had trickled yelling we charged.
To stop, stupidly.
The door was wide, contemptuous.
Worse, there were no booby-traps.

They must have smelt our purpose, slipped the noose
last night, some cryptic way, –
their children briefed, their bright incredible
ikons wrapped against the roving moon.
We had the freedom of their indifference, now.

The halo-drifted air, the pressing text,
grace of absolution, communicable bread, –
all that we'd resolved to loot and lose,
vanished. For crucial nails
picture-marks, unfleshed stigmata; gaping, dry.

So here we sit, morose, leaderless,
picking at knife-handles, desperately cocked
for the next wind of its magnetic settling:
the stanchless chapel-cup of mad legend
still glintingly inviolate.

And with what end to such compulsive piracy?
Marches, marches, circling, waits . . .
storming of woods, abandoned houses . . .
further, barer, till starvation grips, we make
last bestial suppers of each other?

No. This wood's the last.
We must walk out individually, each
to stack and burn his weaponed heart.
Then beneath a white flag
of certain cloud, return in time
to build a silence, kneel, it seems.

Naked, we may surprise a saviour,
hold the stouped blood, be still.

Jim Hovell

A Change of Role

The Brigade's four regiments have had their tanks taken away,
a 'change of role' (as officially described)
greeted with real or feigned fury
by the more heroic or posturing of the officers
and viewed with their customary indifference

by the cynical NCO's and glum other ranks
who profess to not giving a fuck one way or the other.

Now, in place of their former monstrous machines,
they have these romantically named Buffaloes
which roar, rattle and clank on their broad tracks
along the battered and pitted roads,
across churned and muddy fields
and, improbably but effortlessly,
swim across rivers
into which, on exercises, they go boldly,
without a seond's thought or a moment's hesitation,
plop! plop! plop!
one after the other.
When they emerge on the other side
I am sure I have seen these enormous beasts
give themselves a fastidious little shake
to remove some of the water
before they go roaring, rattling and clanking away
to pre-determined destinations.

Eventually, the Brigade's erstwhile
tank commanders, drivers, wireless operators and gunners
will use their ingenious but vulnerable craft
to ferry troops across the Rhine
at various convenient points,
that is if the German Army
Micawber-like, hoping that something will turn up,
that everything, after all, may yet turn out for the best,
is still obstinately resisting
and has blown up the various bridges
with their accustomed Teutonic efficiency.

The Brigadier himself has an intense dislike for the Buffaloes.
But then he never much cared for the tanks either,
being, at heart, still a cavalryman
and dreaming dreams of magnificent and irrestible charges
sweeping thunderously across open country,
sunlight glinting on pennant-ed lances and flashing sabres
and illumining the familiar and venerated colours
borne proudly aloft by a smooth-cheeked, eager-eyed Ensign
riding at his side with practised and aristocratic ease.

Still, when the time comes, the Brigadier,
just like the heroic or posturing officers,
the cynical NCO's and glum troopers,
will, once again, do all that is expected of him
and, indeed, should it prove necessary,
more than reasonably might be expected.

33 Independent Armoured Brigade, Holland, 1945.

Robin Ivy

Before Battle

Girls dancing on the grapes
With eyes like flowers.

Wine that the next day sours.

Guitars by the sea.
Blue dreams in the bay.

Fear in the eyes of the day.

Evening by the lime trees
With scents in the dark.

Dawn lying cold in the heart.

John Jarmain

Tel–El–Eisa

Tel-El-Eisa is Jesus' hill,
Or so they say:
There the bitter guns were never still,

Throwing up yellow plumes of sand by day
And piercing the night across.
There the desert telephone's long lonely line expires,
Ends with a tangle of looping wires
And one last leaning cross.

El Alamein, 26 October 1942

Eric D. Jordan

Egypt: Up the blue

One way in and two ways out.
The giraffe Bofors broods
upon its murderous springs
while servants of the gun toss up
sand castles of artillery precedent.
And as we grave slit trenches,
tumbled bones and skulls
surmise a long forgotten
burial ground, to give us
decorous pause.
Ah well! Civilisation, on!
Move over, mates:
make room for the living.

Denis Knight

Infantryman at Santa Maria[1]

He will move no more from his left side to his right side,
His blood all over the place but mostly in the ditch.
Yet you can see at once he is not dead.
Now something happens in his eyes –
His boots push, and his shoulders twitch.

The trouble is, he can't quite get his head
Out of the universal puddle of his blood,
So waggles a finger of grey hand, instead.

1943

[1] In November 1943 this village above the Sangro river formed part of the German 'Winter Line'.

How Fare the Dead?

How fare the dead? In the green glade
Between two orchards the new wounded
Have been harvested in rows by a young German
MO of the same paleness as his silent patients.

But in this orchard their unquestioning comrades
Dead, look clear-eyed still, and china-cheeked
As dolls. Team-horses lie tangled in the wreck
Of Mark-Fours, trucks, half-trucks and Eighty-Eights.[1]

[1] In mid-August 1944 the greater part of the German seventh army, trapped between Falaise and Argentan in the Falaise 'Gap', was destroyed with exceptionally heavy loss of life.

H. G. Knight (N.Z.)

Christmas in Tobruk

There were six of us that Christmas
(And a war was on in the desert),
A wireless set, six Englishmen the crew;
By the truck two aerial masts,
Gaunt fingers, pointing skywards,
Strained eager at the guy-ropes,
Quivering.

Outside an angry wind,
Sand-laden,
Slashed the sage-clumps
To whirling eddies swirling through the night.
Within
An atmosphere of home, warmth, and light;
The pipes glowing,
Cans of beer (good honest English brew),
Carefully hoarded, ready for the day,
Eked out with captured cognac.
There was food, too –
No turkeys or plum-puddings,
But a biscuit potage
Bubbling on the Primus
Flavoured with apricot jam;
And the sandwiches – sardines from sunny Portugal,
Inevitable bully, persistent, omnipresent,
With cheddar from Australian grasslands
Thick spread on wholemeal biscuits;
And the nuts, too –
Valencian almonds,
Ripe, russet hazels insistently recalling
Rich autumn hedgerows at home.

And when we had feasted
And the mugs were drained,
Our voices lifted in song;
Time-honoured carols praising the wonder of Birth.
And soon we were deep in reminiscence.
Six schoolboys, muddy knees,
The smooth white snow,
Six piping voices shrilling through the crisping air
'While shepherds watched';
The door flung wide,
The cheery glow
Warm-spilt across the threshold,
The pennies clutched by eager, grimy hands –
'Merry Christmas, mum.'
And still outside an angry wind,

Sand-laden,
Slashed the sagey clumps.

There were times we regretted –
That innate yearning for home,
A loving mother, excited children, wondrous-eyed
At some new toy or bulging stocking,
The sweethearts, wives awaiting our return . . .
The little things we missed so much as well –

A cracking log fire, and the roasted chestnuts,
Parties, and the expectant mistletoe,
Clinking glasses,
Cinderella at Drury Lane . . .
Yes, there were moments we regretted!
But it was no time for repining.
So the cognac poured more freely,
As we toasted Benito[1] the donor,
And just as heartily cursed him,
For he it was who made us spend
That Christmas in Tobruk.

[1] Benito Mussolini.

Uys Krige

Before Sidi Rezegh

'– When
will the offensive start?
This time
we won't shove the horse before the cart,
will we?'
'– Not on your life! . . .'

Here
marooned among the sands,
lost for ever it seems

in these grey wastes (haunted by the wind, made spectral by the
    driving dust), dim now, dimmer than dreams,
where no sun shines, nothing gleams,
not even the truck's small squat mirror (still exposed contrary to
    the brigade major's express commands);
in the dead heart of this deadest of dead lands
where nothing, nothing stands
fast or fixed, erect in a horizontal world,
only the sand lifts,
only the sand drifts, shifts,
twirled
by the wind, swirled
by the wild wind's spasmodic eddies, hurled
forward ceaselessly
as over a bone-dry beach the powder of a myriad shells lashed by a
    gale sprung screaming from the sea;

here
in this desertland of wind, sand and dust and a great tank battle
    impending;
in whose vast vacant depths one hears at dawn under the falling
    dew, under a brilliant blood-red sky, no song of lark ascending;
and whose sole song – o soon, too soon! – will be the blast of the
    barrage, a blending
of the dive-bomber's swelling drone, its sudden screech as it
    swoops down, with the thunder of cannon: the crackle
of rapid rifle-fire with the Bofors' steady pounding, slow and
    deep, deliberate: the crazy cackle
of machine-guns spitting their spraying, splaying bullets with the
    reverberate never-ending
roar of the sixty-pounders, shrill whistle of shells, the whine, the
    scream, the crump of bombs descending;

here
somewhere,
nowhere
as in a limbo lost
where till to-day no human tracks have ever crossed,
the long convoy stands in the late afternoon, has somehow got
    stuck
– only the conversation never flags, back of the truck.

'– We loathe
the Ities, hate the Jerries' guts . . .'
'– Do we or don't we?' '– Like hell we don't!'
   '– But, Bill, but . . .' '– But me no buts!
I tell you hate is hard, hate is strong
and hate is very very long.'
'– So we'll make old Rommel chew the dust!'
'– Will we or won't we?'
'– Take an earful of this, young man, take an earful of this. Our
   motto is: Benghazi or bust!
Do you hear? Benghazi or bust,
Benghazi or bust . . .'

Is it the wind's monologue,
muffled, mournful?
Or the sands' patter
falling flatter, flatter
to a low halftone
insistent as the dry scraping of bone upon bone?
Or merely the men's idle chatter
as they stumble about the truck searching for bullybeef, groping
   among the boxes, tins, dixies with a dull clatter?

Who speaks?
What voices are these
rising above the wind's moan,
rising above the truckflaps' jerky drumming, the sands' dull
   drone,
that have as monotonous, as wearied a sound as the slow drip-
   drop of water on worn stone?
Whose voices are these
that though warm and human, chill to the very marrow-bone,
that though coarse and healthy, alive, leave the heart yet more
   forsaken, more forlorn, alone?

'– *Kry end, man, kry end! Skei uit!*' '– Yes, turn it up . . .'
   '– Piet's right, you're getting rattled, Ken . . .
What's biting you? The thought of death? But then death will
   come, *must* come, like measles to all men.
And once it's over and done with, well, you're damn dead and
   there's no more dying then!'
'– Bill, wait, wait! We'll go together! Bill, Bill . . .'

Who calls?
Who speaks?
Who in this half light stumbles
incessantly, again and again
as over rough broken ground? Who fumbles
with clumsy hands as under a leaden, sagging sky daylong the
    tentative rain?
Who in this dim drowned world of sense and thought mumbles
brokenly, back of my brain?

'– So man your gun and fight like fun and let the world go hang,
my son, and let the world go hang, go hang!
Roll on! Roll on, O bloody Death, and let's give the angels a
    bang!'

Are these human voices crying
their curses, oaths, questions, stubborn surmisings into the flying
wind, into the curdled opaqueness of the afternoon that is so
    slow, so long, so endless: Time itself, it seems, is dying,
running down as does the sand in the wind's huge hour-glasses?
    Or the wind sighing?

'– Pull finger, Piet! Pass me the jam . . . Thanks, that's
    wizard . . .'
'Damm! There's grit even in the jam tin . . .'
    '– Just listen to it! It's no blasted wind that, but a
    blizzard . . .'

The wind increases,
the dust, the voices
The men are talking, talking . . .

'– Say, Bill, wake up! You're not in Cairo any longer. Stop
    dreaming of that tart!
Tell me – yes, it's *me* wanting to know now – when's this ruddy
    offensive going to start?
Is this the wind's dialogue with the sand
as on some desolate strand
or just
dust muttering to dust?

Are these the pallid hands of dead men fluttering
out into a vague white tumult as of a thousand broken wings,
    cluttering
up speech and sound, the mind's poise and the desert's vast
    silences?
Are these the reedy voices of dead men muttering
of many murderous wars spawned by the fratricidal centuries
in short staccato phrases, loose scraps of talk, thin strands
of timeless speech seeping through the sands
where here among the crushed shells of snails, the grit, the stones
moulder the old bones
of those who through the ages came this long and cheerless way
now all, all ground into a common clay?

Are these the old voices
muted, meaningless,
long since bereft of sensuous lip or tongue, life's warming tides,
    the ebb and flow of breath,
muttering, muttering interminably of death
and deeper than dark death itself, that dim decay
which wears even the hard strong bone away?

Who speaks? Who questions? Who replies
in this classic and most modern wise?
Alexander's Macedonians? Rome's legionaries?
The Calif's dervishes? or the *vieux grognards* of Napoleon?
Auchinlek's Cockneys with more curses on their smiling lips than
    this desert track has ruts?
Or the tall, hard-accented 'happy warriors' of Jan Smuts?

 This time
we're strong enough to roll 'em up. Maybe, you say, maybe . . .
But aren't we?
This time
we'll drive straight on to Tripoli,
can't we?

This time
we can sling 'em slapbang into the sea . . .
can we – I say yes, we *can* – or can't we?'

Slowly, cumbersomely the long convoy stirs, wakes
to life again and like a sluggish monster that has been a long time
    sleeping, shakes
itself along its entire length, jerks, jolts once, twice, then
    churning up sand takes
to the main track, goes skeetering down the escarpment's
    crumbling slope with a grinding, screeching of brakes.

Now the voices die . . .
Now only the wind and the sand and the slipping, sliding wheels
    reply
and the heart
echoing this one cry
– the dumb, desiccated heart
sunk into its own silences, apart,
without pity, without pain,
drained even of its own despair –
rising to a single spate of sound
as the wheels grip, slip faster over the hard firm ground,
again and again, again:
When will the offensive start?
When will the offensive start?
WHEN
WILL
THE OFFENSIVE
START?

On the Libyan Border, November 194

J.A.K. Lamont

Unsung Hero

He has laboured in the steam of Burmese jungle stream,
    Digging shingle for the concrete of the bridges;
He has wrought with tar and sacking, that the Road
    might have its backing,
He has bored the holes and ironed out the ridges.

On his shoulder is a weal, born of hefting lumps of steel
For the Hamilton, the Stock-span, or the Bailey;
His supplies are poor and rare, and the undue wear and
    tear
Makes his boots and clothes more torn and tattered daily.

If your knowledge of the battle comes from hearing Bren
    guns rattle,
Or by wireless in the comfort of your home,
Please remember we have legions working in these tropic
    regions
Who can build as good a road as those of Rome.

When the Road has reached to Rangoon, and the traffic
    in the monsoon
Goes as swiftly as at other times of year,
Then we'll ask our fighting ranks for a quiet word of
    thanks
For the labours of the humble Pioneer.

26 April 1945

George Lewis

Our First Jerry

stone house as Command Post, by the road we dropped our kit,
When a shout came from the house 'Here is a Jerry!'
His booted feet were outside, his bloodied neck was hit;
The man was waxen, stiff and dead – very.

The knot of us just goggled, silently stood round,
So interesting, the first Boche that we'd seen.
But we've got to get This out of here and buried in the ground;
Yet who among us could be keen?

We knotted some signal wire and looped it round its feet
And, retiring, pulled, just in case it was a trap.
For those novelties of Jerry's he makes 'em very neat;
He loves to leave a booby in your lap.

On the Trigno, October 1943

Somhairle Macgill-eain (Sorley MacLean)

Gluaisibh Gu Deas

Deas, deas gu Bior Haicheim
tancan is gunnachan 'nan deann,
leum agus breab anns a' chridhe
agus seòrsa de mhire –
's e mhire-chatha a bh' ann –
mar a chualas anns an sgial,
gun fhios am b' e bh' ann a'bhriag.

Gabhail gu deas anns a' mhaduinn
an coinneamh an Africa Corps –
chan fhada gun ruig sinn na Frangaich
's gun cuir sinn stad air Roimeal mór!

Roimh mheadhon latha na sligean,
eoin ùr' annasach 'san speur;
cha d' ràinig sinn na Frangaich idir:
chuireadh grabadh grad 'nar réis.

Sorley MacLean

Move South

South, south to Bir Hacheim,
tanks and guns at high speed,
there was a jump and kick in the heart

and a kind of delight —
it was the battle joy —
as one heard in the tale,
not knowing if it was a lie.

Going South in the morning
to meet the Africa Corps —
we'll soon reach the French
and put a stop to big Rommel!

Before midday the shells,
novel birds in the sky;
we did not reach the French at all:
A quick stop was put to our race.

Orain á Bradhagair, á Calanais, 's ás an Rubha
le Calum MacLeòid
no Calum Cuddy á Calanais

El-Alamein

'Se nochd oidhche bhatail mhóir,
'S tha gach aon againn air dòigh,
Le 'rifle' 's biodag thruis nar dòrn
Air bruachan ciùin El-Alamein.

Tha'n t-anmoch nis ri tarraing dlùth,
Tha ghealach togail ceann 's na neuil,
'S tha balaich chalma ri cur cùrs
Air tulaich àrd El-Alamein.

'S beag mo chàil bhith 'n so an dràsd;
'S mór gum b'àill leam a bhith tàmh
An Eilean Leódhais le mo ghràdh
Fo sgàil Fir Bhréige Chalanais.

Ach sud am 'Fifty-first' an sàs,
Seòid na b'fheàrr cha deach gu blàr,
Na Sìphorts, 's Camronaich 's Earr-Ghaidheal
Cur smùid ast' le'n cuid bhiodagan.

Tha nise seachdain agus còrr
Bho chuir mi na rainn-s' air dòigh,
'S tha Rommel le chuid Africa Corp
Air ruaig air falbh bho Alamein.

Cha robh buaidh bha sud gun phrìs,
Phàigh sinn oirr' le fuil ar crìdh;
Tha sinn fàgail mìltean sìnt'
San uaigh an ùir El-Alamein.

Chan eil an so ach dùthaich thruagh,
Chan eil deoch innte na biadh;
'Bully Beef' is brioscaid chruaidh,
'Se sud am biadh tha againne.

Bu shuarach leam bhith greis gun bhiadh,
Greis gun thàmh is greis gun dìon,
Ach tart ro-mhór thug bhuam mo chiall
'S a dh'fhàg mi 'n diugh ri fannachadh.

Is ged tha teas na fàsaich mhóir
Ga mo phianadh 's ga mo leòn,
Na faighinn-s' innte làn mo bheòil
De dh'uisge fuar cha ghearaininn.

Nan robh agam 'n so an dràsd
Cothrom air an Tobair Bhàin
Chan fhàgainn i gum biodh i tràight'
Ged bhiodh innt' na gallanan.

Malcolm MacLeod

El-Alamein

Tonight is the night of the battle,
And each one of us is in good order,
With a rifle and bayonet gripped in our hands
On the line of El Alamein.

Evening is now drawing near;
The moon raises her head in the clouds,
And strong resolute men are setting a course
To the high mounds of Alamein.

Little my appetite to be here;
Now would I were resting
With my love in the Isle of Lewis
Underneath the shade of the Callanish Standing Stones.

But there's the 51st[1] into action,
Better lads never went into battle:
The Seaforths, Camerons and Argylls
Dashing them to pieces with their bayonets.

*   *   *

There is now a week and more
Since I put these verses together,
And Rommel with his Africa Crops
Is in flight from Alamein

That victory was not without price
Paid with the blood of our hearts;
We are leaving thousands prostrate
In graves in the dust of Alamein.

This is but poor country
Without food or drink of its own;
Bully beef² and hard biscuit,
That is the food we carry.

I am indifferent a while to being without food,
A while without rest or without shelter,
But the great thirst has taken my sense away,
Leaving me feebly fatigued.

And though the heat of the wide desert
Pain is wounding to me,
If I could only get a mouthful
Of cold water I would not complain.

But if I had here
One chance to get at the White Well[2]
I wouldn't leave her until she was dry
Though there are gallons upon gallons within her.

[1] 51st Highland Division.
[2] The well at home.

John Manifold

Defensive Position

Cupping her chin and lying there, the Bren
Watches us make her bed the way a queen
Might watch her slaves. The eyes of a machine,
Like those of certain women, now and then

Put an unsettling influence on men,
Making them suddenly feel how they are seen:
Full of too many purposes, hung between
Impulse and impulse like a child of ten.

The careless challenge, issued so offhanded,
Seems like to go unanswered by default –
A strong position, small but not commanded
By other heights, compels direct assault.

The gunner twitches, and unreprimanded
Eases two tensions, running home the bolt.

For the Mercenaries

Forget your regions for a Touareg country
That has no function but to floor a tent,
That has all roads for its indifferent entry
And borders always further on in front,

Forget and do your duty – to suppress
The young and evil for the old and rotten –
Do not make friends, do not expect, do not
Count on remembrance. We have had our lesson.

There is a lot to lose; we must be rid
Of our allegiance – we are not for either;
Of our experience – it will only wither;

Of sympathy – each instant takes its tithe.
Let your achievement be your only myth,
And kill with nothing but a craftsman's pride.

The Deserter

orn with all arms, he sought a separate peace,
esponsibilities loomed up like tanks,
nd since his manhood marked him of our ranks
e threw it off and scrambled for release.

is power of choice he thrust on the police
s if it burnt his hands; he gave the banks
is power to work; then he bestowed with thanks
is power to think on Viscount Candlegrease.

laiming the privileges of the dead
efore his time – the heart no blood runs through,
he undelighted hands, the rotting head –

Strong in his impotence he can safely view
The battlefield of men, and shake his head
And say, 'I know. But then what can I do?'

Geoffrey Matthews

Aubade 1944

Following headlights pierce the hollow cave
Where men cling, dazed as bats,
Lights bright like tigers, eyes that are cruel and have
Strength to assail the Dracula mystery.

Some lean on their rifles like an old witch on a stick,
Eyes greener than cats'.
Propped on the margin
Between devil and man, they turn to answer back
The light's inhuman gleam
With a more pitiless intensity.
Souls forfeit, at the eleventh hour
They plan to cheat the devil by a trick.

Having sucked her blood in a dream
Others are slow to quit the throat of the past.
But the past is a proud virgin,
Her cheeks grow white as chalk
Under their pursed lips and greedy stare.

A few, half-aware,
Sponge sleep out of their heads with randy talk,
Or straphang from the lorry's rafters and in dim little bursts
Of disobedience, light the forbidden cigarettes.

Flat as a negative in the developer
Emerge ruins, gaunt shops, torn rails,
Abrupt and apathetic after the night's bombardment.
A few searchlights still finger the clouds' braille

Fumbling without hope
Where bombers carved verses of judgment.
Perhaps those with an eye for prophecy would run
For the Swiss frontier,
Or lean on the crooked cross like a ship's tiller
To wrench the ship aside;
But they are cut off from the sun
By the vast shadow of the common will,
And like a rebel staring into the barrel of a gun
Sulky but afraid
They stare into the lights that probe and blind.
It is only the next lorry, following on behind.

February 1944

Derek W. McBride

Just a Morbid Thought

Bury the dead
Don't leave them lying,
the Sergeant said.
Its hard enough dying,
Without being left
On the ground where they fell.
Coldy bereft of their commands farewell.
Bury the dead
Its the least you can do,
The Sergeant said,
They'd do it for you.

Return to Kasserine[1]

The rocks are scarred not by rain,
but by the harsh sand, Wind blown,
Yet our fathers, Flanders trained,

None the less would feel at home,
For crater nudges crater once again
Though in this charred earth, no poppies bloom.

Tunisia 194.

[1] North Africa.

Charles McCausland

Gunsong at Alamein

Suns wheel in silence,
Dip and flatten on the desert's western rim.
Cassiopeia, the Great Bear and the dim Pole-star,
A huge and chimeless clock, turn our little time.
We are the subjects of the mad Khamsin,
Swept sandgrains eddied in the whirlwind
Passive as the old white snail-shells
Buried in sand that was limestone.

But also we impose our will:
In the cool morning the air vibrates,
Shells stream cleanly through the orchestrated air
As one by one
Our guns sing
In resilient steel baritone.

Egypt, 1942

L.A. McIntosh

Captain the Lord Lyell. V.C. Scots Guards

The umbered scabrous hills
Enfolded in their threadbare cloaks
The pockmarked nests of death.

Each crimson-flowered its fruit
Whose seeds devoured the skin
And bones and brain.

The slain, in tumbled rush,
Bestowed their ebbing blood
To thirsty sand and rock; – survivors crouched,
In numbing shock, to seek their nerve
And try their fear-filled flesh
Against the throbbing shock of piercing steel.

The gun, its muzzle sniffing, like a hound
From roving pack, for scent of foe,
Recoiled, recoiled again and threw its baying bark
Across the plain.
Its challenge there – to bar the way.

One man, one slender darkling man
Of noble breed, accepting this,
Contemptuous of personal pain
In crouching run with zig-zag step
Slid shadowless across the hazing soil
And forced the way. With bayonet and bomb
He broke the seal,
Through which his raging men
Destroyed the hold and opened wide
The gap into the German line.
The cost? Most certainly too dear.
A single life?
A dark-red ribboned life
Which bears his worldly work;
'For Valour'.

The Stranded Whale (Anzio)

It was all to be so very simple.

Across the sanded beach, into the dunes
We raced that winter's day,

Hell-bent for Rome, Berlin and Blighty.
No blasting flash, no stuttering guns
To bar our way. We found a ray
Of comfort in the pine woods;
Shelter from the rain
And there we stayed, a stranded whale,
And waited, waited, waited
And waited,

Until, in sudden flash of General's wit,
Awakening to what we were about,
He sent us off to force a way against
Some Herman Göring Grenadiers.
A piece of cake you might have said.
It was.
Until the Germans swept around
And forced us, hedgehog, in defence,
Then pushed us back. No Rome today.

Five months of bitter war
'Old Ted'[1] so close we heard him cough,
And he heard us (The old Somme War);
With bayonet, bomb and knife we held him back.
Nowhere to retreat. The sea
swelled right behind.
But Alban Hills they stood so close
And called us.

One storming day we broke the iron band.
But – the lads we left behind
Such brave and gallant men whom
Fractured mind and palsied hand
Bestowed them land within to rest.
And we who went away, still carry
In our secret hearts and in our
Yearnsome minds the love for men
Who never saw our shaking peace.

[1] Germans (short for the Italian, 'Tedesci').

William E. Morris

Strident Strada[1]
(Polish Armoured Brigade Moving Up To Cassino)

Cold 'strada' welcomed a bleak dawn sun silver fortresses
thundered from a nocturnal run as an armoured brigade
moved up to a battleground that was Cassino;
there was an earthly stamp about them, sweat glistened
in hairless shiny domes, dull unimaginative faces
lacking the twinkling eyes of gnomes;
thick pronounced features sensuous lips, stolid bodies
girthed to the hips, stocky soldiers strangely ill
at ease, far from a war-torn homeland trying hard to
release; infantrymen sat haunched 'neath lorrie's drab
canvas hood, there was bending room only, no one could
have stood; at convoy length tyres fled a swan song to
those days of dread, when tired feet in hob-nailed boots
had tread – crumbling skin of blistered heels had bled.
Hanging their heads in peaceful mood, their muzzles hooded
guns roll forward a menacing brood, rude reluctant hosts
lie supine, tin hats tilted all awry, gazing sombrely
at a cotton ball sky;
Sherman tanks squat ungainly creatures amble aimlessly
within the ranks of spaced and patterned convoy file,
leeches of mosquitos festooned themselves on flesh
as mesh of caterpillar tread traced its imprint in the
wave with every mile;
tranquil features had these men never fashioned for
war's bewildering ken, slow of mind as a slothful snail,
with crumbling soil of Italy ingrained 'neath broken
finger nail – unknown future twisted entrails with
torturing fear;
whole forenoon this convoy rumbled on, tidy strada
shuddered to its ceaseless beat – then strangely conglomerate
mass was gone – those who had watched shivered in stifling
heat.

'strada' highway or road; it was the Polish Corps who breached the stalemate of
Cassino when they took Monastery Hill, in the mist, May 1944.

Martin Moynihan

(*Extract from*) *South of Fort Herz, Burma*

Fort Herz is Burma's most northerly post. In this extract, prior to Slim
advance back into Burma over the Chindwin, a Frontier Force colum
(Lt. Col. Hugo commanding) is moving from Imphal through the h
country of the Nagas, to clear out any enemy up to the river.

At last, it comes in sight.
The long file halts. The few advance
And make their swift reconnaissance;
Locate – and chlorinate – the water
Beyond the village; choose a quarter

For one night's stay and site each post;
Then meet their not unwilling host,
The village headman. Soon the rest
Are summoned up and each addressed
To his own task: they dig the trench –
But first, each man makes speed to quench
His raging thirst, his bottle sinks
Into the pool, then lifts and drinks.

They dig the trenches round about,
Cut fire-lanes, put the sentries out,
Prepare, with so much space between
As may be, cookhouse and latrine,
Light fires, draw water, feed the mules
While order in confusion rules,
Then peace in order, aftermath
Of labour long, a standing bath.
Clean socks, a smoke, and last a stroll
A moment to possess one's soul
And view the village.

In a wood,
Bamboo within bamboo, it stood.
Though perched upon a rising mound

Its huts, too, rose above the ground.
Bamboo huts on bamboo stilts,
Their sole upholstery the quilts –
Red-woven, trimmed perhaps with beads –
Which serve both home and owner's needs:
A bedspread now and now the plaid
In which and which alone is clad
Their lord when, more from love of show
Than fear of shame, bedizened so,
He sallies forth. All else, from thatch
To platform or to doorway-hatch:
Furniture: mat, screen and trestle;
Utensils: calabash, pot, pestle;
Weapons, for chase or war: the pike,
The springe, the bow, the *panji's* spike;
Fuel and gear; the shoulder-pole,
Sunhat, sandals, tinder, coal –
One wood alone this bamboo
Whose very shoots when young and sweet
Serve the Naga for his meat.

Far otherwise the mule-borne fare
Of those whom war makes sojourn there
And gives to satisfy their hunger
The messes of an Indian *langar*:
Bannocks, baked in earthen stoves
And – spiced with chillies, saffron, cloves,
With onion, mint and cardomum,
And liquored with a tot of rum
Or else a tea-mug's steaming brew –
Pulse and vegetable stew.
Then, having eaten, drunk enough,
They take to *betel, pan* or snuff –
More likely, some rank cigarette –
The while each man's mosquito net –
For now the fading of the light
Warns them of their double fight
Their double foes: the Japanese
The deadlier anopheles –
Is rigged and strung. Each coats his skin

With cream, to each his mepacrine
Is doled, until, without ado,

All harken to the low 'Stand to'
And man each post and soon Grand Rounds
Inspects the small encampment's bounds
And as he moves, now near, now far,
With orderly and jemadar,
Darkling men hear low voices tell
That all is well, that all is well.
Then silence, immobility,
Till, flooding in, a soundless sea,
The night is on them, sentries drown
And low but clear is heard 'Stand down'.

    Except where watch the sentries keep
Quickly now all turn to sleep
And much they need it. With the day
They must up and far away –
Kasom Khulen, Kasom Khunou –
Stage by stage still pressing through.
Yet not for them their well-earned rest.
Unnumbered bugs and fleas molest,
Infest their slumbers. Where they doss
On bamboo matting there they toss.
One rises (sign for all to rise)
And to his larded skin applies
Not midge- alone but flea-repeller,
A pungent film of citronella.
The others follow. Down again,
Down they lie, but now new bane
Afflicts them: blocked at every pore
Sweat keeps them restless as before.
Uneasily the long night through
They strive to sleep till dawn's Stand-to
Relieves them and incoming day
Laves all the dregs of night away.

William G.R. Oates

Being Bombed in the Open

We are as people that are seen
Waiting in Harley Street front rooms
With paper-gripping dread of who
Shall next be called through the opening door.

Each plane above is a dentist's room,
Unseen through walls of night,
The opening of whose bomb-rack door
Is a butler's call to doom.

Who wouldn't grip now a seat's side-arms
And face the whirring drill
When his fingers dig in the sliding sand
As the line of the 'stick' crumps near
And not the slightest hope we'll hear
Some soothing voice declare –
'Now rinse away your fear'.

North Africa

On the Bombing of Monte Cassino

They did not choose to wash in blood
The lintels of this valley's door,
Who had to die in hell below
To save the hill-top shrine from war.

There is no sense in killing, nor
In war's unplanned destruction:
Nor was it sense that men should die
For heavenly obstruction.

Who shattered centuries in short time
No pride could find in perfect aim:

They only saw below that hill
Was man now crucified again.

Clerics that now condemn are those
Who Franco blessed, and never cried
For German bombs on small Basque towns,
Nor when the Abyssinians died.

Geoff Pearse

Retreat

They limp yet smile
Skins burned dark
No half men these
No black coats ink stained
But fighters war grimed
Grinning thumbs raised
Grinning caps tipped
No half men clerk men
But battle scarred men
Khaki sand dulled
They limp yet smile

Mersa Matruh 1942

Alan Rook

Tank

Lady of Solitude
and evasions!
Lady of Change with
a bellyful of nails,
taking your solitary
path through the desert

under naked stars.
Woman whose voice
is the flood of rivers,
with appetite in your
bitter breath –
Say old lady
what bull was it
punctured you
with the seed of
        death?

Malcolm N. Sharland

L.C.A.

(Landing Craft Assault. Written on landing in Italy in the year 1944)

Waiting,
Squatting beneath the gunwales contemplating
        What lay ahead unknown –
        Three rows of helmets –
And over all the moon looked down,
        Condescending, cold;
And, but for the engine's gentle throb –
        Inevitable, pulsing throb,
Quiet reigned, told
Of lessons remembered – (Sound,
They told us, carries far at sea by night) –
And so we suffered the cold
        And occasional spray, phosphorescent, white,
In silence the more profound,
        Waiting.

Was it smile or sneer on the moon's face?
The moon whose very presence had been sought
To aid us in our task, and grace

With light the blunderings of those who fought,
And why the fear? –
   The strange uneasiness the athlete feels and durst
   Not show; the fear of what? –
Our task was clear,
Co-ordinated, planned, rehearsed,
Every jot
   Thought out; and yet it lurked there hidden,
   Unbidden.

On the hard wet seats we crouched, cramped,
   Legs tucked under us, and damped
   With spray. The soft,
Relentless, throbbing engine driving
Us nearer the shore, depriving
Us of precious minutes, long minutes,
Dragging, lagging minutes. Oft
Our thoughts would stray,
Eager to be away
From the cold and chill of the present,
   To the pleasant
   Warmth and friendliness of home,
Of those who slept
Of those who kept
   Their love for us till we should come.
We thought of them as we sat there,
We fought with time as we sat there
   Waiting.

'Get ready' –
A whisper down the craft –
We tried to gather our thoughts and steady
Our hammering hearts, and concentrate.
In stark reality we stood and almost laughed
As we stretched our cold wet limbs. No hate
   We bore for those we must overrun –
No fear now, as the purring engine ceased,
But relief that our hardest fight was won,
Relief that can only come from pain released
   Or Waiting.

Cassino

Stone by stone they lifted it
  And carried it away;
In basketfuls they shifted it
  A dust-heap where it lay;
With loving care they sifted it
  Their Home, of yesterday.

A. Sinclair

Relics of War

In this valley there was fought a battle.
That was some months ago.
But still the stench of death pervades the hollows,
Odour of decayed matter wrinkles the nostrils;
The earth is pocked with shell-holes
Littered with mud-grimed carcases of mules
Twisted and swol'n poor leather bags of guts.

More fortunate are the bodies of men;
They have had earth thrown o'er their shrivelled forms
True, rain has washed their covering somewhat thin
And here a leg and there an arm protrude;
And that hair plastered boulder was a skull.
But time and heat and rot will decompose
These cast-off remnants of the spirit's case;
And Nature will forget and fling their dust
To fertilize the vineyards on the slopes,
Those gnarled black roots
Soon to take blossom for a vintage year.
'A costly wine', they'll say, 'is that of '44'.
Here a wrecked tank leans perilously awry, –
With drooping gun submissive to the ground
And smashed-in turret.
The German cross is growing faint in rust
And on the ground lie helmets, mess tins, shells,

Heaps of slim, stream-lined, reddened mortar bombs,
And a limp letter
Sodden,
Trampled underfoot,
Addressed to Marlene in the Austrian hills.

Charles Smith

Road Raid

Quietly dawn comes after a pregnant night
of turmoil on the road,
retreat.
Trucks flaming from the lightning Stuka raid
that leaves Larissa sharp in memory.
A sheet
of blurred impressions: transport head to tail
nightlong, climbing the inky mountain road,
a wounded man vainly begging relief,
some heartless swine
has stolen our stolen brandy so he lies
jolting with only staring in his eyes.
So dawn breaks quietly, the column jammed
for mile on mile along the pass and we
wait on this rough plateau for what may be.
Then,
creeping against the gold fleck of the sky,
a dark speck growing to an insect shape,
old Spider-legs again (Henschel to you)
out recceing. The wickedly packed road
sends him about hotfoot the way he came.
'Off to get his cobbers' someone says,
and ack-ack[1] never shot so bloody true.
Presently
comes word the road is clearing so the line
prepares to move, truck engines tick again.
Then distantly a wheeling flock of birds
bat winged and strange: a hostile whine

betrays the engine – Junkers.[2] Every eye
looks to the still blocked road, back to the sky.
Some optimist opines 'They're going past –'
time waits, then suddenly the leader swings
to line his target, and we antlike things
are swift with earthbound scurryings.
'Old Buck! The stretcher! Get him on the ground!'
One to each corner quickly out he comes,
only half sensing 'they' are here again
who last night brought his pain.
'Down with him here!' A shallow trench enough
but deep where any holes at all are few.
'Scatter, they're peeling off'. A winger's try
was never faster. Flatten at the cue
of bomb and bomber screaming from the sky.
Crackle of bullets. Crash. (Christ, that was close!)
Scream catching scream, each on the other's heels.
Bombs wipe even a soldier's thinking clean.
(Can human back be broad as my back feels?)
Still closer. This is It – the scream cut short –
(Oh well, for thirty years of damn good life)
A crowning crash. How tortured eardrums flap.
Blown stones come rattling on the good old tin
and sticking in its camouflaging mesh.
And soon, close by, quietly piercing the din,
slow sobbing out of broken flesh.

Greece, 1941, between Larissa and Lamia

Anti-aircraft.
German Plane.

Richard Spender

Parachute Battalion

Platoon by platoon in formation proudly,
Plane upon plane from the valley's mouth,
Piercing, with their black-winged squadrons
In powerful flight, the dark hill.

To the wild pipe's bidding
Last night they danced reel and jig,
Glad for the light in each other's eyes;
To the wild pipe's bidding
They have sprung at the unknown shadows of the North.

In what lowering mountain range
Will they make their stand and fight,
And which strange-named stream shall be their bed,
Lying quietly together, strong in death?

To-day some silent valley of Tunisia
Shall tremble at their stroke from sky unsheathed,
And, with the night, perhaps some God looking down
With dull, cold eyes, by the near stars, will see
One lonely, grim battalion cut its way
Through agony and death to fame's high crown,
And wonderingly watch the friendless strength
Of little men, who die that the great Truths shall live.

Tunisian Patrol

The Night lies with her body crookedly flung
In agony across the sharp hills;
By the fitful moon her nostrils are taut, quivering;
She is tensed in cold sweat and lonely fear,
Giving sudden birth in dark, sly, trodden places
To her unlawful issue, blind, hideous Death.

Across the pain-jerked body of the Night
We must go, taking the new-born Death in arms,
Holding it close, warmly to us, as our own,
Giving it new games to play, new toys to tear apart.

L.E. Symes

Italy 1944

High in the rain swept Apennines
Picking their way with awkward gait
The Company mules bear to the rear
Their groundsheet shrouded human freight.
They have covered each face so we cannot name
The silent figures bobbing by.
Better for us we do not know
Who rides beneath the weeping sky.

Frank Thompson

Mildly Homeric about Modern War

Helpless. Helpless is one who watches
An attack from air on desert-faring men.
Relentlessly like hawks, like bees in swarm
With steady droning from the morning sky
The black-winged planes draw on, wheel overhead,
Wheel and descend: crash after crash resounds
Dust fountains the horizon: Those who watch
Guess at the pain and death among their friends
Scan the whole sky, wait for the sun to set.

8 December 1941

Andrew Todd

Into the Line

The desert's glazed with the moonlight glow
All the stars are out for this fateful show

And the men string out in a long black row
The Jocks going into the line.

The only sounds are the muffled tread
The whispered order urgently said
The dislodged stone at the *wadi*[1] head
The Jocks going into the line.

The fronds that swayed on the palms by day
Are rigidly still, their arms aspray
Dim black streaks on silver grey
The Jocks going into the line.

The Boche is cursed under laboured breath
The buggers are promised a ling'ring death
Shell smoke hangs like a ghostly wraith
The Jocks going into the line.

What fate's in store on that ridge ahead
Will the welcome be a hail of lead
'Why the hell can't we stay in bed?'
The Jocks going into the line.

The fitful light of a dropping flare
A sentry's 'Halt' and 'Who Goes There?'
A bayonet gleams in the sultry glare
The Jocks going into the line.

Stillness reigns, the stumbling row
Is sited, ready for the foe
Keen eyes search dawn's breaking glow
The Jocks have gone into the line.

February 1943, East of Marsan

[1] dried valley.

Victor West

Crete 20th May, 1941

Our brakes scream to a halt.
Before the jolt in one, common mass of volition
we leap from the van
to sprawl together in the dust,
men and guns mixed in one pile.
Staccato racket of automatic by my ear,
harsh and real, chattering into my dreams,
shatters our own windscreen into a shower
of flashing slivers, grotesque, jagged star.
One second before, we had been speeding
to relieve hard-pressed 'D' Company
when suddenly Chick's Tommy gun roars,
battering us with percussion . . . Ambushed!
A figure jack-knifes in the white road . . .
'Parachutists!' Ahead, a crashed glider
with another in unfamiliar uniform,
spreading a bloodred flag across the sunken lane . . .
Surprised, he runs to a ditch, a streak of blue
from an Impressionist's palette . . . so much
in that instant's flash. Scythed by Spandau
swaithe dull sheen of cactus falls past
the dappled shadows where I lie watching for him
to re-appear. Round the trigger my finger tenses
taking first pressure . . . Curiosity would conquer.
Here, a look *will* kill. Framed by dark foresight
a white face bobs . . . is gone.
I fire miss eject in one movement – Only the ricochet
screams on its banshee way . . . Up he bobs again,
human snap target on the range of reality. I fire,
this time speeding it like an arrow
from the tensed bow of my whole being.
He falls with the dull sheen I had marked
of the aloe frond-yellow cloud of dust rises.
Bereft of an opponent, I find myself alone

undersea with green light flooding through young vines
sharing sudden, angry twinge of grief.
Quiet reasserts. Where's everybody gone? . . .

Phillip Whitfield

Casualties, Normandy, 1944

One

Clouds are failing in the sunset,
feathers in a quiet sky,
above the khaki and the camouflage
and the sun like brass on the trees
and across the far hills;
slate and steel and brimstone
stretching vermilion
at the edge of the world.

They lie in this pastoral
habitation of evening,
the dead soldiers.
A bearable beauty alights
on the foreign effects,
the last sun-rays
glancing their tangents
off crab-apple and walnut trees.

Up and down the stream goes
a smudge of gnats,
nettle seeds, the skittering
of brilliant insects;
a guilty donkey
with depressed ears,
snapping at passing thistles,
teased by staccato French
and the French flies.

Clouds move and melt
till the delicate cirrus is a kiss
or a word, day gives to darkness
the gaping cottages,
the fluted fields.

Two

Stretched out under canvas
they lie in the shadows,
not smoking nor talking
but getting cool in the rough wool,
their wounds unhealed for ever
and the pain elsewhere.
Slowly their singleness is reaffirmed.

Babies and girls often
look beautiful being dead
and over the old and sick,
clutching their bedclothes closer,
sinks a common expression
almost of gratitude.

Yet which is better: to go down
with these unlucky soldiers,
unnatural heroes, clowns;
or to have once been young
and end in failure, pious attitude,
bent like a question?

Here I drag on behind an army,
no hero nor a likely one for dying,
and yet I hope I too,
with such weapons as I have,
may spend eventual breath
in some such makeshift place
where battle rumbles on.

Donald Williamson

To any Batman

You were there when the battle raged,
You gave me tea, and we talked of dogs
In England, and the prisoners caged
In the house at the foot of the hill.

You said that all was well from what you heard
From a visitor on the right.
You gave me water, and a bed prepared
That in a lull, I might rest in the night.

Your thoughts I know, were of days
With a gun of a different kind,
Chasing game in the morning haze
Where a pale sun tardily shined.
I'll remember the sight of your arm upraised,
Though the flash of the guns made me blind.

Peter Young

Recce in Bocage Country[1]

Pinned down in the sunken lane we waited
pressed into the hedgerow's shadows
and carefully encoded our location
reporting back to base our sit rep
hull-down in dead ground
in range enemy S P, mortar and machinegun fire
with their O P 2 kilometres distant in church with spire.

For the landscape of war is different
admitting no valleys but re-entrants
no hollows but dead ground
churches neither gothic nor romanesque only with spire or tower;
but not lying there or sitting on our arses
we kept our head down in radio silence
dozing in the drone of bees and flies and scent of grasses.

Until we heard the beat of feet
and the soft lilt of breathy whistling
and saw the laddie with his shepherd's thumbstick
lead his dust-caked platoon snaking up the side of the lane
and halt only long enough for us to explain,
'From here you're out in the open',
and mark his map with the O P in the church with spire
and he never spoke, just nodded,
and walked on out into the searing sun
and the busy stitching of steel needles from the machinegun
with his platoon plodding behind at an easy walk
across the line of the mortar's crunching stalk.

The whistling stopped
branches broke, the lane gave a groan
and the hedgerows returned to their buzzing drone
until there came the jagged detonation of grenades
and a bren gun spoke.
Uncertain, we waited,
as boots rang out coming down the hill.

Seven came back
and threw themselves down in the shade.
'What're ye waitin' for?' one demanded.
'We've cleaned 'em out.'

So we climbed in and drove up the lane
past the laddie with his thumbstick lying under a cloud of flies
and the rest of the platoon sprawled untidily
where they'd been dropped.
'Guts,' I said. 'He must have known.'
And the reply came, flatly, 'Guts, either theirs or our own'.

For the language of war is different
and admits to no words for bravery
courage or victory
in friend or rival –
only survival.

1944

---

[1] The bocage is the rolling and wooded countryside of lower Normandy, with endless hidden lanes and concealed tracks.

4. Action: Sea/Air

Anderton and Fieldsend

Ode to a Blackout

Which of their Lordships could have devised
Knicks of such a colossal size
That even when the wind blows free
And lifts a skirt above the knee
The most sensuous sailor will hardly stare
At such passion-damping underwear.

Now when a Wren climbs from a boat
All the crew stand by to gloat
Hoping against hope that they may see
Something a little more than knee
But their hopes are soon rejected
So well are the legs of Wrens protected

Now in war time when morals slip now and then
Tis well to protect our little Wren
For if she wore some delicate panty
The protection of which was only scanty
Half of the girls would soon be mothers
And I wouldn't give very much hope for the others
Yet blackouts why do you hide from me
So much that I should like to see.

June, 1944

Geoffrey Ball

On being measured in wartime for a naval Midshipman's uniform, February 1944

'Never been fitted before Sir
always ready-made – off the peg?
Weaver to Wearer or Fifty Shilling Tailors?
Well I never Sir . . . you're the first I've met.'

Deadened by the white-tacked canvas
the words hang in the models
of their future youthful masters
headless, armless, soulless corpses
suspended navy blue and gold
awaiting life or renewed death.

Yellowed life in shuttered cubicles
where tungsten lamps augment
the north sky light
or blue-white open watery death
where cut and fit are tailored
by a sea and swell.

'I'll be with you in moment Sir
a lovely cloth that is you know
it comes complete with tabs and buttons
. . . Were you far away Sir? Just feel the nap.'
                    HMS King Alfred, Hove, Sussex

Red Watch[1]

From 'derry[2] out to Moville[3]
from Moville on to St John's
red watch[4] – call the red watch
red watch all to muster.

Get fell in then red watch
pull yer fingers out then
detail – starboard bridge lookout
off yer go then chop chop.

Coxswain on the wheel Sir
full ahead and starboard ten
object in the water green five oh
set the pattern traps and throwers

Commodore convoy flashing Sir
Iddy Umpty Iddy Umpty Iddy[5]

contact bearing red two five
charges gone and sweep astern.

Sippers[6], gulpers[7], pusser's[8] kie
who's the Buffer's[9] Oppo'[10] then?
red watch – 'ands off cocks – on socks
red watch all to muster.

[1] HMS Duncan, destroyer escort in North Atlantic Convoys July–October 1943.
[2] 'derry = Londonderry.
[3] Moville is on the republic side of Loch Foyle, St John's, Newfoundland.
[4] On destroyers three watches: red, white and blue.
[5] Iddy Umpty etc. The sound made by manually operated signal lamps sending morse code.
[6] Sippers. A 'sip' of rum.
[7] Gulpers. A 'gulp' of a tot of rum.
[8] Pusser's kie (pronounced as in 'aye aye') = ship's cocoa.
[9] Buffer. The Chief Bosun's Mate.
[10] Oppo' = opposite number. i.e. who's the Buffer's favourite.

S.C. Bateman

Many Mansions
(In My Father's House Are Many Mansions. . . .)

Above the azure void which was their battlefield and playground,
Higher than highest cirrus, beyond the vapour trails,
I know They're all there, happy in the flying men's Valhalla,
– Still laughing, boasting, nattering, and telling far-fetched tales.

They'll speak of flak[1] and bandits, ditchings, prangs[2] and sticky
    Ops,
Of how they diced Cologne, Berlin; of dog fights over Malta,
For hours They'll talk of glycol leaks and single engine landings,
Of beer at Little Rissington and popsies[3] in Gibraltar.

'The Lanc's a wizard aircraft. – I'd rather have a Mossie'.
'Have you types ever rolled a Spit 14 at thirty thou?'
'Well then the other engine out, I really thought we'd had it.'
'When I joined up at first, but then things are so different now.'

I know They'll stand and chat like this, or sprawl around
    grotesquely,
In scruffy boots and brilliant scarves, – hair long o'erdue for
    clipping –
Sporting beloved battered hats, worn at fantastic angles. –
'Let's press on for a session chaps' – 'Oh, absolutely ripping.'

Frank will be there, still whistling jive and drumming on a tin.
Jock will be planning mischief and chuckling while he schemes.
Mac, Tubby, Harry, grinning Bert, and Johnny, in a huddle.
– And Guy – wistful and silent, happy among his dreams.

Some day perhaps we'll join the boys, another grand reunion,
– Occasion for a party, lusty singing, noisy laughter.
They were the finest lads on earth, the Greatest now in Heaven,
In their own exclusive corner of the flying men's Hereafter.

1944

[1] Anti-air craft fire.
[2] Crashes.
[3] Girls.

Roy Baume

Menu

It's bacon and eggs
for those who get back;
for those who don't, perhaps
a shovel and sack.

Night Out

Tonight I'd have been with Suzy,
A kiss and a cuddle for sure.
Back seat at the Ritz, she's not choosy;
But tonight I'm over the Ruhr.

At the Ritz I'm her Errol Flynn
Though at first she'd play coy and pure;
But now I've soared to a bigger sin,
In a turret over the Ruhr.
Suzy is soft and warm to hold,
Sighing love that's a cert to endure;
Back of this Lanc I'm alone and cold
In the mad sky over the Ruhr.
And strangely, I hear my Suzy say,
'The boy I loved, he just flew away'.

Harry Beard

Burial at Sea

The sun was climbing through the cloud
on the horizon, when they wrapped him in his shroud.
No ripple chiselled out his name
upon the vast tombstone of that common grave,
where many million glorious without fame
have found eternal rest. . . . Where many brave
must fight with their own epitaph, and die
digging the waters under which they'll lie.
They play the sexton thinking they can save
themselves; but go without a wave.

At sea, December 1940

Eversley Belfield

Green Plovers on the Aerodrome, 1943

Winter through they stood silently,
Almost dejectedly, rising only slowly
To avoid an incoming plane,
To settle on the glistening grass.

Now spring has come again
And they rise in wheeling, screaming
Close-knit formations, or in pairs,
Swooping and diving almost to the ground
To show their aerobatic skills.
I see them as long dead airmen,
Ghosts come to watch and be with us.

Rosalie Seddon Carey (NZ)

What You Can Get Used To

When I sacrificed my freedom for that 'Patriotic urge,'
And joined the WAAF's in 1943,
I'd never learnt to type or add, or anything like that,
But s'posed they'd find some 'special' job for me.
I knew they might expect me to do things like 'washing up,'
But they would find out I'd jolly well refuse to.
But soon I learnt my best friend was a washing-up machine –
It's great the things you find you must get used to.

I was taken to a dormit'ry where twenty girls or so
Were scrapping like a lot of silly cats.
Black blankets in a bed-pack looked the oddest sight to me,
Especially on a bed of wooden slats.
The place looked like a night-mare and I couldn't stand the girls –
(As many as I had been introduced to).
But now they're just like sisters, and that dormit'ry's my home –
It's wonderful the things you can get used to.

I thought myself just 'Xmas' when I got my uniform,
Despite the rows I had about the hem,
But when they spoke of berets, I went all conservative
And refused to see what need we'd have of them,
A few of us went 'Bolshie' when they first came on the scene,
We said, to wear them, we would just refuse to.

I never wear my felt hat now (I don't know where it is),
It's funny the things you can get used to.

The other day we were relieved to find some gear had come
To reinforce our crockery supplies,
When we saw the half-inch cups that weigh some sixteen ounces
    each,
We wondered if we should believe our eyes.
But these were but the first of various atrocities
That in due course we've all been introduced to.
And now we use enamel cups and plates at every meal,
It's great how much you can get used to.

According to the rumours that are buzzing round just now,
Many WAAF's will be demobilised this year.
We used to mourn our 'civvy' days and wish them back again
But now the situation looks so queer –
Will I enjoy those crazy hats and fine accessories;
Silk stockings and the fancy high-heeled shoes too?
I guess it will be pretty good in many ways – but gosh!
It will take an awful lot of getting used to!

Peter Clissold

Benghazi Pilot
*(Benghazi, captured by both sides, bombarded by each, harbour choked
with wrecks, a vital supply port for the advancing 8th Army.)*

There rides the ship. Her pennants level fly,
Her funnel-smoke streaks straight across the sky
Caught in the wind. (Already the salt seas
Have soused me with their spray the rising breeze
Slaps at the boat.) Out here the onshore swell
Rolls past her sides, fresh peak succeeding dell.
The boat sinks down beside the sheer steel wall,
Soars skywards, now it tops the bulwarks tall.

Quick leaping for the ladder, holding fast,
(Down falls the boat and surges slowly past),
A leg across the rail – I've gained the deck.

No easy task today within the wreck-
Strewn harbour where the great sea wall
Is bombed and blasted to a ruinous fall
Of jumbled rocks where every wild wave hurls
Its weight and, checking, breaks in spumy swirls.
No room for error here but judgement true
Of how her head will cant, her stern how slew
Into the wind. As we the entrance near
No signs of passage through the wrecks appear
Save past the foaming wounds within the mole
To where a blockship, failing in her role
Yet bars the way. We must have good speed here
Lest we should sag to leeward and not steer;
Yet not too much or else the threshing screw
Will never check her way when we are through
The narrow gap – for there we have to turn
Sharply to starboard and so swing the stern
Into the wind and past (*just* past) the bow
Of poor wrecked *Hannah*. We must not allow
Too wide a margin, for to leeward lies
A reef too close for comfort, so she plies
Astern again to where a rusting hulk,
A much-bombed wreck, gives shelter with her bulk
And does afford a berth. Our boat with speed
Must run away our stern line with due heed
(For one may put a ship where one's a mind
But never *keep* her there against the wind.)
Now all have played their part, the rope is fast.
Heave gently now – the haven's gained at last.

August 1943

English Madrigals Broadcast in the BBC African Service

'In spring time, in spring time . . .'
The ship is oven-hot,
Great drops of sweat befoul each rusting plate
And perspiration soils the crew's bare backs,
All 's close and dark and dank, in evil state.
   'In spring time, the only pretty ring time . . .'

'It was a lover and his lass . . .'
But never here:
A world as masculine as close-confined,
Lovers do not exist except in dreams
(Sweet dreams!) or dwell in memories called to mind
   'In spring time, the only pretty ring time . . .'

'Hey ding-a-ding-a-ding . . .'
Pure voices raised
in English music, hope and promise crammed.
Lovers will love and songs will still be sung
When wars are done and those that made them damned.

George E. Cocker

The 31st Operation . . .

We might have known
That there would be a catch . . .
To match the occasion . . .
Thirty ops they said
Completes a 'tour' . . .
Sounds like a picnic . . .
Or a leisurely perambulation
Around the scenic margins of the coast . . .
Where teas with Hovis

Are the major hazard . . .
And rural deans preside
To serve the host in splendid isolation . . .

'Sorry, chaps,' the Flight Commander droned . . .
'But Group stress maximum effort . . .
Every kite to go. . . .
It should be quite a show. . . .'
He spoke his awkward lines
Without conviction . . .
His words struck like a shower of ice . . .
To freeze our hearts
And add a weight of doom to inner thoughts . . .

'You have my word . . .'
His twitching eye-lid froze
For just an instant. . . .
'Your passes will be waiting on my desk . . .
Signed for your sure return . . .
First thing . . . tomorrow . . .'

There was nothing more to say . . .
Tomorrow was a night of fear away . . .
And sure returns
Were not the order of the day. . . .

'Good show, chaps . . .'

'Good show, chaps . . .' the Wingco drawled . . .
He fumbled for the score . . .
A heavy silence drowned his words . . .
He was a very charming man . . .
The very essence of elan . . .
True blue to the core . . .
He never took an easy trip . . .
He did his share, and more . . .

'I thought I ought to say a word
About the ops last night . . .'

Dawn grey faces met his gaze . . .
He stumbled on without support,
Longing to be gone. . . .

'Our casualties last night were grim . . .
But war is war . . . I wont say more . . .
My thanks to everyone . . .'
And glancing quickly at his watch,
He made his getaway . . .
'Good show, chaps . . .' an Aussie mimed,
To raise a weary laugh . . .
We grimly thought of trips to come . . .
Of more good shows to match this one . . .
And lumbered out to meet the day . . .
Red eyed and sleepless from the fray . . .

With Tommy lying in the morgue . . .
All but cut in two . . .
As though a scythe had done its work,
To slice him cleanly through . . .
While standing by the pilot's seat
To watch the grand attack . . .
He fell a victim to Fate's whim . . .
A shell of heavy flak
Cut through his taut spare youthful frame . . .
And in a trice sniffed out his flame . . .
To leave the plane a wreck . . .
The wonder is they nursed it home . . .
To pancake on a bed of foam . . .

The second victim of the night
Lay like a crumpled bird . . .
The evidence of shot and shell
For all to see, and some to tell,
Of a brief encounter that went well
For an intruding '88'[1] . . .
He stalked them coming from the coast . . .
Had them on a piece of toast . . .
Raked them from below . . .

The first they knew that he was there,
Was when his burst hit fair and square . . .
And almost laid them low . . .

The Kiwi, Mac, shared in the fun,
With three nine-millies in the bum . . .
Which caused no end of mirth . . .
As standing on his blood stained legs,
He tucked into his breakfast eggs . . .
Before they carted him away . . .
To live and die another day . . .

[1] Junkers plane.

James Coldwell

The Long Song of the Sea

The sea has a long song
    As tides flow by,
It's a low and a strong song
    With a long-drawn sigh.

The waves sing a slow tune
    As the waters rise;
Perhaps there is no tune
    So sad and wise.

For the sea is an old sea,
    And the waves are long,
It's a deep and a cold sea,
    And a dreary song.

Herbert Corby

Missing

They told me, when they cut the ready wheat
the hares are suddenly homeless and afraid,
and aimlessly circle the stubble with scared feet
finding no homes in sunlight or in shade.
– It's morning, and the Hampdens have returned,
the crews are home, have stretched and laughed and gone:
whence the planes came and the bright neon burned,
the sun has ridden the sky and made the dawn.
He walks distraught, circling the landing ground,
waiting the last one in that won't come back,
and like those hares he wanders round and round,
bereft and desolate on the close-cropped track.

Olivia Fitzroy

Night Flying

'Night flying has commenced.'
From a comfortable arm-chair in the mess
I look up at the clock.
20.45.
No one else pays any attention, but one man
Shovels a little more coke on the stove.
And returns to the 'Daily Mirror'.
Overhead
The first aircraft roars past.
I can so well imagine it.
A black graceful shape against a grey sky,
Port and starboard lights gleaming, rear light like a star.
He drones past in the circuit,
The only one so far.
Past the edge of the blackout I can see a grey strip of sky,
Perfect for dusk landings.

He comes round again.
Somebody buys me a beer
And I think of another clue in 'The Times' crossword.

After the first hour or so it must be dark outside,
And they are still there, three of them now,
Orbiting low over the Nissen Huts.
It is impossible to stay in any longer.
The night outside is cool,
And sweet.
There are many stars between the trees
And a red and green one now and then,
Moving swiftly.
It is very still and silent but for the interminable drone of engines.
I am drawn, half unwillingly to the end of the runway,
To share the darkness and the spangled flat Christmas Tree effect
Of the lighting,
Red, green, blue, yellow and the lit bats.
Silence and the night, silence but for the crackling of the ground
    set
And the approaching roar of an aircraft,
'D for Dog coming in now.'
Bats are flung out, modelled on the wing tips,
A voice from the runway speaks, gently, encouragingly,
'Down a bit, down a bit,' no hurry no panic,
'Cut!' and the bats cross.
The roar of the engine is almost deafening,
Instinctively we duck
As the air sweeps past us.
On, on along the flare path,
Up and the next one comes in.
I watch and wait.
A for Able is on his nose,
C for Charlie is nervous,
You can hear his voice quiver.
'Round again, C for Charlie, round again.'
We have to duck several times.
Slowly, slowly the moon rises.
Far overhead bombers drone
But we take no notice,

Our whole minds are on the aircraft in the circuit.
The bombers are remote, distant,
They belong to another war.

It is nearly over now,
Everyone is getting tired
And the edges of tempers frayed.
Back in the camp the milk is boiling for cocoa.
I stoke the fire and find things to eat,
Listening to the last circuits,
Waiting, waiting.
'Night flying has ceased.'

Fleet Fighter

'Good show!' he said, leaned his head back and laughed.
'They're wizard types!' he said, and held his beer
Steadily, looked at it and gulped it down
Out of its jamjar, took a cigarette
And blew a neat smoke-ring into the air.
'After this morning's prang I've got the twitch;
'I thought I'd had it in that teased-out kite.'
His eyes were blue and older than his face,
His single stripe had known a lonely war,
But all his talk and movements showed his age,
His jargon was of aircraft and of beer.
'And what will you do afterwards?' I said.
Then saw his puzzled face and caught my breath.
There was no afterwards for him but death.

When He Is Flying

When I was young I thought that if Death came
He would come suddenly, and with a swift hand kill,
Taking all feeling;
Want, laughter and fear;

Leaving a cold and soulless shell on earth
While the small winged soul
Flew on,
At peace.
I used to think those things when I was young,
But now I know.
I know
Death stands beside me, never very far,
An unseen shadow, just beyond my view
And if I hear an engine throb and fade
Or see a neat formation pass
Or a lone fighter soar, hover and dart,
He takes another step more near
And lays his cold unhurried hand on my heart.

D.S. Goodbrand

Port of Dreams

After the duels of the Barents Sea,
The ice, the Arctic gales, the messdeck sludge,
The laggard convoy, wolf-pack's strategy,

Our boat turned south away from bomb and gun
And sped we wondering to the remote Azores,
For rendezvous with the all healing sun.

Fayal the isle, Horta the dreaming port
Which drove the Northern capes far from our minds,
Towered in greenery we long had sought.

Tied up, we roamed ashore with gleaming eyes
And paced old-fashioned pathways into town,
Each scented breeze telling of paradise.

Gardens there were and folk of olive face
Who on the fringe of war made us forget
The black streets and the slag-heaps of our race.

Pipe-smoking fishermen in simple guise,
Contented farmers with their ample crops,
Cheap wine and señoritas with dark eyes.

All these we saw, and lotus-eating, woke
The worm that nestles in Arcadia's bud,
And soon the liquored gangs from all restraint had broke.

Young women fled the incautious word,
Aghast shopkeepers laid their loud complaint –
The Mayor and Skipper hastily conferred.

The Skipper's wrathful writ cancelled our ease,
And with shamed faces we rolled back to ship
Under the pale gaze of the Portuguese.

Five days we swung off that forbidden shore,
Hangdog and yearning for our port of dreams
Like Bounty folk torn from Tahitian lore,

Then slung our hook for home . . . But this I know:
Paradise is not in some Shangri-la
Nor where sweet winds over Avalon do blow –

Long lost it lies, and ever shall, for me,
In Fayal's lovely isle in the far Azores,
When we were young, in the Spring of '43.

Bombed-Out

Pity is wasted where the roof gapes,
And the whole house crumbles in a gutted obscenity
Of earth and bricks, where lies filthily strewn
The kitchen's intimate debris.

Last night bombs fell and sheets of flame relieved
Disintegrating bodies, the sickening rapture of screams

Punctuating gunfire.
     White rods of dawn disclosed
The bitter magic of loss, scraps of the dead.

We, the pathetic group.
We stand on the pavement, looking at our bombed house
With a sombre wistfulness. In a doorway a little girl softly cries,
She is crying for her mother who has been killed.

Pity is not enough: nor is anger enough:
This was our home, this pathetic, scarred wretchedness . . .
We lived here, but bombs struck the house
It was razed to the ground;
Something mingles its decay with the steaming, exposed entrails.

The grey machinery of death,
Fits us for the new agony of being man.

1941

Mary E. Harrison

My Hands[1]

Do you know what it is like to have death in your hands
when you haven't a murderer's mind?
Do you know how it feels when you could be the cause
of a child being blind?
How many people have died through me
From the skill in my finger tips?
For I fashion the clay and portray the landscape
As the fliers are briefed for their trips

Do those young men in blue feel as I do
The destruction
The pain.
Let me cover my eyes as you cover the skies
Let me pray it can't happen again.

Don't show me the pictures you take as you fly,
They're ruins and scape – little more.

Is all this part
Of the madness we choose to call War?
If there is a God up above who listens at all
Does he know why this has to be.
Did he give me my hands just to fashion the plans
That my own land may always be free?

[1] Mary E. Harrison, topographical model maker in the WAAF making models to brief air crews for bombing raids, wrote the poem after being shown the photographs after a raid and then remembering the photographs from which she had worked.

L.F. Hurle

Readiness at Dispersal – RAF 1940

They lounge in chairs made for the beach,
Helmet and goggles within their reach.
Awaiting the call to climb high above,
In defence of the country they love.
Uncertain if they'll survive the day,
When the Heinkel gunner makes his play.
Mae Wests rubbing the back of their necks,
Boots loose, unzipped to stay the sweat.
'Chutes on mainplanes, hoods back wide,
Chocks in place and roped to slide.
Ops' 'phone tinkles breaking the calm,
All eyes turn, some in alarm.
'The Squadrons' released from readiness state,
You can go back to meet your fate.
Feet up in the mess with open book,
Taking your chances, to be killed by the cook.'

Robin Jackson

Atlantic Convoy

Grey silhouettes on glinting sea
in wide formation spread;
all steady on a western course
for England, homeward bound.

Heavy laden cargo ships,
the centre of the flock –
while round them race the watch-dogs,
destroyers, sleek and swift.

A swirl amid the driving foam –
a periscope appears,
and all unseen slides down below;
the 'U' boat's single eye.

A siren hoots, an Aldis winks,
the screen increases speed,
as four 'white fish' streak on their way
toward the convoy's heart.

Flash of red, a booming thud,
torpedoes find their mark –
a black-hulled merchantman is doomed,
her listing decks ablaze.

While far out on the convoy's wing
destroyers, the avenger;
with foaming bows and streaming stacks
they track the foe below.

With depth-charge patterns jettisoned,
they wait the thunderclap,
circling round the echo-fix
in grim expectation.

The hidden quarry waits also
below with bated breath –
while straddled charges mesh
her round in menace.

The sea explodes in flattened foam,
while escorts watch and wait.
So search for tell-tale slicks of oil
from submarine below.

Then, like some steel leviathan,
the German's bows appear;
rising straight and vertical,
plunging down once more.

No need now for signs of oil –
the escort's job is done.
One 'U' boat less to sink our ships;
the convoy presses on.

Norman G. Jones

Spitfire

Set upon a Kent hardstanding,
Nose up, knock kneed, neat and trim,
Eight oiled guns within the edges,
Lean and swift of limb.

One fine day a sneak air-raid,
Sirens screamed a sad alert,
From the blue skies bombs descended
Leaving death among the dirt.

Wheel and chock with my Red-leader,
Formed close by him as he soared,

Skidded to maintain position
While the Rolls-Royce engines roared.

With the gold of sun behind me,
Front a black Luftwaffe cross,
Coated bullet spitting at it
Saw the solid Stuka toss.

In the shambles lost Red-leader,
Received a stern command 'Return!',
Shocked I saw his aircraft halted
Watched the Spitty split and burn.

Below me I could see his victor,
Hidden face behind a mask,
My shots ripped a path across him
Then fire finished off the task.

Ted Lane

Troopship

We've sung the song so many times. . . .
'They say there's a troopship just leaving Bombay. . . .'
But now there's a troopship just leaving the Clyde
And we are on our way!

It's like walking round a city!
What keeps this thing afloat?
There's a sharp end and a blunt end
And you call it a ship, not a boat.

She's known as The Drunken Duchess
Due to the way that she rolls,
Soon her creaks and vibrations are rivalled
By the moans of suffering souls.

Meals are served but twice a day
On first or second sitting.
We also queue for booster jabs
With a needle used for knitting!

So this is the North Atlantic?
This heaving, grey–green terror?
Someone up there doesn't like me,
I'm sure I've been posted in error!

Jack D. Lavers

Day's End

Browns and blues,
A thousand hues
As seen by day
Must now give way
To black and white.
The moon tonight
Is rising still
Serene but chill.
In clear relief
Each rocky reef,
Each truck, each tent
To some extent
Throws a dark shadow.

A bomber's moon!
The droning soon
Will warn us all
Of Jerry's call.
He roams in space
To find this place.
No light must show
Our camp below.
He spots the road,

He drops his load.
His trip's in vain –
He's missed again
And now I'll go to sleep.
                    7 May 1942

Pauline Lendon

Returned Airman

Die peacefully brave boy I do not know
O God please hear my prayer and help you now
Morphia calms the pain of but a while ago
And smoothes the fear wracked furrows from your brow

The morning star that lately was your guide
That served in place of navigator lost
Is waiting now for you in humble pride
Who saved friends' lives and didn't count the cost

Your blood that stains my battle-dress grows chill
The flames light up the pallor of your lips
Your breath comes fainter pulse is almost still
The hand that clasps my own goes limp and slips

Die peacefully young hero yet unnamed
Neath fading bomber's moon on grass dew wet
We who remain may live to feel ashamed
But even so we never can forget

William E. Morris

B25 Strike[1]

Mostly we saw them as a silver pencil-thread
cross-stitching an arc of sky nudging clouds
on their missions of death and destruction
to known targets across Adriatic Sea;
American air bases of some magnitude camouflaged
themselves across miles of country in toe of Italy;
All this might went on display one day
when B25s struck at oil-fields across way
somewhere in belly of Europe; heavens throbbed
to massive V formations wave on wave, we watched
them out of sight – and saw them return, not
neat echelons that were there before – stragglers
trailing smoke, flying low, and one just knew
that there were gaps that didn't show;
mission accomplished oil-fields out of commission
for a long while – memorial to the young American
dream, boys who had seen little of war who died
in blazing bombers – even before they'd emptied a
bomb bay – died in a pitiless holocaust of flame
their bodies just a charred remain.

Italy, 1944

[1] B25: American Bomber.

Convoy at Night

Moontrack silhouettes of ships gliding on the trackless deep,
pennants of white foam stealing in their wake
as the log-line reels the miles with every breath they take;
low down in deep troughs churned by surging might
bulk of a cruiser cleaves a wave in watching convoy
sight; mother to a brood of 'grey ducklings'
in the 'Med', with a waning quarter moon beaming approval
overhead.

Stoke-hold bars are banked and black, wisps of smoke
drift from the stack. Vapour-like it idles high
dissolving sea and sky – leaving no tell-tale lie
to mark a convoy's passing by.
Sweat and turn beneath subdued glow, down 'tween decks
among a huddled row, on table form, and on cabin floor
men lie in sleep, confiding themselves to a trysting
watch crew above must keep;
spilling its human cargo on its wooded strand
as shipwrecked mariners upon island's sand, out
beneath the stars where night breezes band, through
the questing night cheerful souls dream of land;
one by one 'lanterns' die in a dimpled dawning sky,
watch is alert for dawn attack, smoke no longer filters
from the stack, to the convoy on its urgent way –
friendly night has fled, another hostile day.

Arthur E. Newall

Before the Thirteenth. Hamburg, May 1942

Now I have done twelve.
If I could shelve tonight's affair
And not be there
When the clouded moon
Lights up the Alster;
But could instead go home
And sleep
Certain to see tomorrow's day
Then I could live
Grow young
Someday turn grey
But now I feel that this is my last day.
It seems that I shall never do
The things I planned.
Smell no more new cut grass
Touch falling water
Stand cliff high

Facing wind swept sea rain
Or walk those meadows
Holding a smooth hand.
And will she with the fair tumbling hair
Say white haired,
'I knew an airman once. Loved him, too.'
And then she'll shake her head the way I know so well
And say, 'He loved me, too.'
She'll know I'm there.
Watching from every cloud
Carried along in dreams and memories
Trailing the bright stars in Summer;
Perhaps in Autumn
She'll watch the leaves dancing
In every wayward breeze.
Leaves falling from boughs traced lace black
Against the glooming sky.
She'll see me – saying – half aloud,
'He came this way. Look how the old leaves flutter
Sighing for old friends
That living cannot last.'
But in the Spring
When all the hedgerows light up
With May blossom
And the lilacs bloom
I may be found in each new jewelled field
Tasting the sweet drops from new reaching blades
Then she'll run to me
And call my name.
Cry it across the shouting wind
Across our fields
In rain or in the lightning flash
She'll find me there.
And we shall find sweet, solitary bliss
Without the sadness of a parting kiss.

                              57 Squadron, Methwold

(Back from Leave) Methwold, July 1942

Back from leave.
To Methwold.
The Mess, Glebe House,
Still there
Three hundred yards, or more,
From the Cock Inn.
Across the road
The Airfield.
Bomb trolleys winding
Five hundred pounders.
And in the Mess
Some changes have been made
Some new ghosts made
But there are still the old ghosts
That never fade.
New faces having tea
Scanning papers
New voices sound
Subdued
As well becomes new crews
Unused as we chaps are
To Norfolk's booze.

'Jack' Frost was there
Alone
Remote
Sweating – twenty trips done
Just gazing
Thinking
'Ten to do at most'
Two thirds towards the winning post.

Cup in hand –
Sat next to Frost
Tapped 'Jack's' shoulder.
Saw him jump
'Where's Johnny?'
New heads nodded

Old ones shook.
Like Frost.
'Essen' he said. 'Tuesday night.
Bloody flak and fighters.'

'Ten tenths flak,' a new one muttered.
'We only got nine back,' said Frost.

A record blared.
The Andrews Sisters.
'I'm in love with you, Honey!'

'That's Johnny's record!
Grabbed Frost's arm.
'What happened?'
Shook him roughly.
'That's funny,' 'Jack' said.

'Loved you from the start, Honey!'

A new voice said
'That bloody tree.' Heads turned.
'Should have been cut down'

That record. Johnny.

'No one else will do, Honey!'

'What happened?'
Shouting now.
'Where's Johnny?'

A boy said
'That old elm
Near A Flight'

'Undershot –' a wise one said.
'No bloody flaps. Two bombs hung up
Hit the tree. Not a bad landing
Otherwise.'

Someone laughed.
Frost said,
'It takes some understanding.
No future in it.
All those squares chalked up
And only two to go.'

That record again
'It's funny but it's true!'

He must have lost his grip.
But spared the trembling
Of the final
Thirtieth trip.

William H. Proctor

The Ruddy 'Ead of Airman Khayyam

Awake. The bugler in the early light
Hath blown a note which sets my head alight;
That makes the sawmill in my skull revolve.
It seems that, last night, I was very tight.

Dreaming, when dawn's left hand was in the sky,
I heard a bugle by the flag-staff cry,
'Awake my little ones, come on, get up'.
Dear God, the aloes in my mouth were dry.

Happiness is as the wind-blown grain.
A moment's pleasure must be bought with pain.
'A pint of bitter, what will you have, Miss?',
May bring us dreams, but morning comes again.

And with the heartless breaking of the dawn,
The mighty hero, who, last night, was born,
Shrivels again into a half-wrecked man;
A man, forsooth, whose very head is torn.

Flight Mech.

Tea, too weak to stain
Green-mottled oilcloth on the table tops
And stories growing weirder by the hour,
Frankly, I think that Joe abandoned even basic truth
In that last yarn about the half-caste dame.
Twenty to nine. I'll wait until the news is on,
Then try to get some sleep.
'd none last night, and it will be the same,
Tomorrow.
Funny to think that here, so far from all the tense excitement and
    the rage
We are the basis of the Victory.
Yet we can say, we have fought Britain's battle here,
With spanners in our hands, on Naafi tea,
And old loved jokes, and boastings about girls.
We who have lived and worked two lives in one
These latter days;
We who have worried over what was not, by rights,
Our can to carry,
We who have seen the glory pass us without glance
And taken for our share, the mud, the strafings[1]
And the joy of good work done;
Why, if we only knew it, we
Are the Victors of the bloody skies.

Machine-gun attack from the air.

Molly Repard

Poem

Beside his aircraft,
Twisted lies my love,
Charred are the limbs that once lay close to me

No doubt some German woman weeps
For him that you shot down.

For all of Woman
War is agony.

To Every Tide

You, who know not where your lover died –
Search where the wind blows free
The hundred thousand miles of open sea
And weep your longing out to every tide.

Peter Roberts

Frayed End

'Frayed End' remembers a funeral. It was the only one I attended. Th
curious thing was that although losses in Bomber Command were so high
one's friends normally just disappeared. It was strange on this occasion t
be standing at a grave.

'. . . till he hath put all enemies under his feet. . . .'

What a strange, awkward ritual is this –
The sullen, leaden grey
Of a winter sky drooped low with unshed snow,
And here below
The rough-dug clay,
The wind-frisked play
Of a Padre's flapping surplice.

'. . . Death is swallowed up in victory. O death, where is th
sting?. . . .'

Death, where is thy sting?
A row of us here with our minds astray. . . .
Off to the right a little way
Are the riflemen,
With three rounds each.

. . . Man that is born of a woman hath but a short time to live,
    and is full of misery. . . .'

I can't connect that rigid shape
Under the flag's flat drape
With someone quite so full of life as Mike.
The loping walk and the sideways grin
And a car that was hell to travel in,
Mike. . . .

. . . We therefore commit his body to the ground; earth to earth,
    ashes to ashes, dust to dust. . . .'

When did I last see Mike alive?
Briefing before the Hamburg trip –
No, later on – that bumpy drive
Along the uneven perimeter track
In the rattling, jolting Flight Dispersal Van.
We stood together in the back
And clung, with the usual desperate grip,
To the things that brace the tarpaulin top.
That was how Mike's last trip began –
Just as on any other night. . . .
After a while he peered outside
And muttered, 'Hell! He's passed our kite,'
And shouted, 'Stop!'
But nothing happened – it never does –
The drivers are always half asleep

. . the miseries of this sinful world. . . .'

The sun was low and watery;
Wan blue sky;
Hangars and trees a sharpened silhouette

In the translucent moment before night.
Frost was a flashing dance of tinsel light,
Sputtering white,
Leaping until the sun slipped down and set.
With the last slanting rays of it
Burning across the tarmac underfoot.
Mike was standing there,
Muffled to the ears in flying kit –
Brown leather jacket, sweater, spotted scarf,
Parachute harness – legs set rather wide,
With a curl of frost along each flying boot.
He gave a sudden laugh,
Stepped to the van and reached inside –
'Hey – shift your arse!' he said. 'You're on my parachute.'

'. . . that we, with all those that are departed. . . .'

It was bitter cold that night,
Over the bleak North Sea to the German shore,
Doped in the drumming engine-roar
Of long, straight, level flight. . . .
Then the weaving climb –
The sudden plunging swerves –
Seconds when the flow of time
Was dammed by tautened nerves
And stopped, to hold us there eternally. . . .
A jerk which shook us free
Out of the Flak and searchlights' clinging hold –
And then again the dark, unbroken sea,
The bitter cold. . . .
. . .

At last the warm caress of England's coast
Sighted across the water, far ahead –
Some beacon flashing red,
And a thin white whisp of surf like a fading ghost!

'. . . prepared for you from the beginning of the world. . . .'

A little after one we taxied in,
Motors kicked a last time round
And stuck. . . .

A strange, unearthly sound
Replaced their steady eight-hour din –
Silence. . . .
Then, in the stillness, just as Tony's hand
Fingered the switch, the earphones' hissing crack
Was broken, for the last of many times,
By Mike's voice cutting in, asking his turn to land.
I looked at Tony – 'S-for-SUGAR's back!'

'. . . and Redeemer. Amen. . . .'

Strange how completely unaware,
How casual and easy in our mind
Were we who listened, in the stillness there,
Listened to that brief message down the air.
It meant for their crew, as it had for ours,
Dark laboured miles of flying put behind,
Bringing an end to seeming-endless hours –
That message – 'May we land?'

'. . . evermore. Amen. . . .'

Why was that night's performance of the fantasy,
Which Mike had played before,
Given so poor a tragic epilogue?
There was a time somewhere among the roar
Of steady barrage, and the lash and flog
Of vicious tracer flailing up the sky –
There was a time for climax, for the stroke
Which severs all the close-knit earthly ties
Of earthly folk,
And hurls us,
Into the vast unknown.
But to be home – to see the winking lights –
The good, firm, solid earth
Spread comfortingly out on either hand –
To hear the order telling you to land,
And know the nearness of a blazing hearth,
Of food and drink, and common daily sights. . . .
And then –

'. . . Load. . . . Pre-sent. . . . Fire! . . .'

They found S-SUGAR strewn across three fields
A mile or two from here.
Some farmer heard the rumble as they hit,
Or saw the glare,
And guided by the lurid flare of it
He hurried there –
To find a pair of wheels,
An engine and a section of the wings
Littered about the molten fuselage.
. . . thin-drawn brazen notes shiver on the wind. . . .

Last Post, Reveille, die away. . . .
Rifles and bugles, voices, all are mute.
One after one we face the fresh-turned clay,
Pause and salute.
The snow has turned to rain,
Whipping in clammy fingers, full of hate.
We pass out slowly to the lane
Beyond the wicket gate.
To-morrow night there will be Ops again.

Written during a Met. Lecture

With apologies to our Met. man, who is invaluable

Oh, why are Met. men always glum?
And why so melancholy?
In endless soporific hum
Their words fall soft and slowly . . .
'Cumulonimbus,' and again
'Warm Front,' and then 'Occlusion,'
Including 'Orographic Rain'
To add to the confusion –
'Deep Depressions,' 'Anvil Tops,'
'Fohn Winds' and 'Cirrostratus';
And here the droning chanting stops –
And Morpheus charges at us!

Return

The darkened mess was silent. Nothing stirred.
The sounds which drifted in were muffled, blurred,
And often lost before they could be heard.
Two white-clad figures stood, without a word,
And listened to the whispering voice of night
Around the walls which hid the moon from sight.
The moonlight strayed across the hangar doors
And splashed in patches on the concrete floors;
A flarepath glimmered on the aerodrome;
The beacon flashed to guide the bombers home . . .
And then the rustling night wind brought a sound
That muttered softly, swelled and then was drowned,
And for an endless moment silence reigned,
While in the silver darkness ears were strained
To catch that long expected sound anew . . .
At last it came again, and quickly grew,
Its surging waves became a steady drone,
The world seemed filled with it, and it alone –
Gliding across the darkness overhead,
With lights at wing-tips gleaming, green and red,
The first dark shape of the returning band,
With motors throttled back, came in to land.

Now, warmly lit, the mess was flooded through
With cheerful noise. Young men in dusty blue,
Bright scarves and heavy sweaters, eager-eyed,
Sat round the table. Everybody tried
To speak at once, and laughter strong and clear
Rang out across the room. Pint pots of beer
Were raised to thirsty lips, and once again
Nerves, braced against the threat of death and pain,
Relaxed, until the things that mattered most
Were eggs and bacon, jam and buttered toast,
And these the two white figures soon supplied.
But when at last, with hunger satisfied,
They rose and stretched themselves, and made for bed,
'Where's Jimmy? I've not seen him,' someone said.
And then the talking ceased, they looked around,

As if, by seeking, Jimmy could be found.
One saw the clock. 'Still half an hour to go.
He often cuts it pretty fine, you know.'

The lights were out, the tables in the room
Once more retreated deep into the gloom.
Again the very walls were listening,
And waiting for the stealthy wind to bring
Some murmur of the last returning crew.
The curtains fluttered gently, letting through
A sudden glimpse of swiftly setting moon.
And when the shadowed ridge of Sandham Hill
Turned purple in the dawning, all too soon,
The silent room was listening, listening still.

William C. Roberts

Duff Gen,[1] Or Is It?

We're heading for the breaker's yards
With bags of postings on the cards;
Marchant's dishing out the kit,
Zeigey doesn't like his pit.
Waafs will soon be working here;
We'll see Blighty at New Year.
All domestic trades will go,
210 Group will run the show.
Someone's candid, personal views
Soon become the latest news
And spread with such alarming pace
To check would mean to lose the race
And if by chance one does prove true
The others are accepted too.
Take for instance that great day
When two new diesels came our way;
They'd both been on the way for years
And when they came they raised new fears –

A rumour had proved true at last,
The duff gen days, it seemed, were past.
To celebrate new tales were told
And we resumed the life of old,
To live on rumours day and night
But still the boat is not in sight.

Algeria, 1943

False information and rumour: prevalent in the services.

Trevor M.L. Smith

Prune's Prang

Hark to the tale of PO Prune
Who pressed the rudder-bar too soon,
An action that resulted in
A sort of double inside spin.

The engine made a funny sound
And dug a large hole in the ground,
The fitters said a silent prayer
As chunks of airscrew filled the air.

And one, with muffled sort of squeal
Was flattened by the starboard wheel,
But PO Prune in sorry plight
Was taking yet another flight.

And ultimately came to rest
Upon the CO's manly chest,
Who, with a startled cry of pain
Adroitly shoved him off again.

Forgiving Prune this awful slip
He let him take another trip,

'Twas then, observant airmen say
He turned the duty pilot grey.

The PO screamed across the drome
Removing half the watch tower dome,
And just to show how well he flew
He split the wind sock right in two.

And, thinking they required some more
He badly bent a hangar door,
Then with retracted undercart
He finished off this work of art.

By landing with a fearful sound
Upon an aircraft on the ground,
And that was how Prune came to be
A common AC2 GD.[1]

And sitting round the fire at night
He tells of his amazing flight,
Explaining sadly all along
'I still can't think what I did wrong'.

[1] Low-rank General Duty.

Barry Sutton

Hurricane

Breathe, its heady mist of hot
oil, hot glycol,
The musky tang of those
snarling pipes
Ranging the blunted snout.

Now, the fluttering of silk
above, this swooning

through space –
In silence.

Silence, except for the sound
of a bird. Unashamed I
babble and pray, and hold
aloft hands from which
already hang
long skeins of flesh.
The smell of this singed
oxygen mask and my cheeks
sickens me.

1940

Frank Thompson

London, 1940

After fourteen hours clearing they came to him
Under the twisted girders and the rubble.
They would not let me see his face.
Now I sit shiftlessly on the tube platforms
Or huddle, a little tipsy, in brick-built shelters.

I can see with an indifferent eye
The red glare over by the docks and hear
Impassively the bomb-thuds in the distance.

For me, a man with not many interests
And no pretensions to fame, that was my world,
My son of fifteen, my only concrete achievement,
Whom they could not protect. Stepping aside
From the Great Crusade, I will play the idiot's part.
You, if you like, may wave your fists and crash
On the wrong doorsteps brash retaliation.

October 20, 1940

Michael Thwaites

Coming into the Clyde

Part of me for ever is the January morning
Coming into the Clyde in the frosty moonlight
And the land under snow and the snow under moonlight,
Fall upon fall, a soundless ecstasy.

I alone on the bridge, below me the helmsman
Whistling softly to the listening voicepipe,
And no sound else but the washing of the bow-wave
As the buoys go by like marching pylons.

I gaze from the glory of the bared universe
To the guarded secret of the winter world
Rapt, and the helmsman now is silent,
And I wait for the time to alter course.

To port lift the magic scenario mountains
White above the shoulders of Holy Island,
And nearer, clear as a square-lined coverlet,
All the fields and hedges on the slopes of Arran.

But further and smaller, away to starboard,
The plaited hills of Ayrshire gleam,
And I in thought am over them all
Away to my darling and my little son.

Beyond the moonlit hills that morning
My darling lay, and my little son;
But she in her cold bed lone and waking,
And he in the frozen ground asleep.

The Jervis Bay

(The Jervis Bay, a passenger liner plying between Australia and Britain, was converted to an armed merchant cruiser on the outbreak of war, the sole escort of Convoy HX 84 when attacked in mid-Atlantic by the German pocket battleship Admiral Scheer, on 5 November 1940. Sunk with three-quarters of her company, including her Captain, Fogarty Fegen, she enabled 32 of the 37 ships in her charge to escape under cover of darkness)

The fifth day of November, Fifty North and Forty West,
Was edging to its departure, like an undecided guest,
When under the tented edge of cloud slanted a golden ray
That tippled the wavetops, and lighted on the convoy as it lay.
The convoy lay rolling in the steep Atlantic swell
Like a becalmed Armada. You would scarcely tell
They had a port or purpose or power or moved at all
Over the vast ocean. Ships great and small,
Huge pot-bellied tankers, trim, with yellow funnels aft,
Class-conscious liners stepping by with cynical smutty craft,
All shapes and shades of merchant-ship, with multifarious
    freights,
Their holds laden to the hatches, their decks piled high with
    crates,
And the sun on their yellow upperworks gleamed, and on the
    grey
Hull and bridge of the escort, HMS *Jervis Bay*.

In the dusk of the evening the wolf is abroad,
He crouches in the valley at the lonely ford
Where the sheep come down. What help have the sheep?
They must all be slaughtered when the wolf shall leap.
The sheep have the sheepdog. But what can he do,

With his slow old legs and his teeth so few?
He could meet the jackal and never fear,
Or the slinking fox, but the wolf is here
- That steely strength, that merciless art.
He has few old teeth, but a lion's heart.

On either side the *Jervis Bay* the convoy was dipping,
And the Captain as he paced the bridge paused, one hand gripping
A stanchion, to study them against the amber rim
Of sky – the ships whose safety was entrusted to him.
They spread, a broad battalion, massed in columns nine abreast,
There *Trewellard, Cornish City, San Demetrio* – North-by-West
Was it smoke or cloud? – *Castillian, Rangitiki,* and the rest.
Satisfied, he turned to go below; when a sudden gleam
Flickered in the north, and a shout from the lookout, 'Ship on the
    port beam.'
Two seconds, and Captain Fegen's glasses rake the horizon to
    norrard,
Two more, and the bells ring Action Stations. Aft, amidships,
    forrard,
The guns are manned, loaded and trained – the crews were
    standing by –
And the men below are running to their stations, and every pulse
    beats high.
And Fegen's pulse is racing hard, but his eye is steady and clear,
And the smudge on the horizon shimmers into shape, and is the
    Admiral Scheer.

The telegraph clangs to 'Full Ahead'. Her great heart pounding
The *Jervis Bay* trembles and surges forward, sounding
The alarm on her siren. From her bridge the Aldis chatters
To an answering flicker from where the Commodore scatters
The foaming seas, awaiting his orders for the convoy.
'Warship, thought hostile, my port beam.' An envoy
Of wrath, a white column spouts sudden and high
Topping the mast. A detonation shakes the sea and sky.

'Scatter under smoke.' – Fluttering flags and sirens blowing
Down the columns of the convoy. – But the *Jervis Bay* is going
Steady onward as they turn. From the smoke floats are flowing
Streams of velvet solid smoke drifting over the ocean swell,
But the enemy gunners know their job. A salvo of shell
Roars in the sea – one, two, three – by the *Rangitiki*'s bow
As she twists in flight. Already they have found for line. And now
A salvo spouts alongside – the iron jaws closing
On the vulnerable spine. Now the convoy are nosing

East, south, west, away fanwise are scattering,
But the shells fall like drops in thunder ominously pattering,
And Captain Fegen had that day a second, or maybe two,
As he stood on the bridge of the *Jervis Bay*, to choose what he
    would do.
Astern of him the convoy, labouring heavily in flight,
And one long hour till they could win to cover of the night.
To port the Nazi battleship, with six eleven-inch guns
Secure in triple turrets ranged to hurl their angry tons
Of blasting steel across the miles his guns could never span,
With twice his speed, with a Naval crew, trained, expert to a man,
With armour-plated sides and a deck, a warship through and
    through,
The pride of the German builders' craft. All this Fegen knew,
Knew his foeman as he came in overmastering might,
Knew well there was no hope at all in such unequal fight,
Knew his own unarmoured sides, his few old six-inch guns,
His fourteen meagre knots, his men, their country's sturdy sons,
But hasty-trained and still untried in the shock and din of action.
To starboard were the merchantmen, and he was their protection.

Rarely it comes, and unforeseen,
In the life of a man, a community, a nation,
The moment that knits up struggling diversity
In one, the changing transverse lights
Focussed to a pin-point's burning intensity
Rarely and unforeseen.
But in the minute is the timeless and absolute
Fulfilment of centuries and civilisations,
When the temporal skin lays bare the eternal bone,
And this mortal puts on immortality.
In that stark flash the unregarding universe
Is a hushed agony. The suns and planets
Stay: the dewdrop dares not tremble:
The dead leaf in the electric air
Waits: and the waterfall still as a photograph
Hangs in that intolerable minute.
And the dead and the living, all are there
With those that shall be, all Creation
Pausing poised in the ticking of Eternity,

Held at one white point of crisis.
But what does he know, he at the focus,
The man or the nation? Joy and terror knows,
But chiefly a blessèd sweet release,
The complex equation at a stroke resolved
To simple terms, a single choice,
Rarely and unforeseen.
So Fegen stood, and Time dissolved,
And Cradock with his ships steamed out
From Coronel, and in the pass
Of Roncesvalles a horn was sounding,
And Oates went stumbling out alone
Into that Antarctic night,
And Socrates the hemlock drank
And paid his debts and laid him down,
And through the fifty-three, *Revenge*
Ran on, as in Thermopylæ
The cool-eyed Spartans looked about,
Childe Roland, trembling, took and blew,
The *Jervis Bay* went hard-a-port.

'Hard-a-port' and 'Hard-a-port, sir.' The white spray flying,
She heeled and turned and steadied her course for where the foe
    was lying,
And not a man but knew the fate that he had turned to meet
And yet was stirred to fight till death and never know retreat.
'Salvoes, fire.' Her guns speak, but they are old and worn,
The shots fall in the water, short. The raider as in scorn
Keeps his fire on the convoy still, now veiled in smoke, now
    clear,
But the *Jervis Bay* is closing fast and her shots are creeping near.
And now he swings on her his turrets, as a thief surprised might
    turn.
His anger thunders near, ahead. She trembles from stem to stern.
A flash, and she staggers, as through her egg-shell plates
Tear the eleven-inch projectiles, malevolent as the Fates,
And smoke pouring and wreckage flying as the shells fall like rain,
But she fights, and the convoy are scattering fast, and every
    minute is gain.

'Am closing the enemy,' Fegen signals. She heaves, and is hit
    again.

Now the wolf is among the flock,
The sheep are leaping to ledge and rock
Like scattered clouds. To left and right
The wolf is at work and his teeth are white,
His teeth are white and quick is he.
Soon the flock will cease to be
That grazed along so peaceably.

But suddenly the sheepdog comes
With growling as a roll of drums,
Stiff and heavy, eyes a-blear,
But he knows the wolf is near
And within the agèd brain
One thought only may remain,
Headlong as he hurls himself
At the grey throat of the wolf
Where his old teeth sink and stay.

But he, with fury and dismay,
Drops his kill and turns to tear
The creature that affronts him there.

This way and that he rends and claws
But cannot break those ancient jaws
That never while they live relax,
While flanks are torn and sinew cracks
And haunch a mangled tatter lies
And the blood runs in his eyes
And hanging so, he dies.

And it is cold and it is night
Before the finish of the fight
When the panting wolf shakes free
From the bloody corpse, and he
Lies like a sack, defaced and dead,
And the sheep into the hills are fled
And the wolf slinks to his bed.

Now the *Jervis Bay* is ablaze. The fo'c'sle is blown away.
Splinters rive her decks to ribbons and bury her under spray,
And her burning hull as she plunged on was a bright torch that
    day.
She shudders. With the clearing smoke her main bridge is gone,
And Fegen's arm is a shredded stump, and he fights on.
He staggers aft to the docking bridge. Another blinding blast.
The Ensign down. 'Another Ensign! Nail it to the mast.'
A seaman climbs and nails it there, where the House Flag used to
    fly,
And there it speaks defiance to the shaker of the sky.
He strives to climb to the after bridge, but it is unavailing,
One arm and half the shoulder gone, and strength fast failing.
But there is still the after gun that he can bring to bear.
'Independent fire!' he cries, as heaves into the air
The after bridge. He lives, and staggers forrard again, before
The rolling smoke envelops him, and he is seen no more.
Now her engines had ceased to turn, but still the shells came
    pouring,
Till with a roar her boilers burst, and the white steam went
    soaring
Away to the sky. Her back was broken, and she was settling fast,
And the fire blazed, and the smoke-pall brooded like a banyan
    vast,
But still the torn Ensign flew from the black stump mast,
And the after gun was firing still and asking no quarter
When the hot barrel hissed into the wild grey water.

So ended the fight of the *Scheer* and the *Jervis Bay*
That for twenty vital minutes drew the raider's fire that day,
When of the convoy's thirty-seven, thirty-two went safe away
And home at last to England came, without the *Jervis Bay*.

But now thick night was over the sea, and a wind from the west
    blew keen,
And the hopeless waters tossed their heads where the *Jervis Bay*
    had been,
And the raider was lost in the rain and the night, and low clouds
    hid the seas,

But high above sea and storm and cloud appeared the galaxies,
The Bear, Orion, myriad stars that timeless vigil keep,
A glimmering host the stars came out across the heaving deep,
And they shone bright over the good shepherd of sheep.

Donald E. Vincent

Empty Tent

The tent next door is empty
The flap so tightly laced
Protecting scattered clothing
In that littered living space.

The shaving kit
The fresh–darned socks
The knick-knacks on
The upturned box

And there amidst the photographs
A letter ready, to be sent
Should this just be
An empty tent.

Silly Sort of Past-Time

It's a silly sort of past-time
As a wise old bird once said
To spend the whole night flying
Whilst others are in bed.

You spend four hours looking
For a pin-point on the ground
But no-one wants to see you
When the object has been found.

They only show displeasure
When you spoil their forty winks
So they throw the whole lot at you
Which includes the kitchen sink.

Then, if you're really lucky
And you've not come out the worst
You spend four hours looking
For the place you came from, first.

Bertram Warr

Stepney 1941

Much as though some one had sung
'House, house, house, house,'
Row after row of times;
And each time one more sprung up
To shiver in the line.
Shall we knock? Shall we get their reactions to the war?
This one will do. But it's empty; no door even
To knock at. And this too; the whole row
And not a soul, all empty and windowless,
With walls standing around regarding one another
Naked, as they bear the weight of shocked ceilings.
Let us not speak, for we look into hearts
That are drained and stilled, as though
God had . . . Hell, like a lot of tarts
They are, with their legs cocked, showing the works.
Let's get out of this. Look, there's a cat lurking
In that debris! See, beside that smashed divan.
Here, puss, pretty puss, here. Why, look at it run!
Crazed, and that savage eye, already it has forgotten.

Kenneth Wilson

Atlantic Convoy

(Written in HMS Bideford, August, 1941)

Zig. . . .
      Zag. . . .
Zig. . . .
    Zag. . . .
Zig to port;
    Zag to starboard;
Follow the wake of the ship ahead.
    Zig. . . .
      Zag. . . .
All peaceful men should be in bed.
    Zig. . . .
      Zag. . . .
Phosphorus gleams upon the water,
A ghostly light inviting slaughter.
    Zig. . . .
      Zag. . . .
Pin–n–n–n–n–g. Pin–n–n–n–n–n–g.
No echo from the Asdic dome
within the arc it has to roam.
Pin–n–n–n–n–g. Pin–n–n–n–n–n–g.
Thrump! Thrump! Thrump! Thrump!
The twisting, churning of the screw
drowning the talk from 'B' gun's crew.
Thrump! Thrump! Thrump! Thrump!
The watch has two more hours to go.
    Zig. . . .
Zag. . . .
The time crawls on, so slow, so slow.
Pin–n–n–n–n–n–g. Pin–n–n–n–n–n–g.
Tired eyes straining without hope
of ever sighting a periscope.
Two more hours, then to my bunk –
Providing we have not been sunk!

Thrump! Thrump!
Pin–n–n–n–n–g. Pin–n–n–n–n–g.
Zig. . . .
            Zag. . . .
Nothing yet to be seen
upon the moving radar screen.
Thrump! Thrump!
The night is cold with sings of snow.
Smells permeate from the decks below.

PING! PING! PING! PING!

Contact . . . contact. . . .
Range and bearing. . . .

ACTION STATIONS!

Men tumble from their hammocks swearing.
Short sharp rings on the alarm bell.

'A' GUN LOAD WITH STAR SHELL.

A tiny dot on the radar screen:
a U–boat on the surface?
   Crash-dived . . . now no longer seen.

INCREASE SPEED TO TWENTY KNOTS.

Thrump! Thrump! Thrump! Thrump!
Ping! Ping! Ping! Ping!
Range closing.
Bows nosing.
Closing fast.
Shadowy vessels streaming past.

Ping! Ping! Ping! Ping!

SET THE CHARGES!

   The pinging stops. . . .
Target right below.

Press hard the knob.
Depth-charges go. . . .
   Boom-m-m-m-m
      Boom-m-m-m-m
         Boom-m-m-m-m
            Boom-m-m-m-m
Dropped astern, thrown to each quarter;
brilliant flashes on the water;
flashes making night like day,
decks awash with falling spray.

Turn through an arc of one-eight-o
over the spot where down below
men are dying.

Silence.

Then crunch . . . crunch . . . crunch upon the hydrophone.
She's breaking up down there alone.
The reek of oil invades the night.

STOP ENGINES! BURN A SEARCHLIGHT!

Some tangled wreckage, a leg or two:
of oily corpses there's a few;
enough evidence of a kill.
So this night's score is now one-nil!

Thrump! Thrump! Thrump! Thrump!

Back on station.

SLOW AHEAD!

And in Greenhow they're still abed.

Pin-n-n-n-n-g. Pin-n-n-n-n-g.
Zig. . . .
        Zag. . . .
Leave the bloated bodies torn.

It's lighter now, here comes the dawn,
morning for us, who have come through,
but never again for the U-boat's crew.
Yet in killing I find no delight;
perhaps I'll be dead before tonight.

Zig. . . .
Zag. . . .
Zig. . . .
Zag. . . .

Anonymous

In Answer to a Sonnet from a Wren Hall Porter at Machrihanish

(Prose Poem)

Darling – To me you write in verse; that I cannot do,
I never could, a curse, but still perhaps I'll try another
line, and write in prose that rhyme; as Rupert Brooke or Keats
or Shelley; and so display emotion whil'st I eats, and fills
with starch my patient uncomplaining belly.
Beloved – You came to me just now, and with your eyes, your
lips, completely spoilt my taste for fish and chips.

What is the use of trying to hide my wish, my thoughts are
not for charm of any culinary dish, but of you in your office
still, at ease, your body slack, relaxed by effort that must
will your brain to do its utmost, even if in vain, to keep appeased
the stream of deadly queries flowing through the narrow entry of
  the
hatch that is your only contact with that wild unruly bath of men
that stand and wait, and wait, and wait, for transport that is
  always bloody late.

God what a station – what a place, what rain, can you wonder that a
man must steel himself to keep his brain from slipping into
      thoughts
removed from cold and mist, to lips that look as though they
      must be kissed.

Do not pride yourself beloved that 'tis only you and all your
      charm
that makes me be so rash and lose my head; you are but the field
      within
the farm to which the bull must dash to get his normal instincts
      fed.

God what a farm! But Darling what a field!!

Anonymous

The Last Posting

'Lor love a duck,' said the Mech,[1] 'that's done it!
Just me alone with the gear to run it,
The TO's[2] off on an admin. course
The WO's[3] posted to Stoke Holy Cross,
Corporal Plum is in dock with the measles, –
No one to give me a hand with the Diesels![4]
We had two Canadians, but ain't that a laugh,
Last Friday they posted them to Second TAF[5]
No more mechanical personnel
Left on the station. Ain't war Hell!
Saw the CO and he's rang up Wing,
All of them say they can't do a thing,
They blame it all on to Records,[6] Gloucester.
Looks like I go on a one watch roster!'[7]

He beats on his breast and he rages at Fate
Till a signal comes – '*You're* posted, Mate.'

Posted! The very last mechanic!
None on the station – bags of panic – !

Nobody ventured to touch the set,
But it went all right, and it's going yet,
Just as it did in the days of yore
When it had maintenance galore.
So if they post every Mech. from your station
Don't let it fill you with consternation,
Don't be downhearted, never moan,
Just leave the God-darn stuff alone!

[1] Radar Mechanic.
[2] Technical Officer.
[3] Warrant Officer, Tech.
[4] Diesel electric generator sets.
[5] 2nd TAF for D-day Landings: Tactical Air Force.
[6] RAF Records Office.
[7] 24 hours duty per day!

5. Leave

Leave – A Personal View
by Gavin Ewart

For every serving soldier, sailor and airman – and their female counterparts – nothing was more important than leave. In wartime it was particularly prized, as the one temporary escape from the danger and boredom involved in the conduct of war.

Leave came, when operational necessity didn't interfere with it, in two forms: 48 hours' leave and 7 days' leave. The first was rare, the second very rare indeed, and to many known only in the form of Embarkation Leave.

In every theatre of war, there were Rest Camps for troops temporarily withdrawn from the battle, and leave centres of one kind or another for the officers and men. Hotels tended to be requisitioned for the officers; the other ranks more often, I think, had camps. In the Middle East the main centre was Cairo. In North Africa leave was taken in Algiers, Tunis and Hammamet, as I remember it. In Italy I had spells of leave in Naples, Rome and the island of Ischia, at Amalfi and even at Cortina (the only time in my life I have ever attempted to ski). There was a camp or centre at Sorrento for officers; whether this operated for the other ranks too, I don't know.

If the servicemen had no well-defined activity to indulge in, such as ski-ing or sea-bathing, it was inevitable that the hours of leave should be spent in drinking or fornication. Sight-seeing came very low down the list and could end in frustration; Michelangelo's 'Moses' in Rome, for example, was bricked up 'for the duration' when I finally found it in S. Pietro in Vincoli in 1944. The troops, mostly, didn't want to know. On an afternoon expedition to Pompeii, organised I suppose as a cultural recreation for men off-duty when my unit was based at Torre Annunziata, nobody of the whole truckful wanted to see the *Scavi*. So I went round the excavations myself with an Italian guide (paid with a tin of corned beef), while the rest of the party, in charge of a Sergeant, occupied themselves in the wine bars, with the local church, and going round the souvenir shops that sold pious trinkets and lava ashtrays. I thought this showed a very British lack of interest, but perhaps the idea of a sight-seeing tour with an officer present wasn't very attractive.

Certainly, getting drunk with their mates was a favourite

occupation, and very naturally so. Yet it was sad to see British soldiers, completely drunk, wandering about a town in a homesick sort of way. In Ischia many of the shops had been boarded up, as today they are against football hooligans. It's nice to have free time, but not so nice if you don't really know what to do with it.

Editor's Note: See 'Structure of Book' and references in previous *Oasis* series to troops on leave filling the Middle East arts clubs and opera houses in Italy.

Harry Beard

Bar Sonnet

But what is this that to'rds my table sails?
Seductive undulations seem to bear
her 'cross the floor. Bright auburn is her hair,
cerise her lips, and crimson are her nails.
Her gown is not unlike the seven veils.
Her face is paled with powder, caked with care
(concealing creases). Scents are in the air.
God! Put this craft about with friendly gales!

Et Deus flebit, causing her to tack.
She singles out a sergeant for her raid;
A corporal's stripes might mean a trade too slack,
And she's a very mercenary maid.
But how I laugh behind the lady's back;
Her sergeant's local, acting, and unpaid.

Malta, February 1940

William G. Burrell

Night Leave

I know there's a farmer who lives
  On his farm on the edge of the drome;
I know that he's gone into town,
  And I know that his daughter's at home.

'I know that his daughter's at home,'
  For my calendar's ringed on that date.
I know its his night at his lodge,
  That he will not be home until late.

'That he will not be home until late,'
  That she's waiting and watching for me.
For 'Gin and platonic?' Perhaps:
  For 'Whisky and sofa?' Could be.

For 'Whisky and sofa?' Could be.
  That were more a pursuit than a goal.
Though just at the moment I think,
  She would squander both body and soul.

'She would squander both body and soul.'
  But according to low squadron wit,
A man has too much of a load,
  When he's packing a soul in his kit.

'When he's packing a soul in his kit.'
  (It is strange how embarrassment mounts)
Like wearing one's heart on one's sleeve,
  When it's only the body that counts.

'When it's only the body that counts,'
  What a sobering thing to confess.
So I think I'll just fill in the night
  Drinking beer in the NCO's mess.

'Drinking beer in the NCO's mess.'
In that stupid 'Kill-time' on the drome,
Because a fool farmer's in town;
And because his fool daughter's at home.

Narromine 1940–41

John Buxton

Leave

If for a single hour I might be free
  And that one hour might all be spent with you,
  What should we say, my love? what should we do
In such a little hour as that would be?
Words, after so long, would not come to me;
  Kisses would be but torture, being so few
  And yet recalling all the joy we knew
Before I went to war beyond the sea.
But if I took you to the edge of land
  Where we might watch the sea spread wide away
  And the slant waves along the pebbles creep,
Then by the white brink of the tide we'd stand
  And press each other's hand, and nothing say,
  But know the silence coming from the deep.

Lisbeth David

Forty-Eight Hours

Quick, catch the bus from Pompey and the war
And with faint morning eyes begin to find
Green oaks along the road, and hedges twined
With clematis unrecognised before;
Fleet wary foals, carts loaded high with straw,

And sunburnt village houses, while behind
Night watch retreats into a distant mind
And newly woken eyes look on for more.
Then seek this city where the grey stone grows,
A place where peace can never leave unblessed
Dishevelled allies sprawling in the Close
Or cold crusaders in their stately rest;
And as the sands of stand-off swiftly spill
Cling to this ecstasy where time stands still.

Frank Dossetor

Rest Period, Autumn 1944

We had shared the den of a gun,
Several weeks in a dull smoke-screen,
In a valley of liquid mud,
With all shapes blurred
By liver-blue light of the sun.

And at last it was time to scud
To the south of the bent Gothic line,[1]
Around buttress of cold indigo,
Under enemy-shell-carved corbel

Then I shake myself free of the herd
And force my grim way through the hedge
Which encloses three neat gravel squares
With enormous blocks of oak-green.

And I stroll to the garden's edge
To stare at the opulent roll
Of the hills on the Arno plain

Which unwinds in a golden scroll,
With its silver message of peace
And a stampe of streets and towers.

The ground falls down in tiers;
I see oxen unstitch the black fleece

Now I gaze at the opposite hill,
Whose body is netted in silk,
While her shoulders are quiet bracken-brown.

To the odorous dark lower layers
Through the broom and the cypress bowers
To the vines whose out-stretched wings
Are kept taut by half-hidden wires,
Recalling Dante's rings
And Perugino's choirs.

Now I notice the river's coil,
By dividing the plain into halves
Provides either bank with a foil;
As a tumbler of wine
Might balance a beaker of milk.

Sun-bubbled mists rise like yeast
Over knolls that pine forests have furred,
To disperse in the dimly blue sky.

As I take in the scene through the eye
I can feel some coarse shreds blow away
From my turgid belligerent mind.

I stare and smilingly sigh
To be rid of the attitude-lie.
By the group all perceptions are blurred;
The soul, in solitude, is refined.

[1] German defence line, North Italy.

Gavin Ewart

Oxford Leave

'The Lamb and Flag' was closed, so I went to the Randolph Hotel
And saw there several faces that I remember too well,
War-time and peace-time faces, RAF operational types,
Girls who were arty and tarty – and several blokes with pipes.
Young undergraduate faces and over there by the door
Under a smart and once fashionable hat which might (perhaps) be
    a whore.

I stood there like Charles Madge, observing, with the ginger beer
    I had bought
(The war had done away with the beer) and to myself I thought
Et ego in Arcadia vixi and wore undergraduate clothes,
No one here is different from me essentially, I suppose . . .
Plus ça change . . . and a donnish type, a rather middle-aged queen,
Gave me a look, not a dirty look, I knew what that look could
    mean.

Behind my back was a shocker with a handlebar moustache
Treating a blonde to a *Dubonnet sec* and his laugh was loud and
    harsh.
A rather passé arty woman invited a boy to her home
'We're going to have fish and chips, my dear, really we'd like you
    to come.'
On my left two rich young men were busy discussing the tart,
Two well-fed minds without, I should say, a single constructive
    thought.

Ah, youth! and how time passes! Was it really five years ago
That I left my Alma Mater? Yes, time is not so slow.
It takes the loves and the parties but nostalgically in the brain
And even in the Army, their memories remain
And these are all real people, not the distortions of dream,
And though one might not believe it, they're all of them what
    they seem.

                                                    1942

Roy Fuller

The End of a Leave

Out of the damp black light,
The noise of locomotives,
A thousand whispering,
Sharp-nailed, sinewed, slight,
I meet that alien thing
Your hand, with all its motives.

Far from the roof of night
And iron these encounter;
In the gigantic hall
As the severing light
Menaces, human, small,
These hands exchange their counters.

Suddenly our relation
Is terrifyingly simple
Against our wretched times,
Like a hand which mimes
Love in this anguished station
Against a whole world's pull.

Jim Hovell

Alien Country

Coming on leave,
while the world goes up in flames,
is to come, not home,
but to an alien and mysterious country,
where the language and pre-occupations
are remote from one's own
and difficult to interpret.

Family talk is all of food.
'This is short, that is shorter.
We're supposed to get offal
but I never see any.
Expect the butcher gives it to his fancy woman.
They say we'll get a bit more cheese next week.
That'll please your father
but I'll believe it when I see it.
But, even if we get more cheese,
we'll get less of something else
so it'll be all the same in the long run.'

In Brewer Street, just after the rowdy and dangerous Soho pubs,
where I'd been drinking, closed for the night,
a shabby old man in a fawn mackintosh
and a battered trilby hat
materialised out of the darkness,
whispered a furtive invitation.
Not to see a dirty film-show.
Not to an orgy.
Not to enjoy two women simultaneously
or even one on her own.
'Fancy a nice juicy steak, guv, the real thing,' he muttered.
'Rump or fillet. As much as you can eat.
Chips and peas as well.
Not far from 'ere. Just a few minutes' walk,' he wheedled.
'You only got to follow me. But, if you see a copper,
just pretend you ain't nothing to do with me.'

Clearly, the fate of western civilisation depends
upon tins of Spam and packets of dried egg
and draconian measures to ensure that the butchers
do not reserve their offal for their fancy women.

The talk of my friends is guarded.
I come and go on leave and (as they see it)
am uncommitted, disinterested, uninvolved, transient,
a tourist, circumspectly welcomed
temporarily among them but not, now, one of them,
not, now, one of the natives of the place.

When, Barbara, I was last on leave,
Peter (still in his reserved occupation)
had moved in with you
and, over the quart bottles filled with draught bitter
brought from The Flask just before closing time,
there was talk about books and there were the latest issues
of Horizon and Poetry London to discuss.
This time, perhaps, your husband, the Mad Major,
will have returned and, as once before,
will talk a lot of balls to me
about battle training with the Bren gun,
while you, Barbara, having earlier made sure
that all copies of Horizon and Poetry London
and all other evidence of Peter's recent occupation
have been removed, will look on, warily and uneasily,
in case, in some forgetful, unguarded or, even,
treacherous moment, I let slip a reference
to previous visits and the conversations
over the bottles of draught bitter.

And, Sylvia, this time you have offered
no invitations to your loud and vulgar parties
in your house in The Grove,
nor any hint that any such ever occurred.
Something, obviously, has happened to curb your goings-on
but, native Sylvia, you clearly do not intend
to confide in a mere tourist about such matters.

And, Brenda, will you be asking me back, as before,
to lie with you beneath the shiny eiderdown,
to make love while Geraldo plays on the wireless
on your bedside table?
Or, on the other hand, when I meet you in the pub,
will you, by a casual gesture, a dismissive glance,
indicate that someone else has replaced me
under the shiny eiderdown and that Geraldo no longer plays for
    me
on your wireless.

I venture with trepidation into this alien country
with its ambiguous landscape, obscure pre-occupations
and shifting relationships.

Jack. D. Lavers

The Morning After

Piastres, lire, francs, BMA.[1]
That's what we're used to in drawing our pay.
Drachma, millieme, centime and fils,
Copper coin, silver coin, rich looking bills.
Money, more money, so easy it flows.
I've not the faintest idea where the hell it all goes,
But go it does and quickly, leaving no trace
Of how it was spent, the time or the place.

Piastres, lire, francs, BMA.[1]
I've nothing to show how I've thrown them away
But in Alex. the bar-owner's wives bathe in milk
And all the hostesses wear nothing but silk.
In Tel Aviv, Cairo, in Tunis or Bari
The owner of any disreputable gharri
Who can jog around town on a tour of the dives
Can take diamond bracelets home to their wives.

Piastres, lire, francs, BMA.
Maleesh how much the cost while we were gay.
Ten akkers a glass for the hostess's drink,
Ten akkers for beer fit to pour down the sink.
Next morning, a headache is all I can show
For twenty weeks back-pay blued in one go.
In all of the currencies I've saved not a dime
A poor show indeed – but oh boy what a time!'

19th November 1943

[1] British military currency.

Louis Lawler

Ein Karem

Dodgy the god-gift on the thymey hillside
Under olive trees and won't last long.
What was whispered's been belied.

Laughters in cypresses across the valley
Do not doubt its going wrong.
Lizards move impatiently in the stony wadi.

God-licked however and holy the afternoon lovers
Are fortunate in harmonies and sing their song
Without rehearsing, though each afterwards discovers

What the trick was in the harebrained
Caper and the convent gong
None expected or explained:

These were the performance and no run-through.
Each knows that to such belong
Their chances of being beautiful and true.

Charles Edward Naylor

*The Japanese Government has agreed to unconditional
surrender following the dropping of the second atomic bomb.*

Burma Leave

We were seven, a seven insisting and sure
Of re-unions, jobs for the boys when the war
Rolled its bleak bloody course. Only now there are four
So we all drank arak in Mingaladon.

We had whored in the houses and sank in the ruts
Of the glorious Vino . . . consorted with sluts
For we knew of the fear that had spewed in our guts,
And we all drank arak in Mingaladon.

We had seen death at home in the slow passing hearse,
But here was the fountain of death at its worst,
With the last fleeting seconds, a whimper, a curse,
So we all drank arak in Mingaladon.

For the dead in their fox-holes, corrupting and vile
With the drawn yellow flesh and the teeth set in smile
Will be tumbling round in our heads for a while,
So we all drank arak in Mingaladon.

The cold and the heat, and your courage that shrank,
And your woman at home in the arms of a Yank,
The thing that was Phillip. Your mind goes a blank
When you all drink arak in Mingaladon.

So drink and be damned. More whiskey you swine.
We'll all get a woman and have a good time,
For better the pox than return to the line.
So we all drank arak in Mingaladon.

Richard M. Roberts

Alexandria

Three days leave
In Alexandria's teeming streets.
The pleasure of the hard pavement
After the soft dusty sand
To sleep between the white cool sheets
The fresh water shower
Boots that remain clean,
The twice daily change

Of pressed and laundered khaki
The cafe's long-stemmed drink
The luxury of the full course meal
The gharries and the gardens of the Bourse.
The nearness of the sea . . .
This . . . a near heaven to us
Who have been so long away
From the sidewalks and the trams,
The shops, the banks, the cinemas,
The busy people.
The pretty frocks that flutter in the breeze
Like butterflies in this garden
Of concrete, chrome and steel.
We have not walked within
A city, town, or village
Since Capetown.
There is no welcome here
From smart-dressed Europeans
Nor do we seek one,
Sufficient is the freedom that we've won
To shop and buy and stroll
And jostle with the crowds
In the shafted sunlight
Of a sea-washed sun.
We know of the squalid Arab quarters
That cling to the city's skirts
The awful stench of tannery
That greets the western approach,
And the festering coloured beauties
The flowers of Sister Street.[1]
Of ugliness and hardship
Of dirt we've seen enough.
So deliberately we turn our backs
On the sewers of this glittering delta port
Privileged as we are to choose
And turn to the fuller pleasures
Of a saner life.

[1] Brothel area.

Russell Sage

48-Hour Pass

Meeting

And now hello my love for we have met and kissed
As wife and husband after parting should
And said how much each has the other missed
And said how much meeting again is good

And I said you looked as beautiful or more
Than when I saw you last and you said 'Well
You're looking fitter than you did before
You joined the army' – And I said 'Am I hell!'
But that was empty talk. 'Unfix your hair
The time for these polite remarks is past.
Slip off your clothes. Shall I help you? There!
Hello, my love. We meet again – at last.'

Parting

Let us forget all matters else but this
For one short hour the world is you and I
And time the endless moment of our kiss
And space each other's arms in which we lie.

For us no future. Time to come is dead.
This one short hour, and love itself will die.
Leave no caress unmade, no word unsaid.
To-morrow you are you and I am I.

No, no. Don't stir. An unreal world awakes.
Lie still and close your eyes: it is still night.
Let us pretend a night when no dawn breaks
For having love, what need have we of light?

Patrick Stewart

On returning to the Desert after being wounded

Cairo after rain, and the bough in blossom;
do not forget them utterly
and wholly,
nor regret too bitterly
the not fully
appreciated moment; the lost bloom
from the skin of the dream.

Thin mud on the roads. And on men's faces,
smiling, shafts of sunlight
in the open;
but behind intimate
windows deepen
the shadows that lie in corners, in the creases
where no light reposes;

which rest upon the debris of my staying,
the half-packed suitcase, the litter
of departure;
the broken paper, the letter
promising a future,
the scattered floor, and the chair-back showing
your stockings drying;

but do not warm the blank stare of the room
and the grey desperate chill
within me.
I think I shall recall
them even though,
cold with absence, it may never be the same
in Cairo after rain, the bough in blossom.

February 1942

Frank Thompson

Weekend Leave

When the year lumbers round again
And sleep lies leaden on field and hill
Drizzled with mist; when the green ballet-skirt
Of the aconite hoops up through the brown earth,
The only thing awake; when the melting snow
Banks like white violets along the ditches,
And lilac-buds are dreamers at the window
Shall I be here? Or will you think
'A year ago this was his death-weather,
This the last time he sojourned with us,
Before he found, as the Greek poets say,
The gayer meadows of Persephone'?

28 January 1941

Victor West

Austerity: Love in War-Time

With only the regulation Five Inches of Water,
We make love in the bath; obeying one stricture,
Ignoring others. And when the strange air-raid sirens
Bawl their first unearthly wail one night,
We lie close together, naked in the dark,
Hearts pounding close together, frightened, listening . . .
'The windows are pushed right down
To minimise the effects of blast'.
Fear and love cements us together.
It was a phoney *war*, they say . . .

Lyall Wilkes

Reflections on Leave

Standing in front of rich Bavarian Baroque
I am too aware that
under this too splendid gilded ceiling
earnest Nazis bent their necks and knees
in prayer. Walking in the hills around Jerusalem
I reflect on what Christianity has meant for the Jews
(if the Roman Empire had been Judaised
the fate of the Christians would have been just as terrible).
In Toledo's San Bartolomeo I think
Of the auto da fé and the smell of burning flesh
As occasions for religious celebration.

In Egypt and all around the Mediterranean
the sun, day after day, becomes an enemy,
drying the mouth and the soil, nourishing only
insects, scorpions, flies and malaria.
In Cairo beggars lie and die in the street,
no-one approaches and asks, 'What is the matter
my friend?' because everyone knows precisely
what is the matter.

The Parthenon is beautiful, but the cruelty
of Greek to Greek is not. What is the point
if only the buildings show a sense of proportion?

So in spite of the paintings, the ornate pilasters
and the plasterwork, I return oppressed,
and find release, not in the scorching sun
and the brilliant colours, but in the paler blue
of a Peploe landscape
and the beauty of working ports
like Tobermory and Tarbert,
the bays ringed with white houses and mountains,
and cattle in small fields –
although it would be dishonest to pretend
that fish are not being murdered

merely because they cannot scream.
Apart from this, there is no crime,
people pay their debts,
old people are listened to,
questions are answered without derision.

In the morning the boats return,
the herring is cooked and eaten within the hour
at the harbour side,
and, for me, Civilisation
means this temperate landscape and people,
the grey light and the rain and the broken clouds
behind the mountains, and the promise of islands beyond
and begins somewhere just North of Perth.

6. Behind the Wire

Poetry Behind Barbed Wire

by John Brookes

I dare say that for the soldier at the front the possibility of being killed or wounded is taken for granted. What never enters his head is being taken prisoner. An unforeseen accident for which no mental preparation has been made. The exhilarating nightmare of battle replaced by the impotent nightmare of submission. Suddenly the enemy has become gaoler. Suddenly survival has a different context! But men are resilient and composing poetry has the advantage that it can be done anywhere. Just pencil and paper or, failing that, a memory like those chess experts who can play games in their heads. Every community, however deprived, has its poets, known or unknown. They write as an emotional reaction to events, to summarise the common lot, or simply to leave a personal thumb-print on the passage of time. Those of us who landed up in a German Stalag instead of a concentration camp or in the hands of the Japanese were fortunate. Those in Far East POW camps had to hide what they wrote – given that they found paper to write on. One of our POW poets acquired Jap officer loo paper to bind into a book, miraculously concealed from endless searches.

But for us in Europe with a football pitch, some cultural facilities such as a library provided by the Red Cross and the intermittent distribution of Red Cross food parcels, all we lacked under the circumstances was the pleasure of women and the dignity of freedom. We knew that victory would be ours, but when? With time on our hands, frustrated energies were devoted to sport, forming clubs, lectures from experts on every subject under the sun, theatrical productions, tournaments for chess and bridge and I remember that we even played a series of Test Matches England v. Australia.

Doubtless many others wrote poetry in Stalag VII A, but poets are inclined to be 'loners', and I did not come across any or seek them out. Those who wrote had no privacy and their few possessions were either carried or concealed in a bunk bed, few kept mss. They seemed of little worth at the time, in the same way that in moving house we throw out encumbrances that foresight might have prompted us to keep. Just carelessness! And many of us 'moved house' often, not only as forced or voluntary labour in outside camps (which provided better opportunities for escape) but, as the Allies advanced into Germany, marched from one place to another, whereupon a full belly, an army paybook, and the imminent prospect of freedom were more precious than the products of a full mind. And after? Those poems we kept were either lost or forgotten, relics of the past. That some poetry written by men who endured the sharp end of that mighty conflict survived, to appear in print half a century afterwards, is an abiding miracle. The pen IS mightier than the sword!

Background of Poems

Note by John Durnford POW, SE Asia

One of the largest convoys of troopships left the Clyde in March, 1941. At Capetown, most of the ships were sent to Aden for the Middle East Campaigns. Ours reached Bombay in May.

In July, we sailed again from Bombay, round Ceylon and Dondra Head, across the Andaman Ocean, landing at Port Swettenham in North Malaya that August. The campaign that followed took us from Kedah, near the frontier with Thailand, the whole way down the peninsula from December 1941 to February 1942, when the island and city of Singapore capitulated.

More than 20,000 of us were sent up to Thailand in October 1942 to begin building the strategic railway in the film *The Bridge on the River Kwai*.

The poems relate to experience which almost defies description. No love-letters were written from the Railway Camps. Letters from home did not arrive until 1943, and thereafter at six-monthly intervals.

Barely more than 3,000 men survived. The tragedy is not surprising as the Allied armies had been out-numbered by three to one. And for the previous ten years, intelligence reports from Malaysia had been almost ignored by officials in Delhi and Whitehall. Thanks to untiring efforts by Lord Mountbatten and

14th Army in Burma, the first convoy of survivors left Rangoon in September, 1945, arriving at Southampton on 8 October.

It was an interesting home-coming. Neither medical experts, families nor friends knew what to make of those they had last seen four years before.

We scarcely knew what to expect of docks, railways, cars, buses, radios, houses and telephones ourselves, having spent most of the interval working as native labourers in a tropical climate for a twelve-hour day. Most terrible of ironies, wives had re-married and sweethearts had not waited, regarding those they loved as not only missing, but probably dead.

E. G. C. Beckwith

The Admiral's Daughter

(Note: the 'Admiral' was a German Naval Petty Officer; the scene portrayed below was witnessed from a window in the Lower Camp.)

It was all over in less time that it takes to tell.
It was so simple, so delightful,
so unexpected,
yet, if you like, so downright immodest,
that I cannot but chuckle at the recollection.

It was yesterday morning,
August – and as perfect an August as I can remember –
the sun blazing on the roof tiles,
throwing deep purple shadows under the eaves,
making the road cobbles and the plastered walls of the houses
dance with the heat.

Outside the Guardhouse
three soldiers sat, bareheaded,
field-grey tunics open at the neck,

feet planted in the dust; off duty.
Nobody else about –
the children not yet back from school,
the others all up in the fields, haymaking.

At the Admiral's farm the front door stood open,
a black rectangular gash against the criss-cross of the timbering.
At one moment an empty rectangle,
the next – a frame for a picture.
And what a picture!
In the doorway stood The Admiral's daughter,
the breeze playing with her curls,
a smile of complete satisfaction shining in her eyes,
hovering at the corners of her mouth
and radiating out upon the world at large.
It said, without any doubt whatever,
'I've fooled 'em'.
For the rest, she hadn't a stitch on –
not a stitch.

From the crown of her head to the soles of her pretty feet
she was naked as she was born.

And she liked it.
She liked it immensely.
But she wouldn't stay in the doorway –
not she.
She wanted to show the world.
She stepped out into the sunshine,
crossed the road to the water,
said 'Boo!' to a goose
– and saw the soldiers by the Guardhouse.

Did she blush?
Did she cry out?
She did not.
Without hesitation she advanced,
unhurriedly,
you might say brazenly,
and seated herself without more ado on the knee of the nearest.

But Nemesis was at hand.

An old lady,
a properly scandalized and purposeful old lady,
appeared in the doorway,
advanced in her turn to the Guardhouse,
removed her granddaughter from the embraces of the brutal and
    licentious soldiery,
tucked the little beggar under her arm
and disappeared indoors.

Aonghas Caimbeul (Am Puilean)

*Earrannan a 'Smuaintean am Braighdeanas: Poland
1943–44'*

Togaidh mi ri monadh liath, slat is driamlach air dòigh
A sheòl air dubh bhreac a' chòmhraig le seòltachd na làimh;
Loch is òb, gil is brialoch, feadan, riag-allt is òs
Badan chaorach ri am bòrd, lachan seòladh nan tonn;
Loinn ghréin air gualainn an tuim, gormadh air bheann a' cheò;
Canach 's fianach air lòin, liath-gheàrr nan còs is cearc dhonn;
Colmadh corcur a' fhraoich: sgaoilt-bhrat na mòintich mhóir
Air riasg an aonaich 'na chnòd is raineach ri bòidhcheadh nan
    gleann.

Chì mi rithist fir-chlis oidhche phriob-rionnag reòdht'
Dannsadh ruidhleadh 's a' spreodadh á seòmar na h-àirde tuath:
Boillsgeadh á dachaidh an t-sìor-shneachd, uinneag na mìle
    lòchran,
Rìomhach le dathan a' bhogha sitheadh 's a' croiseadh 'nan dual:
Lainntireachd rìoghail nam buadh, cleasaich luaineach nan neòil,
Smàladh gloinne na cruinne, solus sìdhe 'na ruaig;
Neamhnaidean crùn na Tuath air geal-chathair fhuar a' Phòil
Dealbhadh gruaidh 'na mòrachd 's a' cur bòidhchead air snuadh.

O faire faire na dh'fhalbh! thoir á tasgadh clàr-dealbh mo smuain,

Gu siubhail mi rithist na raointean gu h-aotrom an cuideachd
  òigh,
Gum blais mi cìr-mheala na h-òig, gun òl mi á tobair a' ghaoil,
'S gu lùb mi meangan á craoibh, ri sireadh meas-draoidheadh na
  toil;
Bha geàrr-rathaidean sìochail ri 'n coiseachd am preas-fhlùr
  taitneach do'n t-sùil,
Gàirdeachas gràidh fo m' ùidh ri fàth air cuireadh gu pòg,
Sainnsearach brìodail an t-sòlais, faoineasan gòrach nan leannan,
A bha, a bhitheas, 's a tha gean milis feal-dhà na sògh.

Angus Campbell

From *Thoughts in Captivity, Poland 1943–44* (Stalag XXA)

(Prose poem. English rendering by Dr John MacInnes)

I shall set out and make for the grey moor
Rod and line made ready to fight with brown trout through
  cunning of hand
Loch and inlet, narrow glen and waterfall, darting stream and
  outlet of a tarn
Clusters of sheep by their banks, wild duck sailing on the waves
Beauty of sunlight on the hills' shoulder, the misty mountains
  glowing green
Bog-cotton and moor-grass on the water meadows; grey hare
  and heath-fowl,
Purple blend of heathers; spreading mantle of the great moorland
  on the mountain peat-moss
Turf and bracken making pretty the glens.

I shall see again the Merry Dancers on an icy night of twinkling
  stars
Dancing, reeling, thrusting upwards from the chamber of the
  North
Gleaming from the home of everlasting snow,

Windows of a thousand lamps, beautiful with the colours of the
    rainbow
Darting and winding into plaits, powerful royal cantering,
    restless play of the skies
The glass of the universe dims, fairy light in flight
Pearls of the crown of the North on the cold white throne of the
    Pole
Forming a profile of majesty, making beautiful its complexion
    and its hue.

Alas for all that is gone! Bring out of safe-keeping the image-
    hoard of my thought
So that I may roam the open fields again in the company of maidens
That I may taste the honey-comb of youth, that I may drink from
    the well of love
that I may bend a twig from a tree, seeking the magic fruit of
    desire.
There were peaceful short paths to walk amidst flowering bushes
    pleasant to the eye
My thoughts rejoicing in love, waiting for an invitation to kiss
Happy whispering love-play, innocent foolishnesses of youth
That were and will be; there is a sweet good humour in their
    luxury.

John Durnford

V.J. Day. Kanburi

'Gentlemen!' he said in tears, 'the war is over'
Looking towards a yellow hurricane light,
Held up by someone in the struggling crowd,
I glimpsed your face, its usual smile
Checked in bewilderment at so much joy,
So you must once have looked, when, as a boy,
They give us gifts at Christmas – now, this Freedom.
Silent, the men sat on in darkness, bowed and still,
As though at prayers, or sleeping after death.

Then slowly, one by one, as a great crowd
Of ransomed spirits might attend their Lord,
Began impulsive movements towards the door.
Stars filled the jagged hills, the village slept.
The shuffling feet paused. Then someone sang,
Timid at first, their voices, gathered in strength,
Sounding a great hymn from the ragged lines,
While, all night long, drums beat in darkened shrines.

16 August, 1945[1]

[1] V.J. Day was 14 August.

The Camp Cobbler

Taking one's hat off savours of a church:
Cooler inside, out of the sun! the flies hang round
Cracked pots and reeking dressings. Quiet in here!
Expecting sadder visitors perhaps.
The long dark ward leads like a narrow nave
To what vile altar and what sacrifice?

The bed is somewhere near the centre post.
Dreaming in all six-foot of him, he lies,
Dreaming of arched foot, set in its separate hole,
Body a bow for stringing, or a hound
In leash for coursing, waiting for the start,
Of how the arrow, and the dog, and all fleet things,
Seed of Pheidippides, all messengers, springing up
To demonstrate their swift perfection with fierce joy.

That slow, relentless stride, like the last throw
Of a piston over rolling crank; being caught
At corners like loose strings in some great hand
And scattered in the straight; meeting the wind;
Seeing like ribbons of print the lines being drawn
Towards one's eager and impossible self. . . .

The runners spin like ballet-dancers in the sun,
This dance-motif is older than they know

The first race run was so, by the forgotten slips
That launched their high-prowed, painted, resolute ships!
So raced the Argives for their mortal olive crowns,
And so raced he at Fenners, five years since. . . .

How to find conversation? How to take
One's eye from this? 'I'd several friends up there,
You must have known them, what a term that was!'
Yes – war-spring haste of the reluctant years,
When every stroke, shot, sprint had in themselves
A singular quality, being the last. And after all,
What things we did not many years ago,
Coming from old rooms moated by the river,
Where roistered Marlowe and his favourite crew,
And bridges like soft eyebrows hinted where
The empurpled crocus hid the spacious lawns. . . .
Only the great bones show the former man,
Or the futility of bringing to him shoes
He does not know he will not want again.

> Former Oxford Triple Blue, dying
> of tropical ulcers in the feet.
> *Chungkan, December 1943.*

Frederick Rackstraw

Bed Bugs

*(Written in a POW Camp in Singapore within sound of the clock tower
in Raffles Square, Singapore. May 1942.)*

You are awake all night my friend
You heard the bell,
You have my sympathy
My night was hell!

I too, heard the chimes
Nor can I count how many times

I shifted in my hammock.
It was the heat of course and BUGS.

I lay there sullenly
I knew their evil bloated bodies were about.
Imagination drew the pictures of them
Crawling on the floor and in the beam
Soon they would pour with quivering antennae along my
    creosoted ropes.
Like a tip of feathered grass there is a touch upon my arm
I hold my sleeve over a tiny mound, and with a grimace crush it.

The smell of blood sickens, I turn my face
In the attap roof, a lizard nestles and a cricket chirps,
And on my cluttered shelf, a lean rat bustles, drawn
No doubt himself to scraps of coconut;
Or strains his muscles to reach and nibble hanging bananas.

No use, I cannot sleep! Funny the other men can keep so quiet,
Perhaps they lie like me waiting and listening? Waiting, what for?
To see if you can count to ten before the next man coughs, or
    mutters in his sleep?

Or for the next quick prick that shows a bug is sucking?
How long can you bear this intolerable itching?
Waiting for the next chime of that clock?
Four times I've heard it mock me
With the closing of an hour
I wish it was in hell
That lovely clear toned English pealing bell!

Last Post

(Written while working on the Burma Railway 1942-44.)

The camp is noisy, with the shouts of mens' laughter and curses,
With the whining grumble about the orders, the food and the lice!
From every attap hut the steady mumble of a thousand discus-
    sions of the stale news.

The clop of wooden slippers, the rattle of a pail, and someone
   banging bamboo slats for bugs.
The slither of impatient feet in meal queues
And the clanging din of tin plates, mess tins and mugs.
Suddenly, from the graveyard the clear arresting bugle races
   through the uproar,
Like a summer breeze that bends the golden wheatear in the field,
So that the inattentive stalks are by their neighbours bent over
   with a shudder,
All straighten and are still!
In the camp with notes come loud and clear –
'Psst! Quiet there! Last post!'
Hot words are left unspoken, a hand half way arrested –
Hurrying feet freeze into immobility,
Then a deep and awful silence settles
Now the camp is still –
Only the clear notes of the bugle go soaring above the jungle to
   the sky . . .
Then with a loud sigh the spell is broken
There is a shuffle of feet on sand
A rustle and a bustle, a growing hustle, laughs, shouts and
   arguments,
And clanking billy cans!

Penry M. Rees

Hell's Railway

To the south of Pakan Baru
   where the nightly tiger prowls
And the Simians greet the morning
   with their ululating howls,
Through the Kampong Katabulu
   and the district of Kuban
There runs a single railway track
   a monument to man.

In a short and fretful period
    that was eighteen months of hell,
Through the tangle of the tropics
    and the oozing swamps as well,
Through the cuttings that they hollowed
    and embankments that they built
They have laid a modern railway line
    on jungle trees and silt.

And in spite of tropic noonday
    and a host of wasting ills,
Ever southward went the railway
    to Muara and the hills.
Every sleeper claimed a body
    every rail a dozen more.
'Twas the hand of Fate that marked them
    as it tallied up the score.

Thirty times a score of prisoners
    fell asleep upon their back,
Thirty times a score of prisoners
    fell to sleep beside the track,
Thirty times a score of times
    the sum of one immortal man,
Thirty times a score of ciphers
    in the Councils of Japan.

On their ulcerated shoulders
    they transported rough-hewn wood,
With a dying desperation
    carried more than humans should,
On their suppurating feet
    with beri-beri swollen tight,
From the rising of the sun
    until the welcome fall of night.

From the rising of the sun
    until the setting of the same,
Theirs was just to grin and bear it
    and pretend it was a game;

Theirs was just to laugh and say
   they'd have a grill when it was done
And the cooling breath of ev'ning
   took the place of scorching sun

With the cooling breath of even
   came a leaven of repose,
And a narrow hard unyielding bed
   on which to rest their woes.
Just a width of rotten bedboard
   for a shrunken, rotten frame,
Where the bliss of sweet oblivion
   might eradicate the shame.

Yet the bliss of sleep's oblivion
   tarried long upon its way
While the bedbugs left their havens
   for a drying, dying prey,
And the ants and the mosquitoes
   and the scorpions and the lice
Joined the rats and noisy chikchaks
   and the jungle's lesser mice.

So another day was over
   and another day was done,
so another day of misery
   was all too soon begun,
But the mighty Tenno Haika
   and the power of Japan
Can't recall a day that's done with
   – and Thank God there's no one can!

'Show a leg, my sleeping hearties!
   Oh, get up and rise and shine!
For the sky is blue and cloudless' –
   and they feared it would be fine.
There was breakfast for the hungry
   if their stomachs weren't too sour
Made of boiling, swampy water
   and of tapioca flour.

Back in England, paperhangers
  would refuse to use the mess
But Japan must give them something
  and it couldn't give them less.
So they thought of those who loved them
  and with far, unseeing eyes
They consumed their mess of pottage,
  and the maggots and the flies.

There was someone trusting somewhere
  that a husband would return,
There were sweethearts praying softly
  there were candle lights aburn.
There was God up in His Heaven
  and he knew about it all,
And He heard their falt'ring whispers
  and He listened to their call.

And they drew new strength from somewhere
  and they battled for their life,
Though the odds were overweighted
  in this too-unequal strife;
But they kept on carrying sleepers
  and they struggled with the rail,
And they still persisted hopeful
  when it seemed of no avail.

It was 'Kura!' and 'Canero!' –
  if you straighten up you shirk,
And the one excuse for living
  is a finished job of work.
'Twas the mercy of the Emperor
  that saved them from the gun,
There was nothing now to save them
  from the task they had begun.

There was nothing then to save them
  from the toiling and the sweat
But the saving grace of illness
  that was more exacting yet.

So they welcomed their malaria
   with its vomit and its ache
So they welcomed their malaria
   for its semi-torpor's sake.

There was dysentery, pellagra,
   and a host of sister ills,
Beri-beri and Bush Typhus,
   but no medicines or pills.
There was every cause for dying
   and but few for hanging on
When so many fell asleep and
   followed comrades who had gone.

It was tie them in a hurry
   in an old discarded sack,
With a plank of rough-cut timber
   to support them in the back.
It was lower them as gently
   as a withered muscle may,
And commend them to their Maker
   and remain a while to pray.

But for those they left behind them
   there were brutish things to bear
At the hands of brutish beings
   who were only well aware
Of the primitive upsurging
   of an animal delight
That enjoyed the thrills of torture
   and the quiverings of fright.

They could drag their aching bodies
   to their grass and timber huts.
They could rub the salt of impotence
   in open weals and cuts.
They could steel their will to conquer,
   to forget, perhaps forgive,
But they found it mighty difficult
   to force themselves to live.

They had open huts of atap
   loosely tied to wooden poles,
And the roof and the partitions
   gaped and yawned in rotting holes.
Either side were filthy bedboards
   but a yard above the ground
With a floor of earth and water
   and with refuse all around.

And to rest their weary bodies,
   overworked and underfed,
Sixty centis of this planking
   was their homestead and their bed.
Sixty centis night and morning,
   sixty centis well or ill
Sixty centis for each body
   and it had to fill the bill.

Many talked of playing cricket;
   many said they played the game,
But they let the devil rider
   take the honest and the lame.
There are many will be tongue-tied
   when the trump of doom shall burst
On the ears of waiting sleepers,
   on the blessed and the cursed.

On the twenty-ninth of April
   there was nothing to be done.
On the birthday of the Emperor
   they rose to greet the sun,
And his Clemency Imperial
   made a fatherly decree
That the slaves might send a postcard
   to their wives across the sea.

When the Day at last arrived
   and when the rest of them were free
They devised a Union Jack
   and they displayed it on a tree,

And they thanked the God that made them
    that He let them live again,
And they prayed they might be better
    for the suffering and pain.

There they left their friends behind them
    thirty times a score and more,
Left them sleeping in the shadows
    on a distant tropic shore,
And I pray that God Almighty,
    in the evening of their lives,
Will be gentle to their parents
    and their children and their wives.

Pakan Baru, Sumatra, 1944

Joy W. Trindles

Until Belsen

We thought we had seen it all.

Our cheeks bloomed like peaches,
Bright eyes, Quick light movement.
Flashes of scarlet, snow white caps,

We thought we had seen it all.

The London Blitz, bombs, fires, headless corpses,
Screaming children: Yankee Doodle Dandy!

We thought we had seen it all.

Scabies, Lice, and Impetigo, T.B., Polio
and unmentionable V.D.

We thought we had seen it all.

Then France.
Day followed night and then another day
Of mangled broken boys.
Irish, Welsh and Scots
Jerries, Poles and French –
They cried in many tongues as needles long and sharp
Advanced.
Their blood ran very red and so they died.

We thought we had seen it all.

Our souls shrank deep and deeper still,
Until with nowhere else to go, soft hearts
Hardened and cocooned themselves.
Laughter broke like glass over fields and orchards
And from tent to tent.
We tried; we really tried, but some they died.

We thought we had seen it all.

Until Belsen

There are no words to speak.
We hid within our souls, deep and silent.
We clung together trying to understand,
The smell pervaded the mind and the sights and sounds
Reached those souls buried deep within and for so long
Encased in rock.
Bitter, scalding tears melted the rock
Our hearts were broken.

We had seen it all.

1945

Victor West

Never to Return
(An Incident of the Liberation 1945)

Sharpen your little knives, Russian Brothers,
on your soft leather boots;
Sit expectant, waiting patiently for Justice.
One of your number was shot on the march
you claim, by the one-eyed German guard.
We hold them all, prisoners in the farm,
And you want him – Must have him.
Justice will be done.

In control of the enemy village now, we are armed
with captured German weapons, all sorts . . .
. . . Sharpening done, patience gone, as one
the ragged Russkies rise, and press for the culprit.
Justice must be done.

I wave my Russian friends back . . , with unfamiliar Luger
which in truth I do not know how to cock . . .
The five of us cannot bring ourselves to administer
allow, witness . . . summary lynching.
Hasn't there been enough killing already?
If only Ivan were here to explain!

Ivan Knak, Red Army man, schoolteacher, Chernigov . . .
Yesterday you shared potatoes, mouldy cheese, last fag
and tea. Even held Allied 'Conference'.
Where is he now?

Your fellow escapees, the Russkies, impatient now,
advance in slow menace, determined on retribution;
They want the messy murder of an insignificant man
. . . to die the death with blunt tinplate knives.

We stand in the way, two Yanks, Canuck, Percy and I,
But we could never bring ourselves to fire

at our Russian comrades for the sake of any one-eyed Nazi!
Only the fact we hold the weapons . . .
(What is keeping Ivan Knak?) . . . protect
the cowering Kraut, as Brooky calls him.

Impasse.

But Decision, bloody crisis cut short, averted
by the rumbling arrival of white-starred tanks.
Liberation! . . . At last! We all run to greet . . .
Only faithful Canuck remains on guard,
but drawn ten yards from the door . . .
Hoarse cheer from inside the farmhouse
The Germans feel liberated too!
Even the little one-eyed guard, yclept war-criminal.
As in any Western film,
The 3rd Cavalry have arrived . . . in the nick
and in the heat the joy of the moment
all is forgotten – crisis, vengeance
. . . and Ivan Knak.

So the Americans take your prisoners, probably
to shoot them everyone, despite the safe-conduct
you had given the Feldwebel.[1] These GIs
were in white fury – they had seen the death camps.

Your Russian brothers bring you a young boy
in the purple grey striped pajamas of the death lager:
'Russian . . . sixteen . . . Dachau', they tell you.
You note hands clawlike with famine, black with grime.

'Take him and wash him' I hear myself say,
and almost as an after-thought . . . 'Feed him well'
You whitened Englishman of a petty-bourgeois sepulchure!
To be disgusted with a little dirt, before common humanity
You yourself had just spent a week starving on dandelions
Strange how soon you revert to snobbish type!

So the little one-eyed guard got off. Or did he?
Do the sound of American Brownings down the road

hammer out justice, execution or genocide?
That same thing you had tried to prevent.

And what happened to your friend, Ivan Knak,
Schoolteacher, Chernigov? Would he have said,
'Lest one murderer should go scot free, innocent men should
or rather 'give the benefit of the doubt . . .'
'Lest the innocent should stand condemned too?'
But – wave of panic – supposing that same one-eyed object
had done for my comrade, Ivan . . . how would I feel then?
And I had let him go! Perhaps by now our prisoners
were safely inside the POW Cage at Herzbruck?

And Ivan Knak?
What is guilt in war? And in Peace, what is shame?
You write Ivan a year later – through the diplomatic bag,
But no answer . . . Wipe badly rehabilitated chalk
from the background of unmarked grave.

The next morning they are all gone, the ghosts,
never to return. And Justice?
We shall never know.

Brunn, 23 April 1945

[1] Sergeant Major

Prophecy

In the Grubbé cookhouse
steam billows down.
Bending over a soup boiler
a sack for an apron
the old Frau grumbles
speaks out like Cassandra
– words cleaving the steam clouds
like clean, bright sword –
treasonable sympathy
for the ragged Russians,
'It is not right
to treat them so.

God will punish us.
You will see,
God will punish us all!'

But everyone around pretends
not to have heard.

Grubbé Wiednitz,
Arbeitskommando, November 1941.

Snapshots in the Woods

Slender and white as silver birch
the women stand by sombre heaps
of their discarded clothes,
eyes lowered in peasant shame.
Stealing fingers of soft breezes
caress unexpected places;
one is free of encumbrance,
captivity, elemental self.
Yet hissed through clenched teeth
the quiet threat of rape or worse,
and one girl is startled into flight –
her last defence – across the grass . . .
in and out the bare trunks
she runs barefoot, bounding
gracefully at first, a dryad
desperate for speed, doelike eyes
almond shaped with fright,
ever askance at pursuers
over shoulders, form dappled
in sunlight, swanning in green
panic, panting over hard patches
between the trees, until a shot
ends the chase. And then another . . .
Without pity reload automatic
camera, voyeur. Come again

next summer. Silver birch
will still stand trembling,
weeping, never forgetting
– ever.

Poland, 1943

Phillip Whitfield

Day of Liberation, Bergen–Belsen, May 1945

We build our own prison walls
but that day the doors fell open,
it was holiday time
in the death camp.

Lift him with courtesy,
this silent survivor.
Battle-dress doctors,
we took him from the truck
and put him to bed.

The moving skeleton
had crippled hands,
his skinny palms held secrets:
when I undid the joints I found
five wheat grains huddled there.
In the faces of other people
I witness my distress.

I close my eyes:
ten thousand wasted people
still piled in the flesh-pits.
Death of one is the death of all.
It is not the dead I pity.

Anonymous

The Fortress of the East[1]

A MIGHTY ISLAND FORTRESS
THE GUARDIAN OF THE EAST
IMPREGNABLE AS GIBRALTER A
THOUSAND PLANES AT LEAST
IT SIMPLY CAN'T BE TAKEN
IT'LL STAND A SIEGE FOR YEARS
WE'LL HOLD THE PLACE FOREVER
IT WILL BRING THE JAPS TO TEARS
OUR MEN ARE THERE IN THOUSANDS
DEFENCES ARE UNIQUE
THE JAPS DID NOT BELIEVE IT
AND TOOK IT IN A WEEK

[1] Singapore.

7. Reflection/Aftermath

Reflection and Aftermath

A poet reflects. Those caught up in war reflected on separation, on service life, on chance, the unpredictable – a recurring theme. Above all, in a war in which they believed, men and women would be killed, not neatly and clinically but roughly and left to be collected.

This was a literate and caring generation. If asked, 'Am I my brother's keeper?' the answer could only be 'Yes'. And so we got poems of conscience – feeling too for the dead enemy even after treatment from the Japanese.

Yet, as written in our Introduction, *the* cry of conscience in this anthology comes earlier in ACTION: SEA/AIR by the WAAF who modelled towns from maps and photographs to brief the bomber crews. She sees the photographs before and after and is overcome with guilt – the work of her hands. For that is war and the reality cannot be switched off like a television set. She must live with it.

This final Face includes the aftermath, demobilisation, leaving the security of the services which prompts thoughts of an uncertain future, in one case realised for an Australian, writing when he got back.

The poems provide a social insight of the time: the woman poet on a course in civilian life envies the fortunate girl assured of security. She is to marry an electrician earning £5 per week. That was 1945.

Victor Selwyn

Drummond Allison

A Funeral Oration

For Douglas whom the cloud and eddy ejected,
Though clad in dark Wellington he had deserved
Perpetual fellowship with those aerish beasts
Whom the eloquent eagle introduced to Chaucer;
But now the North Sea separates his bones
– Douglas who cocked an incessant snook at Death –
And crab and plaice make love wherever his soul
Shrived by a Messerschmidt cannon began to be sand,
They make light of his non-watertight prowess.

For Robert whom the wrath of the Atlantic
And untiring fire proved by the mouth of the River
Plate, but later the Mediterranean
Whose vaults he visited tricked and shut securely
In, and he penetrates forever the palaces of Atlantis.

For Colin last seen within sight of Greenland,
Who disagreed with all the gods and went down
The gradual stairs of the sea with the 'Hood', until
He could have used vacated shells for tankards
A vigorous white worm for a cigarette
And girl friends having swords upon their snouts.

'Almendro'

Scorn

I laugh at death, accuse her whore,
for she seduced, while in the mirth
of life, my comrades, when she tore
their fragile plants from out the earth.
So, if her finger beckons me,
enticing, luring me to go
in meekness to her skirts, and be

enfolded in their pleats, I know
my parting will be well-content,
since neither rot, nor all decay,
erases those few moments lent
by many years to one who spent
his life compiling just one perfect day.

Michael Armstrong

The Meadow

Reaching for a book I am reminded –
a spark illuminates a picture.
A meadow like a summer frock,
the sky a blue saucer,
the wind my mother's hand
and the sun
sketching lines of grass
on my outstretched arm.

An arm that gained full strength in Italy,
killed ruthlessly
beneath the shadow of an olive branch.

Now it reaches for a book
and I wonder about the meadow
and what went wrong.

Stephanie Batstone

After

They have swivelled their chairs, and with cups of tea on their
    knees,
And starkly fruitless buns balanced on their typewriter keys,
They embrace this brief respite,
As their jaws wag industriously in gossip between each bite.

And they talk about cod and perch,
And atom-bomb research,
And gas-pressure, and foreign delegates,
And the marital entanglements overseas of the fighting Forces of
    the United States;
But I sit aloof, withdrawn,
I have the demise of my little world to mourn.

For oh! I have done strange fantastic things in the Hebrides,
Where the thundering seas
Shake the little houses until their teeth rattle,
And those magnificently sombre Highland cattle
Stand near,
Gazing, in melancholy absorption, after Landseer.

Of course, it would be much worse if I had seen
The Taj Mahal by moonlight, or the lean-
ing Tower of Pisa, or, of course, the Acropolis,
Or even, I suppose, the Sphinx; but I must stop all this,
And return to the argument
Of this lament.

I have found seagulls' eggs in the soft springing turf
Of uninhabited islands, watched the mottled surf
Leaping with abandoned glee up the patient rocks –
I have sailed by night on little secret lochs.

And then there were all the enchantingly romantic
People; tall Free Frenchmen, and positively gigantic
Russians, and pale interesting punctilious Poles,
And, of course, Uncle Sam's nephews in shoals and shoals.

And round my heart, like a shawl,
I gather the blue, blue hills of Donegal,
And how heartbreakingly sweet
On the evening air, the faint, sharp smell of peat.

Now even the memory of those glad and golden days is waning,
But I would not be complaining
If only they would for one moment disengage themselves from

those intolerable cups of tea,
And show even the very slightest interest
In me.

Angela Bolton

The Generals

Generals seven[1] from Singapore
  Netted in the tide of war,
Left to rot in Nippon's jails
  Four long years, like stranded whales.

Pale of eye and grey of face,
  Staring blankly into space,
Slumped in attitudes of care
  Each wrapped in his own despair.

Travel-stained but wearing still
  Crushed and threadbare khaki drill.
Here at last they join the quota
  In the battered old Dakota.

Generals of advancing years,
  Prey to memories and fears,
Cheated of post-mortem glory.
  I at least shall tell your story.

Loving you across the plane
  As you face the world again.
Generals seven from Singapore
  Netted in the tide of war.

7 September, 1945
(Returning on the same plane)

[1] Major General Callaghan, Major General Key, Major General Macrae, Major General Maltby, Lt. General Sir Louis Heath, Major General Keith Simmonds, Major General Stilwell.

John Brookes

War Games

When we joined up to fight the war it seemed
a glorious adventure. Had we not
by reading books of war in boyhood dreamed
of our becoming heroes braving shot
and shell in Flanders, or with wooden swords
and dustbin lids as knights in armour played
at being Richard Lionheart slaying hordes
of Turks at Acre in the Third Crusade?
And had we not vicariously fought
the French with Wellington at Waterloo
and Nelson at Trafalgar, therefore thought,
as veterans, we knew a thing or two
of strategy and tactics? But stripped off
in draughty drill-halls with our private parts
man-handled when the MO murmured 'Cough!'
and mastering the military arts
(that officers were all addressed as 'Sir',
and NCOs according to their rank,
that Regimental Sergeant-majors were
as God Almighty and, indeed, as frank)
we thereby lost our innocence and came
to the enlightening conclusion war
was not a sort of mock-heroic game
('You're dead, I shot you first!' 'I'm not, YOU are!')
and afterwards all going home to tea,
but deadly serious. We could have come
to an additional conclusion we
had not discussed in detail, that for some
it could prove fatal. Doubtless that was why
we wore around our necks that little disc
with army number on it, to imply
that though enlistment justified the risk,
if we were killed in action then despite
the personal misfortune, as we died
we could at least take comfort that we might,

if posthumously, be identified.
But once the time for argument is past
and we go into action for the first,
and what for some of us will prove the last
and only time, we find by far the worst
of possibilities is not the fear
of being killed or wounded but the much
more pressing matter, that it might appear
to all and sundry that we are not such
a splendid fellow after all. In fact,
although we wonder how we came to place
ourselves in this predicament we act
the part of veteran to save our face.
Except for that fine character who ends
his life in battle to protect his friends.

John Buxton

On Reading Some War Poems

These foul-breathed men who chew their fetid hate
    And scorn the enemy they never saw,
    Who answer to the distant bombers' roar
With curses mouthed in their best Billingsgate, –
How dare they speak for England, who prate and prate
    As if we only had a creed or bore
    Brave arms in battle, and who claim (once more)
'Thou shalt not kill' for us is out of date.
It makes me sick, this smug self-righteousness,
    This certainty that we can kill with right
Denied our enemies, as if we bless
    Their towns with blood smeared on the walls at night!
God help us! for their faith is nothing less,
    And who shall judge between us in His sight?

William Clarke

Dunkirk (June 1940)

War can be funny – strange to say.
What I can most recall that day
Was someone with a winning hand
Playing poker on the sand
Just when a bomb from a Stuka burst:
'How's that for rotten luck?' he cursed.

And later, on the jetty, when
We marched in squads of fifty men,
Somebody had his haversack
Blown literally from off his back
With his wife's photograph and letters:
'All,' he said, 'that really matters.'

But what intrigued me most, I think,
Was queuing up for a hot drink
At bottom of a boat before
It sank a mile or two off-shore.
One chap stood waiting for his tea
While all the rest dived in the sea.

What Hitler lacked that favoured us
Just when it seemed we'd missed the bus
Was any sense of humour or
He wouldn't have pursued the War.
And if he'd won it after all
Ours would have driven him up the wall.

Ken Clift

Who Are You?

A soldier bitterly asks a question of God following death of loved comrades in battle in the Western Desert, Greece and Crete.

Who are you? A Superior Being known as
God. If you exist, who then created you?
You are worshipped by all classes and colours –
Christians, Moslems, Buddhists, even Pagans
believe that you are out there in the vast space –
way beyond the Universe.
Perhaps, without the actual intent, mere mortals
have taken their first hesitant steps into the
atmosphere – just exactly as a baby learns to
make its unsteady way toward a beckoning parent.
Why, if you love man and have power of life and
death over every living or breathing creature or
plant, as the scriptures assure, are you so
bountiful and generous with your right hand – so
utterly ruthless and cruel with your left? Is
this a balance demanded or necessary by nature?
Or are both hands producing lessons which must be
assimilated, to punish or to gain favour in your
home called Heaven?
I'm curious, I want to know – so does almost every
thinking creature in your Kingdom. A mortal waving
a book of psalms from a pulpit assuring me of your
existence is not sufficient. Even if this smacks of
sheer blasphemy, I still want to know – a real sign
that you exist, and if these thoughts displease you,
I'll still hold my head up high when you pass
judgement, but remember as you do so, this is the
way you created me. – Who are you?

George E. Cocker

Epitaph

Remember us not by a day
Extolling war's horror and blight . . .
No prayers will restore us from clay . . .
No anthems will shorten death's night . . .

In the dust we are brothers in dust . . .
Death treats us the same, friend and foe . . .
Our weapons are soon turned to rust . . .
On our graves the same grasses grow . . .

Remember our youth at the dawn . . .
At twilight remember our pain . . .
Plead not that we fought the good fight . . .
For we are all brothers of Cain . . .

Let the word prevail o'er the sword . . .
And the lowly and meek have their say . . .
The future is yours . . . we are dead . . .
Remember us not by a day . . .

Joy Corfield

Budget for Romance

I fell in love with a sergeant
So took a course in domestic virtues
In Bad Oeynhausen.
The girls in the class
Were drawn from different units
But we shared romantic dreams
Of being super wives and mothers.

They taught us to cook, to clean and mend,
They lectured us on health, on sex and children:
They pointed out the problems
Of finding a home and how to equip it
Worst of all was 'The Budget'.
From our future husband's income
We deducted rent, food and heating,
With other essentials.
Only one girl could make it balance.
Her future husband was an electrician
And would earn £5 a week.
We were envious of her good luck.
We thought her life free from care.

Lisbeth David

Solemn Occasion

Gay blows the flamboyant, green flutter the palms,
The winds of Colombo stretch longing their arms,
But hey nonny nonny the lark and the wren
I trow we shall never be meeting agin.

Now Gavin can cling to his bottle and glass
(Assisted by Dai) as the centuries pass,
And Layton will join them (regardless of cost)
Lamenting the love that they think they have lost,
And hey nonny nonny the lark and the wren
I trow we shall never be meeting again.

Now Steuart and Ted and the Vicar and all
Can devote their attention to hearing the call
And plough through the Hymnal in pious collusion
Without a disturbing soprano intrusion,
And hey nonny nonny, hey nonny nonny!

Now Gwilym and Ifor and Hari and Glyn
May return to the days before wrens butted in,
And Alun may sit at his desk in the sun,
Immersed in the trains he is trying to run,
And hey nonny nonny the lark and the wren
I trow we shall never be meeting agin.

Now Bob can perform undisturbed by his neighbour
And Julian live with Debussy and Weber,
And Gervase may dream with the masters long dead
And nothing but music will enter his head;
And hey nonny nonny the lark and the wren
I trow we shall never be meeting again.

And whether I like it and whether I choose
Good friends I have made and good friends I must lose,
So hey nonny nonny the lark and the wren,
I trow we shall never be meeting again.

Norman Maxwell Dunn

Let's Go Back

(This was written in a moment of cynicism shortly after arriving home)

Do you think, if we asked nicely, for a passage back
    To the German prison camps we know so well,
That the Gov'ment would allow it – or would they still insist
    We endure our homeland's 'welcome' from that Hell.

For years in those surroundings, we dreamed of our return,
    And we built our simple castles in the air:
We'd buy a home and furnish, or we'd rent a little flat,
    And we'd find goodwill a-plenty everywhere.

We've heard so many speeches, and read so many plans,
    We're sure our sons are going to be alright:

But it's so draughty reading papers in the street,
   Right now we're more concerned with our own plight.

The Germans gave us shelter, crowded though it was,
   While Australia gives us nothing – 'cept some cheers.
She's very glad to see us, and hopes we'll hang around,
   'We may need you boys again in future years!'

We're coming in our thousands, from the fronts and camps,
   From Jap and German strongholds far away:
And we find you've failed us badly – as you have failed before,
   Seems like you didn't expect us back to stay!

So when you give your welcomes, and when you play your
      bands,
   Forgive us if we smile a little, please,
You can call us little heroes, and tell us what you've done,
   But we did have huts to live in – overseas.

19 September, 1945

Frank Fletcher

'No Blades, or Boot-Laces . . .'

Winter whitened the Ardennes,
soaked, like cotton-wool, the casual blood
that pooled, to sink, anonymous,
on lint-bright surface, layer-gauzed the ground
quick to hide its new-day dead.
Year end;
December bled away.

A hospital train waited,
lay patiently in the Gar' Midi;
I, three days gingling in my pocket,
three days to forget

the boredom and the sweating fear,
the seeping wet of snow,
let myself right in for it.

The bright boy at the Welfare Centre,
complete with Sam Browne and apple-polished face,
had shown me the high spots on the map,
told me my hotel, and –
'Whilst your on your way, old chap,
you pass the station. Could you find time
to drop these for me? I'm terribly busy . . .'
He pointed to a pile of boxes.
'Something for the bomb-happy.
I'll let you have my jeep.
If you want, you can keep it
for the afternoon . . .'
I should have known
he'd worked that one before.

It stood isolate,
tall, as are Continental trains.
As when a stone's thrown in a pond,
around it spread circles of sound,
it, the point of quiet.
Its Orderly had the bonhomie
of one who lives perpetually with insanity,
but knows no one's deceived.
'Something for the lads?
That's good, sir.'
He jerked his head.
They're in their beds;
but . . . no blades,
no boot-laces.'
In battle, one accepts death
as a bird charmed from a tree
by a voice in the night,
as inevitable, for some,
as snow melting from a branch.
Of the wounded, you see little;
they're taken to the FAP, or die quickly;

they inhabit, for a pause in time,
for but a brief moment, 'our' world.
This was another: of neither war
nor yet the civilised scene
where war has been but is no more,
where men and women strive
to put 'today' back into a calendar.

So bright the light; no shadow held
which might contain memories
or forbidden hope.
Valhalla twilight; Götterdämmerung
slept in the eyes of friend and foe alike.
One would fight to rise,
to talk to invisible foe or friend,
oblivious of intrusion.
From here a babble, incoherent;
there, another cried
like a baby whimpered, dry-eyed,
stirred, moaned, sank back,
stank sweet with cloying breath
of communal death:

Row on row
of neat, anonymous lines,
arms shrouded,
tight bound
to their sides . . .

I left the boxes on the step,
unopened.
They contained
neither blades
nor boot-laces.

Ivor George Fletcher

Password

The elemental hunters gathered here tonight,
Were led through wire,
And then went out, beneath the white of stars,
As coughing infantry, without desire.

I feel sick sympathy with those who sleep tonight,
The other side,
And then die out, beneath the fury of great wars,
As bodies bayonetted, as lives denied.

Is sympathy a traitor who would have restored
The linden trees
In dreams too brief to be resented by a cause,
A steadfast patriot, a fickle breeze?

Impression

I thought how beautiful the blue
Of the Impressionistic scene;
Of trees and hills, of all in view
A dusty blue,
Blue fields, and nothing green.

The heavy olive trees were still:
A cypress poised, it seemed, to run
Lightly towards a nearby hill
To see the still
Mediterranean.

And far inland a shadowy blend
Of minute mountains smudged the sky
Where distance floated, at an end.
My friend! My friend!
That was no day to die!

G. S. Fraser

Poem for M.G.

These nervous and golden evenings, under the lamp
You will turn strict and pale to another smile,
And other hands will help you off with your coat,
And other voices will praise and qualify
Discussing a mood or a style
And raised as your sentences die with a jerk in your throat.
And outside at night it will be dark and damp
And against the raw damp sky
Your medallion will offer a scare to the sidling glance.
Oh, perhaps in some house you pass there will be music,
Perhaps people will dance.

Here I am soothed by the sad, the satiable sea,
Here I ride with a trident the blue imperial wave,
Here I am drowned by the hands, voices, and faces,
That move, sound, and behave,
Here I am smiling to think it is not you,
My dear, or your sort that intermit the wars
To root us from our vegetating places,
It's not for you the towers of Troy shall burn;
But you are like that patient Ithaca
To which, from all the headaches of the sea,
After ten years of labouring at their oars,
Some few, the luckier voyagers, return.

'Frolik'

Trial by Fury

'Shoot all the menfolk!' the Daily Blah cries,
'Put all their women in fetters!
Teach all their children a new set of lies,
Teach 'em respect for their betters!'

Careful, my countrymen, guard what you say,
Think twice as you reach for your guns,
Lest history ask in its pertinent way
'I wonder which crowd were the Huns?'

30 May 1945

P. Godwin

Rise and Shine

It was the Day of Judgment, the final crack of Doom,
And every saint and sinner rose, straight up from out his tomb.
It was a very eerie sight to see those sinners rise,
As many Angels took their names and measured them for size
Of wings and nice long night shirts and gave each man a harp,
They thought they'd never finish, so their tempers all were sharp.

The Foreman Angel raised his head and banged upon his cloud.
'There's all that lot of tombs down there' he shouted very loud,
'Why don't you fellows wake 'em up, this slacking's not allowed,
'We've got to get this lot all done, so look alive' he said.
'Come blow your trumpet, Gabriel; come, blow and wake the
    dead'.

The Angel Gabriel looked at him: 'I fear it is no good,
'I've blown and blown like anything, they lie like blocks of wood,
'It's just a lot of Army men, I don't know what to say,
'I'm blowed if I can wake 'em up to meet the Judgment Day.'
The Foreman Angel stared at him, 'They're Army men, you say,
'Well, stand outside, yell "Rise and Shine", you'll find this is the
    way.'

Then Gabriel, he shouted out 'Hey, fellows, rise and shine!'
And slowly one by one they rose, those soldiers all in line,
Yes, all in line they rose and stood, upon the heavenly border,
And to the Angel's great surprise, in alphabetical order.

R.G.A. Gow

For Fallen Oxford Sportsmen

Sometimes it will come to us
Pausing beneath the fan-vaulting of the staircase,
Or in a sudden shadow trailing
Over the brittle pool and aslant the corners
Of ancient buildings.

Sometimes it will come to us
Under the fitting shadow of decline,
When there is sunlight dying on grey stone
And darkness on the lawn below lighted windows
One Oxford evening.

Or it may come to us quickly
In joy of summer, in white figures moving
Far over hazy grass, in the run towards the wicket,
Clopping of ball on bat, brain, eye and hand consenting,
June days in Sussex.

Often it will come to us
Where we have known you – in the great quadrangle,
Upland and field and moor, and we shall honour
Action and strength, for you were strong and are still,
Whom England honours.

Stephen Haggard

So Deep the Pain Lies

So deep the pain lies
Neither love nor sorrow has found it yet,
Hushed in a dryness that defies
Even the unfastidious jet

Of warm, wet
Pity . . . In the guarded eyes
No lifting of vigour, no glint, no wings,
No hope, that springs
So damned eternal in commoner things.

A spirit that dies
In a curtained room,
A pilgrim, for whom
There is no flattery in the lies
Which faith the cheap-jack can devise
To stretch the finality of the tomb.

Spring 1941

J.P Haldane-Stevenson

The Grey Limbo of War-Ravaged Europe

We have fought a crusade
But where's the Holy Land? Where are the ships,
The ancient famous ships, *Jesus of Lübeck*
And *Marigold*, in which when younger we
Fled from the spectre of security?
To unknown lands across the unpredicted sea
We are grown old and
Frightened of freedom, which is ravenous
And devours a man's strength, while slavery
Offers quicker results at smaller cost
And we are in a hurry, being old –
Seeking salvation by devaluation
Of francs and lire and the souls of men
Into a paper currency that we seem
Content to use, unable to redeem.

Bari, 1946

L. Halsey

For T.M.

Now the thunder shakes the world
  And the lightning splits the sky,
And fearful on the precipice
  Are standing you and I,
Rooted on the toppling cliff
  That is today, and gazing down
On futures camouflaged as they
  Are shuffled by the pale-faced clown,
  Time. the tumbler, at play.

Biographies are being flung
  Like confetti at a church:
Lives are interchangeable.
  Through the doorway see Fate lurch
And the certain years retire:
  Time's a clown and Fate a liar:
We are cynical, the young,
  Flotsam on a barren shore
  Washed up by the tide of war.

In the air the stage is set:
  On the sky the searchlights play,
Through the clouds the bombers go.
  I (poor suburban Romeo)
Record the fact in halting verse,
  Though nothing I can think or feel,
Nothing I can do or say,
  Can call the Universe to heel,
  Or make the spheres obey.

The February landscape throbs,
  On her breast the hand of Spring
Hotly presses, and the sap
  Of living things prepares to ring
  The curtain up on May.

Spring, the Italian tenor, sobs
    His liquid sorrows months away,
Sadly, because this year entails
    Mixing guns and nightingales.

John Buxton Hilton

Christian Soldiers

('This is the Lord's doing; it is marvellous in our eyes.' From a
Commander-in-Chief's Order of the Day.)

The Lord is with us, saith the General,
Behold His doing; war is nearly done.
He will bring the Hun to book,
With one last Divine Left Hook;
Fill your soul with Christian courage.
    Clean your gun.

Was it the Lord, then, made things happen thus?
I often wonder – I'm a simple soul.
He, then, who killed my mate outside Falaise?
And brewed that tank up, just beyond St Paul?
    Was that the Lord?

We saw a stiffened hand in khaki sleeve
Protruding from the earth at Templemars.
What did he think, thought I, how did he feel,
Alone and finished, spirit riding far
    To meet his Lord.

I praised the Lord the day He shelled those trees:
A mortar there was making life too hot.
The Lord, He missed, and maimed a dozen kids.
Almighty God, Thou art a rotten shot:
    Wrong bearing, Lord.

We often hear Thee, Lord, about Thy work,
Screaming above us while we wake at night,

We bow before Thy Shrapnel Incarnation,
Thy love sears through the clouds
    And heals our fright.

**And yet, oh Lord, perhaps our General has his lesson
    wrong,
Unless Thy tone has changed since we last met.
I hate to think that Thou wouldst thus unsay
Thy sweet unmartial thoughts
    On Olivet.**

Antwerp, September 1944

Geoffrey Holloway

Heirlooms

The stoup I stole as victim,
from an abandoned Belgian house.
With its head of Christ looking like silver
it lurched with me through to Dunkirk,
shot at, ransomed by the pigswill fog,
to end hung up at home.

The gun was presented to me as victor
by a German Oberleutnant:
an automatic, small and sweet
as a toy, a handshake.
From the Baltic, where its taut
dainty incentive first touched me,
it came in time to the same house,
aired for visitors.

I gave each away –
the stoup to a lame Catholic,
the gun to someone
crossing the Sahara.

Both became enemies.

Frederick Horn

Release Group Blues

In the drab shape of khaki, four dead years
I've spent in this damned place, four bloody years
Of slime and heartbreak, guards and graft and grime,
Of flagrant exploitation all the time,
Of Jacks-in-office, idiots in charge,
Headaches, and tortured limbs, and fools at large,
Administration crazy, cretin's rule,
The nadir of existence – Mar's poor tool.

Dreaming of freedom, scant escape I found
Scourging with pleasures fragments of the day
That discipline discarded; now the ground
Is covered, and escape is sure. The way
To freedom opens. I am glad – I know;
Yet here's the rub – I hate like hell to go!

13 February, 1946

Jim Hovell

Limited Expectations

After the Great War, somebody wrote something
about the soldiers excitedly returning
to the homes fit for heroes that,
in the muddy, bloody trenches of Flanders,
they had dreamed about,
and finding only the same old mean streets,
finding, too, no doubt, the same old pointless routines,
trivial pre-occupations, haphazard inconsequences,
empty longings and unfulfilled expectations.

Still, those of us who are about to return home now,
complete with the eyes and limbs we started out with,

with our wedding tackle still in good condition,
it having been neither shot away nor ruined by venereal disease,
no bits of metal painfully and irremovably embedded
in our sensitive flesh,
no facial or other physical disfigurements,
and, all in all and by and large,
much as we were when it all started,
except for being a few years older, even if not wiser,
must, obviously, be grateful
that we've got through it, got off lightly,
compared with some of the other poor sods.

For a demob suit, I hear, you can choose between
a blue one with a chalk stripe
or a grey one with a pin stripe.
Neither is likely to be as helpful in getting women into bed
as my service uniform with its Lieutenant's pips
proved to be.
But, anyway, I expect, the women now
won't be anything like as keen to be casually bedded
as they were when the war was on
but will, rather, be on the lookout for potential husbands
– steady, decent men with regular jobs and good prospects,
you know what I mean? – with whom to settle down
and raise a family.

Yes, I reckon that'll be about the strength of it.

Robin Ivy

Displaced Persons

These
Mere numbers
Live in camps.
Let us give thanks
We're not like these
DPs.

We
Who are plumbers
Tradesmen and tramps,
Or clerks in banks,
Are not like these
DPs.

Re-
Habilitate
Those who'll work.
The rest are scum
And are covered in fleas,
DPs.

We
Will incarcerate
Those who shirk.
Our task is done
We are not like these
DPs.

Italy to Austria

We knew that peace had come
When driving down the steady tree lined road –
No traffic jams of tanks and guns
Or silent men on foot.
No long delays
When urgent jeeps would slip between:
No bridges blown,
No signs to say that dust brings shells
Or maddening roughly-worn diversions –
We knew that peace had come
Because the convoys one by one
Clocked by at leisured speed,
And in the fields
The trucks were parked in squares,
Patiently awaiting their return
After the dust and thunder of the years.

Kenneth Lang

War

A bang bang war
Doesn't hurt at all,
Though the peace after
Is even better
When Johnny gets up
After being shot dead
And Tommy and he
Play conkers instead;

For all this to them
Seems really for real
And the stories they hear
Of silly grown-ups
Are like those bad dreams,
The bumpers of night,
That disappear
At the first chink of light
And hell's not for these two,
At least not yet . . .

May they never remember
What we hope to forget!

When the drum-beats fade into the distance
All the women weep;
Diminuendos leading to silence
Spell out the fear of no return.

But after the battle, if the battle is won
There is a rare crescendo
For those who wait;
A joy is anticipated
In dance and song:

O dance to the song of Death-gone-by,
Let's sing to the Year-to-come!

If we can see the year out
Another battle is won.

For that was the year
He began to live
On the verge of dying.

Before then it seemed
The opposite was true –
But how was he to know
Which way the wind would blow?
Then suddenly it veered,
Blowing his old ills away
To make room for the new.

One Kind of Courage (Greece 1941)

His like we have not seen before
Amongst the brave ones of this War,
For when the planes scream overhead
And we take cover, he instead
Stands bolt upright, no shade of doubt
He hardly cares if the bombs drop out;
But when they fall half a mile away
This man who stands against a tree
Now falls himself, and so stiffly
We realise he is cold already.

Attitude in War

His arm torn off, our friend,
And then he died –
And though inside we may have bled
We merely shrugged and sighed;
For what in hell could be said,

How could we care?
It scarcely helped if we cried
When the pain was everywhere.

Years later he
Had completely forgotten
The immensity
And enormity
Of it all,
The huge machine of war
Quite capable
Of pounding into dust
A million men or more.
　　But those who escaped,
　　Who were not crushed?
For them sheer desperation
And the deprivation
Of free will.
　　What was it brought
　　This back to him, this thought?
A comparison with
Another power
In which lies strength as great,
But does not lead so easily
To Hell.
　　What power is that?
The power of one body
Over another
Between woman and man.

There was a man
Who had a child,
But that man's children
Never were;
They never lived,
They never died,
It was not for them
To decide
Whether the man
Who had a child

Was right or wrong
To explode that *thing*;

As they never knew,
For it was their lot
Not to be born
And not to die,
They never asked
The reason why –
But others did.

Lilli Marlene

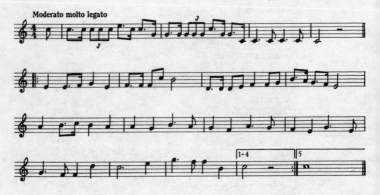

Music by Norbert Schultze

Lilli Marlene, sung by the Germans, sung by the British, a hit too in occupied Europe, became the song of World War Two – much to the disgust of the German Propaganda Minister, Dr Josef Goebbels. It was not martial enough –just a sentimental lyric by Hans Leip, a German Infantryman in World War One, set to music by Norbert Schultze in 1938 and recorded by Lale Andersen, daughter of a Bremerhaven sailor in March 1938.

At first it did not catch on. Then in late spring of 1941 Radio Belgrade – now under German occupation and transmitting to Rommel's forces in the Western Desert – asked for records to be sent from Vienna. Lilli Marlene was one of them.

The armies of the Desert – on both sides – adopted it. Not only was Dr Goebbels apprehensive but the British authorities, fearing the song's popularity might demoralise the troops, commissioned Tommy Connor to write an English version, published in 1942 and recorded by Anne Shelton and the Ambrose Orchestra and by Marlene Dietrich in the USA. The song enjoyed many parodies, including the 'D-Day Dodgers' published in *From Oasis Into Italy* (Shepheard-Walwyn, 1983).

Lili Marleen
(Hans Leip)

1
Vor der Kaserne
vor dem großen Tor
stand eine Laterne,
und steht sie noch davor,
so wolln sir uns da wiedersehn,
bei der Laterne wolln wir stehn
wie einst, Lili Marleen.

2
Unsre beiden Schatten
sahn wie einer aus;
daß wir so lieb uns hatten,
das sah man gleich daraus.
Und alle Leute solln es sehn,
wenn wir bei der Laterne stehn
wie einst, Lili Marleen.

3

Schon rief der Posten:
Sie blasen Zapfenstreich;
es kann drei Tage kosten! –
Kam'rad, ich komm ja gleich.
Da sagten wir auf Wiedersehn.
Wie gerne wollt ich mit dir gehn,
mit dir, Lili Marleen!

4

Deine Schritte kennt sie,
deinen zieren Gang,
alle Abend brennt sie,
mich vergaß sie lang.
Und sollte mir ein Leids geschehn,
wer wird bei der Laterne stehn
mit dir, Lili Marleen?

5

Aus dem stillen Raume,
aus der Erde Grund
hebt mich wie im Traume
dein verliebter Mund.
Wenn sich die späten Nebel drehn,
werd ich bei der Laterne stehn
wie einst, Lili Marleen.

Lily Marlène
(Henry-Lemarchand)

1

Devant la caserne
Quand le jour s'enfuit
La vieille lanterne
Soudain s'allume et luit.
C'est dans çe coin là que le soir

On s'attendait remplis d'espoir
Tous deux Lily Marlène
Tous deux Lily Marlène

2

Et dans la nuit sombre
Nos corps enlacés
Ne faisaient qu'une ombre
Lorsque je t'embrassais
Nous échangions ingénûment
Joue contre joue bien des serments
Tous deux, Lily Marlène.
Tous deux, Lily Marlène.

3

Le temps passe vite
Lorsque l'on est deux
Hélas! on se quitte
Voici le couvre-feu . . .
Te souviens-tu de nos regrets
Lorsqu'il fallait nous séparer?
Dis-moi, Lily Marlène?
Dis-moi, Lily Marlène?

4

La vieille lanterne
S'allume toujours
Devant la caserne
Lorsque finit le jour.
Mais tout me paraît étranger
Aurais-je donc beaucoup changé?
Dis-moi, Lily Marlène
Dis-moi, Lily Marlène.

5

Cette tendre histoire
De nos chers vingt ans
Chante, en ma mémoire
Malgré les jours, les ans

Il me semble entendre ton pas
Et je te serre entre mes bras
Lily . . . Lily Marlène.
Lily . . . Lily Marlène.

Lilli Marlene
(Tommy Connor)

1

Underneath the lantern
By the barrack gate,
Darling I remember
The way you used to wait:
'Twas there that you whispered tenderly,
That you lov'd me,
You'd always be
My Lilli of the lamplight,
My own LILLI MARLENE.

2

Time would come for roll call,
Time for us to part,
Darling I'd caress you;
And press you to my heart;
And there 'neath that far off lantern light,
I'd hold you tight,
We'd kiss 'Good-night',
My Lilli of the lamplight,
My own LILLI MARLENE.

3

Orders came for sailing
Somewhere over there,
All confined to barracks
Was more than I could bear;
I knew you were waiting in the street,
I heard your feet,

But could not meet:
My Lilli of the lamplight
My own LILLI MARLENE.

4

Resting in a billet
Just behind the line,
Even tho' we're parted
Your lips are close to mine;
You wait where that lantern softly gleams,
Your sweet face seems,
To haunt my dreams
My Lilli of the lamplight,
My own LILLI MARLENE.

Charles McCausland

Dead Japanese

Why does your pointing finger accuse,
your black arm, swollen (skin stretched tight
as a surgeon's glove) point, accuse?
Was your cause just
that you accuse me, your enemy?
You the aggressor, I the defender?

Why do you stink so, fouling the air, the grass,
the stagnant pool in the creek?
No other animal stinks so in putrefaction.
Why do you vent your protest against life itself?
Is it seemly for the dead to fight?

Have you not known the sun,
the sweet softness of a woman's breasts,
rest after work?

Then let your arm drop to your side, as in deep sleep;
hasten your decay, sink into the earth,
unloosing your last hold on personality

to know, unknowing, every man's rebirth
in other life; so, when the winds pass, you may be
part of the sweetness of the rippling kunai grass.

New Guinea, 1943

Alexander McKee

The Soldier Speaks

I am a conscientious objector. To killing
I have no objection, although
I can think of more apt targets nearer home.
I will kill for good reason and for none,
Preferably for the former –
There is more enjoyment in it.

I do not mind going to Normandy;
What I object to
Is going to Dunkirk or Stalingrad
On the wrong side. I do not mind dying
In respectable company for a respectable reason;
But I do not want to be thrown away.

All causes, however just – and I have rarely seen
A cause which was wholly just –
Are vapourings in death's presence.
For the dead only the manner of their dying matters;
And I do not desire to die
In the lost, avoidable battle that never could have been won.

(Go away, you wild old men!) I have never been
Defeated; but I have seen
A famous vitory;
And where there is a victory there is also a defeat.
I have seen; and therefore
I repeat: I object.

Hamburg

William E. Morris

Imprint of War (Italy 1943)

[Prose Poem]

Land desolate as a lone sheep lost from flock
in snow storm's hazing; olive trees walk as
grey ghosts hand in hand denuded as sparse
rock strata'd land; land winter clutching at
its throat, manacled by invading armies steel
encircled moat.

A daub in artist's dingy scene child figure
tends a twig-fire green, sketchy garments
rent in every seam cling dejectedly to a body
honed to starvation's rampant paw;
misery oozes from his every being crouched
on feet ridged and raw, his legs as pea-sticks
after you had plucked pods – and left sticks
to weather's unruly nods; child body pregnant
in its import of need – all about war's greed.
Wise eyes that stare apathetically through
an alien in narrow soul destroying life
he always knew; across a curl of coiling
smoky haze a pleading cretin looks with
soul-filled gaze, hope tinged in thrust of a
wizened chin, an old man mask creased in
merest grin; embittered tread of war's rough
shod chariot, firmly imprinted on features
lineated in certain death.

Bernard C.P. Robinson

To Alan

A tumbril full of parsons
And a pulpit full of hay
Might make a holy haystack
But show a man the way.

An ocean full of politics
And a parliament of cod
Might make the seas more turbulent
But bring man nearer God.

Cottages filled with millionaires
And palaces filled with men:
And turn the whole thing upside down
Till one and more make ten.

Colin Sheard

If Your Number's On It

Kids are front-line troops in Antwerp;
Doodle-bugs don't discriminate

Take the three young girls who
Waved to us gaily, daily
From the shop across the street;
So innocent, so sweet, were they.

And taken they were. By a rocket!
We being in God's pocket that night
When the whole row of shops went up.
Leaving us facing carnage. And they

Oblivion. So much for the nuance of chance
Which brought that rocket down behind
Those shops.

And this remains unwritten,
Being etched on instead, in horror,
The tabula rasa of those clean young minds,
Had they looked upon the reverse of what

We saw just the width of a street away.
Of course it could happen any day.
We know, and wish a pox on Hitler
With his ostensible target of the docks.

His fanatical game of Russian Roulette
Based on a V1s erratic flight
Which day and night is triggered off
To drop where and when it will.

As the one that hit the 'Rex', a cinema
Which Bob and I were destined for;
Had not the acquisition of a pot-bellied
Stove, but just two days before,

Engendered heat, and it seemed meet, in the
New-found comfort of our little room
That we should fall asleep and thus delay
Our entrance to the Rex and, as it proved,

Delay our exit from it all.
Since the rocket scored a direct hit,
Where none survived. And as we eyed the
Rubble that had been the Rex, it seemed

That once again chance had troubled itself
On our behalf and we'd notched a double
Within the last few days. And dodged once more
The number it bore for someone else.

Not that it was to last more than a day or two:
At any rate not for Bob, whose job it was to

Pick up rations for our mob.
And in the cause of duty Bob bought a beauty:

Not from 'The other side', but by being trapped
Between the tail-board of his truck and one that
Backed, haphazardly as a doodle-bug, into his
back. And this time Bob was out of luck.

Killed by a bloody truck.
Which brought his number up.

George Shepperson

On the Japanese dead in Tamu, Burma, 1944

O temples now in Tamu tumbled down,
and men and mules mouldy everywhere;
death smelly suppurating from the ground,
and putrefaction poisoning the air.

These were the Sons of Heaven,
sunless now, lying in mud under the dripping trees,
with pallid stupor on each rotting brow:

No sacred ashes for the sacred shrine:
ancestors weep for them, denied access
to Paradise, and wives and sweethearts whine
whilst war, not they, receives the last caress.

But, it is wrong to scorn them. They believed
in destiny divine, were fed on lies,
till Death, illusion's killer, crushed their dreams,
and laid the dust upon their blinded eyes.

Decaying men, may all your fellows fed
like you on lies, find out the false from true,
and Tamu temples tower again to sound

a pacan of peace, proclaiming love anew:
and white chrysanthemums and holy dew
rest on your bodies in this tired ground.

Martin Southall

Aftermath

The battle was long over.
Clothed in hospital-blue
with white shirt, red tie,
he was wheeled across
to face a full-length mirror.

Silently
he took in the trouser-legs
pinned back to just above
knee level.

Jacket sleeves treated
in like manner,
folded back through
one hundred and eighty degrees.
Again, pinned, neat,
Bristol Fashion.

'You'd think,' he said,
glancing at the mirror-imaged nurse,
'You'd think that, with a name like
Cassidy,
they'd have left me just one
sodding leg!'

'Even then though,' he mused,
'Just what would I hold the
sodding reins with?'

It was then his laughter started.
The sound spiralled, shrilled and
curled upwards, then,
suddenly, changed to racking sobs.

His nurse could find nothing
to say.
Quietly, she turned,
wheeled him back
towards his cot.

Memories

On winter walks I hate
The sound a dead branch makes
When I step upon it.

In wartime, infantrymen
nearly always buried
their own
and enemy dead.
And the dead died hard, frozen
into grotesque shapes,
their stiffened arms
wildly semaphoring
for help that could never come.

Purchase was obtained
standing on the chest
of the dead man, whilst
the limbs were manipulated
rather in the manner
of an old-time railwayman
wrenching the huge levers

in a manually-operated
signal-box

Arms and legs were broken,
brought closer to the trunk;
not from respect
but simply to lessen
the burden of digging.

God! How I hate the sound
A dead branch makes
When stepped upon.

Even
The snapping of a stick of celery
Chills my spine,
Calls up old memories,
Makes the hairs
On the nape of my neck
Erectile.

May – 1945

When we entered Venice it was flowers all the way
For the war was almost over, and we had won the day.

'Bellissimo Tenenti!' cried the girls as I drove by
In my Regimental Splendour, waving beret to the sky.

We were wined and we were dined, for Tedesco was no more
And everywhere we went, there were flowers on the floor.

But I knew beneath the flowers, so beautiful, so red,
We had ridden on a carpet of the bodies of the dead.

Requiescat in Pace

Silenced by well-hid sniper
he spreadeagled the slit-trench bottom.

Shed no tears for him, for
he has a resting-place of panoramic view
carefully sited
tactically sound
with excellent field of fire.

For him
no quick-tossed clods of earth
to press him into nothingness.

He shall be exposed
to all the changing seasons
and the gentle soothing rain
and he shall lie at peace – forever.

Or at least, until
the War Graves people
bag him up
move him on.

W.D. Thomas

These I Have Loathed

(With apologies to Rupert Brooke)

These I have loathed:
       Enamel plates and mugs, all greasy,
Ringed with dark lines; and all-pervading dust;
Leaky Bashas in the monsoon; the grimy crust
Of parachuted bread; camouflaged bully;
Dehydrated spuds, onions, cabbage;
Soyas, M & V, chlorinated cha';
Gut-shaking gharry-rides and futile

Trench-digging; pay parades in scorching sun;
TT, TAB, all inoculations;
Flit, Skat, tablets Mepacrine and Vitamin;
Flies and mosquitos, ants, bugs and weevils;
Stink-beetles and aggressive praying mantis.

All these I have loathed. But these shall pass,
Whatever passes not, in that great hour
When, Blighty-bound, I last see Collyer's Quay.

Imphal, Burma 1945

Frank Thompson

Marathonomakh

To Nikoteles the Sophist, now the sun
Is cropping the clover on Hymettus, I send
These words by the friend who will soon pull down my eyelids,
The last words I shall speak in Attika.

I call to mind, Nikoteles, our walks
In the olive-yards, the many things we discussed
And the clever remarks we made – in particular
About Life, which seemed a strange puzzle
Whose point we could not find, – and our similes
Of the fat sailor spitting in the fish-market,
Barouche but full of interest, December rain
Soaking the finger-bones, or the lute-player
Who was drunk and only rarely played good music.
Often we branded it mellow but quite empty
Like a lovely flower that has no pollen.
You were fond of saying that only a dying man
Could give a balanced judgement: for that reason
I hope to amuse you with these observations.

You will get, I'm afraid, no witty sophist answer,
Sharp and one-sided – 'Life is a comic play
Which those in the pit enjoy' – 'a tragedy
Too sordid to be fine.' – 'a school' – 'a struggle'.
Nor can you graft on nature a suspicion
Of point or purpose: that is a human twist
Foreign to life: on this green fennel-field
As the numbness spreads from my feet upwards,
I see it clearly – Life is movement and growth
Of mind and body – Life is movement and growth,
All that is real – Death is not what we hoped,
Not restful, but obscurantist, a foul smoke
That blinds and chokes – growth is supremely good
And in itself an end. Of all my years

I only regret the hours spent dozing in porches
After drinking too much wine, the argument
Shirked out of laziness, the stifled question.

You, Nikoteles, if the gods are kind,
Will spend many years in that strange city of Athens,
Which none of us understand, you will watch the folk
Taking their evening airing on the Pnyx
Or greeting the asphodels on Lykabettos.
You will see, no doubt, a great deal more of destruction
And as much as you can of spring. If you have time
You will probably stop to pose our favourite problem,
'Why?' – but remember 'Why?' is academic,
Irrelevant to life. Do you think the olive
Asks 'Why?' before budding out. Does the fennel ask it?
When you stretch yourself on the dry-scented hillside
And stare at Salamis, – leave off asking 'Why?'.
Remember what I, your friend on my deathbed, saw –
When I died at Marathon, I saw this only:
By my head the fennel was growing, slowly.

Athens, 13 March 1941

To F.D.S.S.M.

Together, my friend,
We smiled at death in the evening,
Recalling the goodness of gray stones and laughter;
Knowing how little either of us mattered,
We found a kind of happiness, if not peace.

You went, my friend,
To spread your wings on the morning;
I to the gun's cold elegance; and one
– Did you feel too the passing of a shadow
Between the glasses? – one will not return.

9 December 1939

R.W. Tuck

The Going Rate

Hardened soldiers eyed a struggling figure,
Thin, unkempt, ill clad against the cold,
Propelling a battered old pram,
Bumping, swaying, over the cobbled road,
Laden with pathetic bundles from a shattered home.
Ribald comment hid their pity,
Low teasing whistles brought a smile
To her strained young face.
'Old' Bob, thought of a daughter safe and sound,
'Young' Fred, a girlish wife,
Tom, a sister far away.
Others reacted to the smile in hope,
Would she?
Would she trade, for chocolate, or soap?

Dennis Uttley

A Changing of Spots

Bob-majoring rehabilitation
Yet almost denying its possibility.
Thousands of us passed through the Drill Hall
At Chatham – O Beautiful Dawning! –
With scarcely a thought
That Great Demobilization Day –
Beyond walking past the Jaunty-Man
(All belt and gaiters and savage scowls)
On the Main Gate at Pembroke Barracks

Like a Victorian Cotillon we waltzed along.
With small presents all around:
A pin-stripe here, a raincoat there.
Shirts, cuff-links, socks . . .
Not forgetting
A collar-stud or two . . .

But that face on the Master-At-Arms
When we'd finished!
Something, it was, fearful and wonderful to see.
Wrinkling the sour old apple, as it were.
Still stuck up there on the tree.

Roger Venables

Spring, 1942

The Spring tide, blossom-foamed, returns once more
To orchard and to field. And no green thing
But serves to swell that flood, except the pines,
Who never bare their boughs nor shed their sorrow,
And whose unenvied wisdom still proclaims
The fallacy of unreflecting Joy

That crowns itself as for eternity
In leaves and flowers that fade.

The lilac fades and the laburnum falls.
The roses are despoiled. The trees are stript.
The rain treads rutted pathways in the mire,
And tramples on the pride of fallen leaves.
In mockery of which,
The Winter raises cenotaphs of snow,
And hangs out banners of ice,
Brittle as his regret.
Brief, too, as his dominion! Ice and snow
Vanish; and Spring returns – until again
The lilac fades and the laburnum falls.

This year, the soldiers march. In the Spring rain,
Under the dripping twigs, they march in threes;
And, at the year's end, you will find them still,
Still marching armed and helmeted with steel,
Past the raw acres where the sheds are building,
And the taut wire is humming in the wind.

So men have marched before, helmeted, with steel;
So men will march again.
– Till the time comes to put their weapons by,
As these will do, and walk abroad to taste
Spring's bitter-sweet and Summer's rounded ripeness
Then overreaching Autumn in his fall
To the renewed assault will leave them naked
Of Winter and of War.

And thus is re-enacted, year by year,
The unrelenting wisdom of the pines!

Edward Venn

Easter and the Broken Churches

Beauty and holiness have been destroyed!
The lovely minsters with their spires that stood
In hallowed spots, proclaiming constant good
To all the city, busily employed;
The churches, crosses and towers that once enjoyed
The clarity of morning air, all so imbued
With heaven-sent glory in their quietude;
These things have fallen, and now lie devoid
Of former loveliness, their stones awry;
Altars and aisles are open to the sky,
Their sanctity disturbed by godless scorn.
Yet, like one other Temple once that died,
They too shall rise upon an Easter morn
Glorious, with all their wounds resanctified.

26 April, 1943

John Warry

War Graves

White galaxies of war graves chalk the way
From Flanders southwards to the Libyan coast.
Quiet neighbours dwell in the disputed clay
And none of them now cares who won or lost.
Young men who killed each other in the sky
Share narrow churchyards under English yews.
No rhetoric can reach them where they lie,
No commentaries appended to the news.
Yet why should I declare them innocent
And lay the blame upon authority
With eulogies of general extent
Slyly contrived to cover you and me?
We are all guilty. Only, don't forget
That they have paid and we have not – not yet.

Victor West

The Victors

They had talked of nothing else
but the fishing to be had.
At the Turn-Off for Bayreuth,
our Jeep stopped and we stood down
on rubbery legs, grateful for the lift.
We gave them the fish that bomb-happy
Major had taken out the Naab with dynamite.

Belting seven bells out the road to Prague,
Yellow Ball expresses hurtled towards us,
beflouring all with dust.
                    The day advanced our drought.
Max indicated where a neat farmhouse lay back
off the road, '*Hier mann trinkt wasser, bitte?*'
Suspicious, the old farmer motioned us to wait
in large room while his frau brought us milk.
This, the scene of many family feasts and jollity –
now austere as workhouse . . . or a shrine, perhaps.
As we drank, smiling faces of the young watched,
each from simple black frame: '*Gefallen für der Führer*'
all around, all gone those past years of madness.
No children scampered before us, as we left
sadly musing, disconcerted victors, tails between legs.

Franconian Jura, 25 April 1945

Phillip Whitfield

Apart in Wartime

This Cornish evening
is full of soft words
but leaves off the oak-trees
like little brown soldiers
are falling.

The advancing winter
threatens destruction.
Some will not know again
the unfolding leaf,
the lengthening days.

Lovely to remember
is my absent love,
but her dark promise
had a constrained look,
as though snow had fallen
and ice might split the trees.

Anonymous: 'G.B.' (Crown Film Unit)

Epigram

*Celebrating the change in our relations with Russia after German
attacked that country*

Once the Kremlin
Set us tremlin;
Now we've a pal in
Stalin.

23 September 19

A Thought

Why
Does the MOI
Dish out propaganda?
We prefer Carmen Miranda
And Alice Faye
Any day.

Holyhead, 27 October 19

Frank Thompson

Polliciti Meliora

As one who, gazing at a vista
  Of beauty, sees the clouds close in,
And turns his back in sorrow, hearing
  The thunderclouds begin,

So we, whose life was all before us,
  Our hearts with sunlight filled,
Left in the hills our books and flowers,
  Descended, and were killed.

Write on the stones no words of sadness –
  Only the gladness due,
That we, who asked the most of living,
  Knew how to give it too.

Editorial Reflections on Oasis and the poetry of World War Two

This critical appraisal of the anthologies of the Salamander Oasis Trust, together with the *Oasis* Anthology in war-time Middle East, serves two functions:

(i) to clear up misconceptions of the origins of *Oasis* and its role in the poetry of World War Two.★

(ii) to show the modus operandi and attitudes of the editorial team of The Salamander Oasis Trust anthologies – a team drawn from those who took part in *Oasis* and writings in the Middle East in World War Two.

Let me begin with the negative. *Oasis*, 'The Middle East Anthology of Poetry from the Forces', was *not* the product of the virtually peace-time enclave in war-time Cairo, where discussions raged between rival schools of poetry represented in such publications as 'Personal Landscape' and 'Salamander'. The War had posted writers to the Middle East, who encountered a civilian literary circle, including Terence Tiller, Bernard Spencer, to be joined by Lawrence Durrell and others. The Salamander Society founded by Head Master, Keith Bullen, was a friendlier place where many service writers and others met and contributed to Salamander publications.

However, *Oasis* did not begin there. It began with a question asked in a Cairo Service Club, by three of us on leave in 1942, one of whom, Denis Saunders (the South African Air Force poet, Almendro) had just taken his poems to Schindler, the publisher in Cairo.

We asked . . . *was it only the War of 1914–18 that produced the poetry? Surely there were poets in this War*. If that question had not been asked there would have been no *Oasis* – and most unlikely our post-War anthologies and the collection of 10,000 mss, which would otherwise been lost to oblivion.

For the answer to our question came in 3,000 manuscripts submitted by 800 would-be contributors – only a few from the recognised poets who appeared in Cairo and home publications. For here was writing from the grass-roots, from the well read,

especially Bergonzi: *Poetry of the Desert War*

thoughtful and literate generation of World War Two. To us, then as now, culture grew from the grass-roots and was not a rare blessing bestowed from a self-appointed élite on high.

The significance of that response was to shape our role when we set up The Salamander Oasis Trust a generation later. We knew the poetry was there to be collected – and not only in the Middle East.

Oasis may not have overflowed with literary masterpieces. However it was well above many collections at home.

The Editors had been dispersed.* So The Salamander Society in Cairo rescued the anthology and published. Their concern centred on literary level. *Oasis* led with Almendro's poem of conscience 'Night Preceding Battle'

> Today I killed a man. God forgive me!
> Tomorrow I shall sow another political corpse.

Poems of conscience would become a hallmark of World War Two writing, an un-warlike and aware generation fighting a war that had to be fought. *Oasis* contained sonnets, lyrical poetry, eight most polished lines of John Rimington *Danse Grotesque*, G.S. Fraser's *Egypt*, Hamish Henderson, John Waller, Erik de Mauny and forty five others. (Paper was rationed.)

Interestingly, we had yet to define war poetry. We had not even considered it and General Sir John Hackett's concept, appended at the end, could not be written until many years *after* the War. For two lessons emerge.

Lesson one: At the time: the startling realisation that so many wrote. The freedom of the desert and Cairo itself moved them as it moved others before. Yet the three thousand mss came from a limited catchment area. The Army had moved up the desert.

Those on leave may have known. Keith Douglas would have been a thousand miles away, days by truck. Militarily he may not have known what was happening in a unit five miles away, let alone of an appeal for poetry in Cairo. This was all before today's instant communications, quite aside from the movement and dust of war.

---

* The great difference between military and civilian in war lies in the fact the service man or woman can be posted at a moment's notice near or far, pleasant or otherwise. He/she is subject to military law.

Lesson Two follows forty years later. *It would have proved impossible to compile a definitive anthology of World War Two in wartime or even soon after.* It takes years to gather in the mss. Each of the appeals produces more poetry. This lapse of time, though, works to our advantage. We can not only judge more objectively – difficult enough when assessing poetry – but also see more clearly the poetry to hand on to future generations.

The world has changed. With it, attitudes and interests, and also appreciation and understanding of past events. We as editors change and this last anthology differs even more from *Oasis* in Cairo. It relates far more to the action in war. Then we took the War for granted. It was all around us. The poetry was an *Oasis* in war. A generation later and we can see poetry, *reporting* war to those who were not there; and for some reason, we cannot explain, the more appeals put out, the more we have received poems of action, of the eye-witness, of wry reflections on aspects of war. They were written then. We check. Yet it has taken the publicity, especially of TV, to draw them in.

Clearly it would not be possible to produce a series of anthologies without an editorial policy and mode of operation. Our late colleague, Professor Ian Fletcher, wrote in the Introduction to our first anthology as a Trust, *Return to Oasis*:

It is to be hoped this anthology is both a document and a memorial. What it is not, unlike some anthologies, is the expression of a temperament, or very much a personal choice. *These poems seem to have selected themselves* (my italics).

The operative word is '*seem*'. True that the anthology comprised poetry from the Middle East, background we all shared, together with our regarding the exercise as a search, the pleasure of discovery, seeking out the writings of unknowns among which were would be many poems demanding a wider audience.

Yet, given a common philosophy, the problem remains of thousands of mss, all of which must be carefully read – for often an apparently unpromising collection conceals a poem of inspiration lower down. We must balance an anthology between established poets and unknowns – usually preference for the latter, as the former have appeared in print, balance between themes and, above all, between content and literary level.

Thanks especially to the late G.S. Fraser, *Return to Oasis* certainly achieved its balance, enjoying both the War's leading poets, Douglas, Keyes, Jarmain, Henderson, Uys Krige, Sorley Mclean, G.S. Fraser, John Waller, Victor West and so many discoveries, the poem *Luck* of Denis McHarrie, or John Brooke (whose poem *Thermopylne '41*, to appear first in the next anthology *From Oasis into Italy*, must rank as unique in war poetry – we can find no parallel).

The end product, though, as with later anthologies, concealed the many selection stages, over a period of two years and more, sometimes, especially as with our later anthologies, challenge and counter-challenge, with the determination . . . *we must get it right*

In all this we are asking four basic questions.

Q.1. What is *war* poetry? Not just poetry, but *war* poetry?
Q.2. By which criteria do we judge?
Q.3. What should we include in an anthology?
Q.4. From where do we draw our material?

As in many walks of life there cannot be hard and fast answers so much is subjective. We begin with definitions. We draw boundary line: only those poems written by those serving and written during World War Two – with a few exceptions listed in our Introductions.

This poetry enjoys an immediacy later writing cannot always re-create. The boundary line gives the poetry a unity. As to what is war poetry can most easily be answered negatively. Not poetry that could be written in peace-time. War poetry is that written under the pressures and inspiration of war. It can take many literary forms and whether it is neo-classical, modernist, neo georgian, or whatever, may be of outstanding interest to certain academics but less so to us. We judge on three counts. Has the poet something to say? Can he/she say it – the mode of expression and literary level? Above all, has it that magic spark of inspiration which any work of art must have? Invention. Creativity. A new twist to an old theme. Content and literary level may conflict and hence we are so indebted to our late colleague Professor Ia

---

* Hardly a commercial proposition, not possible without editors and advisers *giving* their time and the unstinted help from staff at the Imperial War Museum and members of the public in UK and Commonwealth.

Fletcher, not only an authority on twentieth century poetry but also a Middle East war poet, for his reminders of what poetry must be, not just prose chopped into odd lengths. Ian would walk round the room, declaiming the poem – for the poetry must have a sound – its final test.

So to the compilation of an anthology. It must have a structure. 'Theatres of War'. This time by 'Faces of War'. We need a balance of subjects – and styles – and even lengths. As for sources of poetry, as explained, we have drawn on two streams: the established poets, already published, but far more, those moved to write by going to war, whose mss come to us in original form or privately published occasionally. We eschew the term 'amateurs' to describe these poets. It can be derogatory.

Finally, throughout our work we are concerned with authenticity. Hence our rejection of a 'religious' poem purported to have been written by a soldier and placed in a slit-trench at El Agehila, published in *Poems from the Desert* (Harrap), and commended by no less than Montgomery. We sensed no soldier would write that way well before we found the Sunday paper story of a professional, Gerald Kersh, had written from comfort far away.

In the context of authenticity we have always published the poet's version, when reprinting the poems of Keith Douglas and not Desmond Graham's revision (OUP). Before he left for Normandy to be killed in 1944, Keith Douglas, a perfectionist, handed all his mss to Tambimuttu of Editions Poetry London. There were markings where Douglas had a second thought. But the poems Tambi published in *Alamein to Zem-Zem* are those of Keith Douglas, from where the Trust reprints. For the Trust produced its first anthology *Return to Oasis* in conjunction with Editions Poetry London. The book included a piece by Tambi *Last Lunch with Keith Douglas*. It reveals the fate of the Douglas mss and is most critical of the Graham revisions.

For example, *compare* the revision in *How to Kill*, as quoted incidentally in Professor Bergonzi's indifferently researched *Poetry of the Desert War*,

> And look, has made a man of dust
> of a man of flesh. Being damned, I am amused
> to see the centre of love diffused   (O.U.P.)

with the poet's version, we have used,

> And look, has made a man of dust
> of a man of flesh. This sorcery
> I do, Being damned, I am amused
> to see the centre of love diffused

'This sorcery' enjoys a sound, missing in revision. The lines move. The revision, however, is minor compared to other poems. For some strange reason Tambi's article in *Return to Oasis* has been completely ignored, even by academics whom one might expect to be most concerned with the revision of the leading poet of the War. But then, maybe, they have not read the *Oasis* series even if they have pronounced on it and maybe damned it.

Victor Selwyn

For reference:

Return to Oasis (includes the original *Oasis* from Middle East 1942/3) 1980 – Shepheard & Walwyn

From Oasis into Italy 1983 – Shepheard & Walwyn

Poems of the Second World War: The Oasis Selection 1985 – Dent

More Poems of the Second World War: The Oasis Selection 1989 – Dent

Addendum: on War Poetry: From General Sir John Hackett's Foreword to *From Oasis into Italy*, chiefly written for the benefit of critics, who he was sure would take no notice. But it had to be written, a definition of *Oasis* anthology war poetry . . . of poems written under the emotions of war, poems that would not otherwise have been written were it not for war. Poems reflecting the feelings and attitudes of those in war, giving us,

'a collection in all its variety, at all its level of quality, as a glimpse as part of the structure of which the *history* was made, a sort of environmental archive without which all the factual chronicles of events and all the hardware on display have little meaning'.

World War Two History*
1939–1945

In these pages we aim to present a summarised history of World War Two both by theatre of war and chronologically, identifying main events. To keep a chronological sequence The Pacific SE Asia war is divided into two sections, one before Normandy to Germany and one after.

Origins

By the sheer extent of the terrain it eventually covered, and by the vast suffering it inflicted on civilian populations, the Second World War proved a more truly World War than the earlier conflict of 1914–18. The principle belligerents were the Axis powers – Germany, Italy and Japan – and the Allies – Great Britain and the Commonwealth countries, Australia, New Zealand, South Africa and Canada, together with France, the United States, the Soviet Union and to a lesser extent, China. (The Allies are now the permanent members of the United Nations Security Council.)

The 1919 Treaty of Versailles created many of the problems which faced Europe between the wars. Its punitive clauses had several dire consequences in that they

  i. fuelled the Nazi movement in Germany – reparations led to the inflation that wiped out the savings of the thrifty.

* The reader is referred to Field Marshal Lord Carver's 'Historical Review' in *Poems of the Second World War: The Oasis Selection* (Dent). The official British record published by HMSO forms a useful starting point for the student.

It is easy to select documents or choose hearsay evidence to show that what happened did not, especially by those who were not there. One must be wary of certain potted histories from both sides of the Atlantic.

For a one-volume insight read Viscount Alanbrooke's Diary (Arthur Bryant: *Triumph in the West*) and for the diplomatic tangle of the pre-war years A.J.P. Taylor – *The Origins of the Second World War*. There is a wealth of historical background in the records offices in Britain – Kew and the British Library; in Washington DC and in Koblenz in Germany – a great deal 40 years later still untapped and often unsorted. Finally, for German background consult histories by Professor Andreas Hillgruber.

ii. provided a rationale for those in Britain and France who felt the Germans – and Hitler – had a just cause. (The Prussian military claimed they had never been defeated in 1918 – only betrayed on the home front.)

The Treaty re-drew the map of Europe. As ever in history, new frontiers would provide a *casus belli*.

Hitler, elected Chancellor in January 1933, tore up the Treaty of Versailles and ordered conscription two years later. Then, *without firing a shot*, Nazi Germany

i. re-occupied the Rhineland, 10 March 1936.
ii. annexed Austria 11 March 1938, having guaranteed its frontiers two years before (Treaty of 11 July 1936).
iii. cajoled Britain and France into the Munich Agreement of 30 September 1938. The two powers obliged Czechoslovakia to cede the Sudetenland to Germany and stand down 34 divisions. Hitler in return assured the Peace of Europe. 'No more territorial demands'.
iv. marched into Bohemia and Moravia and on 14 March 1939, taking over the rest of Czechoslovakia.
v. forced Lithuania to cede Memel on 23 March 1939.

The occupation of Prague changed British attitudes.

On 29 March a news report of imminent German troop movements towards the Polish frontier (though not from official sources) spurred the British Government into its declaration of unconditional support for Polish independence on 30 March. This declaration[1] shaped subsequent events. Poland faced with a demand on the Polish Corridor and the Free City of Danzig – relics of the Treaty of Versailles – stiffened its resolve not only to resist Germany but also to veto any cooperation with the Soviet Union. However, to implement the British and French undertaking the two powers had to look to Russia, which had a common frontier with Poland, to defend Poland which did not want Soviet help. So began a frustrating 4 months of negotiations. Any Russian plan including a wider range Treaty entailed crossing frontiers.

[1] The declaration also ensured Poland would not fall into Germany's orbit – a British fear.

On 24 August 1939 Nazi Germany signed a pact with Soviet Russia.

The Pact stunned many in the West who assumed the Soviets would not deal with the Nazis. To German historians, though, (as Dr. Seidelmann, our colleague, explains) the Pact accords with what they term 'Territorial Reality'. Central and Eastern Europe comprised smaller countries, which for a century looked to one of the two bigger countries on either side, Germany or Russia, as a protector.

Between the wars Germany drew the Baltic States into its orbit. Poland supported Germany in the September 1938 Czechoslovakia crisis, making its demands on Tešin. (For this support the Russians ended their non-aggression pact with Poland.) Poland also shared German objectives in the Soviet Ukraine. But in 1939 the Poles felt strong enough to assert their independence, balancing Germany against Russia. Germany prepared for war if Poland would not concede their demands. In late July the Germans, aware of every detail of the fruitless Anglo-French-Soviet talks, had used a Moscow trade mission to offer a deal Stalin could hardly resist. In return for a non-aggression pact, keeping out of the imminent war, the Soviets could recover former Czarist territories, lost in the 1917 Revolution and Treaties after World War One: the Baltic States, Eastern Poland, Bessarabia. The Baltic States were especially important. They governed the route to Leningrad, vulnerable to invasion by land or sea. (In World War Two Leningrad would be under siege for three years. The Soviet aim, as Czarist, was to have a protective cordon of neutral or satellite states aligning Russia's open borders.)

The Soviets had another reason to accept. In the Far East the Japanese invasion of Manchuria and China, which began in 1931 at Mukden, led to battles with the Soviet Army on the Mongolian frontier in the summer of 1939. Eventually the Japanese were halted at Nomandhum, having suffered 18,000 casualties. Days later, Foreign Ministers, Ribbentrop and Molotov signed the Pact.[2]

---

[2] In general, foreign policy of most countries stems from a perceived self-interest. Diversions – political or religious – have proved very costly. In the absence or non-availability of Soviet contemporary records, the German interpretation in

Unless Poland gave way the German Army was now ready – but not for a long war. Hitler believed first in threat – and this had worked well up to 1939. Now, committed to war, it had to be a lightning affair, 'blitzkrieg', without even a force in reserve. This would work in Poland and later in the Low Countries and France. In the Middle East it did not in the end and in Russia the strategy finally came unstuck.

1939–1940: From the 'Phoney' War to the Fall of France and Dunkirk

On 1 September 1939 Germany invaded Poland and bombed Warsaw. On 3 September Britain and France declared war. Up to the last minute – and beyond – diplomatic efforts were made to avert war. Public opinion, especially in Britain, decided Hitler had to be stopped. However, while Poland was over-run and the Soviet Union took advantage to move its frontiers westwards, for eight months French and British forces sat in defensive positions – along the Maginot line and in north-eastern France – facing the Germans in the Siegfried Line. This was the 'phoney' war.

On 9 April 1940 Germany invaded Denmark and Norway, forestalling an ill-prepared British and French intervention. On 10 May Churchill replaced Chamberlain as Britain's Prime Minister. On the same day the Nazis invaded the Low Countries and bombed Rotterdam. A German Lieutenant and one hundred and thirty paratroops made their way through Luxembourg and by-passed the Maginot line unopposed, opening the route for German armoured divisions to sweep through to the Channel. The British Expeditionary Force was cut off from its retreating French allies and eventually evacuated from the Dunkirk Beaches. From 26 May to 4 June nine hundred vessels took 338,226 troops across to Britain, including 16,175 French.

terms of 'real-politik' commends itself, though the historian must explore further. French documents merit research. France had a pact both with the Soviet Union and Poland. This did not deter their signing an accord with Germany in December 1938, following British-Franco-German diplomacy at Munich in September. France, at times more ready to see the Soviet view joined Britain in the prolonged Moscow negotiations of Summer 1939. However in assessing this predecessor to World War Two, the Italian proverb . . . one cannot help oneself to a piece of truth with a knife . . . certainly holds. Though on the record, the House of Commons debates showed Churchill and other back-benchers more enthusiastic about reaching an accord with the Soviet Union, than HM Government.

Mussolini's Italy declared war on Britain and France on 10 June. (Italy had already invaded Abyssinia (Ethiopia) in 1936 and Albania at Easter 1939.)

The Germans entered Paris on 14 June and signed an armistice on 22 June, remaining in occupation of the northern half of France. A French Government was set up at Vichy under Marshal Petain to administer the so-called Unoccupied Zone of Central and Southern France.

Japan moved South into Indo-China, a French colony (today Vietnam) on 22 September 1940. Indo-China would become the springboard into Malaya and Burma.

War in the Air 1940–1945

From 22 June 1940 to 22 June 1941, when Germany invaded Soviet Russia, Britain faced Nazi-occupied Western Europe alone.

Whilst German U-Boats in the Atlantic raided British merchant shipping bringing needed supplies from the USA (Lend-Lease), the Luftwaffe began the preparation for the invasion of England, known as Operation Sea-Lion, bombing London first on 10 July and RAF bases in south eastern England. However, RAF fighters defeated the Luftwaffe in air battles over Kent in mid-September. This was the decisive 'Battle of Britain'. The German invasion barges stayed in their Continental ports.

Meanwhile the Luftwaffe stepped-up the bombing of British cities: Coventry 14 November 1940, Birmingham five days later. London churches were hit on 29 December. The RAF were first sent over Berlin 25–26 August 1940 and mounted their first 1,000 bomber raid on Cologne on 30–31 May 1942.

From 1942–45 bombing in Europe was divided between American planes by day and the RAF at night, hitting railway marshalling yards, communication centres and cities.[1]

The German invasion of Russia eased pressure on British cities until June 1944, when the first V1 rockets fell on London and the south east followed by the V2s in September. The RAF shot

---

The chief industrial target struck in Germany was the Krupp steel plant at Essen. The Hamburg shipyards were also devastated. Otherwise, industrial production was maintained, helped by occupied countries and neutrals.

down some of the rockets but the attacks only ceased when British forces over-ran the rocket bases in Belgium and the Netherlands in 1945.

The RAF Bomber Command lost 55,500 killed, 47,268 in operations, out of 125,000 aircrew. Fighter Command lost 3,690 in action. Fighter Command shot down 1,771 V1 bombs over south east England.[1]

The Middle East to North Africa[2] 1940–1943

In the Middle East, the war in the Western Desert proved to be the last major campaign that Britain, with its Commonwealth partners, would direct on its own. Thereafter, the United States exercised supreme command.

In three years of war, fighting ebbed and flowed over two thousand miles of desert. It began with the Italians advancing slowly into Egypt from Libya, reaching Sidi Barrani on 18 September 1940. In a masterly counter-stroke, Wavell's 'Thirty Thousand' routed and encircled the Italians and had taken 24,000 prisoners by 23 December and 30,000 more prisoners at Bardia by January 1941. The Australian troops reached Tobruk on 22 January 1941. The port of Tobruk became a focal point as Australian, Indian and South African forces remained there under siege. (Tobruk changed hands twice. Rommel took it on his third counter-offensive in the desert on 22 June 1942 and held it until 12 November, when Montgomery's forces finally took it after El Alamein. Tobruk proved typical of the see-saw nature of the Desert War.)

Two factors were to shape the campaign. Firstly, British, New Zealand and Australian troops were diverted fruitlessly to Greece

[1] Memo from Wing Commander Derek Martin: In my own command (Coastal), 10,304 aircrew were killed or injured. As regards Bomber Command, with an average loss of 4% per raid and an operational tour of 30 operations, it was statistically impossible to finish a tour. Yet the aircrews went out again and again, knowing their chance of survival was slender.

[2] See Lord Carver's Historical Review in *Poems of the Second World War: The Oasis Selection* (Dent 1985) and Erik de Mauny's Chronology in *Return to Oasis* (Shepheard-Walwyn 1980).

and Crete, where many were taken prisoner. Secondly, the Germans[3] under Rommel, took over from the Italians and their planes dominated the Mediterranean.

In a war of attack and counter-attack the first German offensive took them to Sollum.

A year after pushing the Italians back into Libya, the British and Allied forces reached the same line. Rommel mounted a counter-offensive in January 1942 and a second in May. Notwithstanding heavy damage on German armour inflicted by the Desert Air Force, in June Rommel took Tobruk and advanced into Egypt. The 22 Armoured Brigade and the New Zealanders finally stopped Rommel at Alam Halfa, 3 September 1942.

On 18 August General Sir Harold Alexander had been appointed C-in-C, Middle East and General Sir Bernard Montgomery to command the 8th Army.

On 23 October the Battle of El Alamein ended Rommel's drive to the Suez Canal. It also eliminated any possible link-up between Rommel's forces and the German armies sweeping through the Caucasas, a year after their invasion of the Soviet Union on 22 June 1941.

The 8th Army pursued the Axis forces through Libya and entered Tripoli on 23 January 1943.

Two weeks after the start of the El Alamein battle, a combined force of American and British troops with the British 1st Army under General Anderson, and under the overall command of General Eisenhower, landed in North Africa. The object was to advance to Tunis to link up with the 8th Army from the west. It was a costly campaign through naturally defensive territory and points like Longstop and Kasserine Pass were taken and re-taken with heavy losses.

By 7 May 1943 Allied forces had captured Bizerta and Tunis and five days later all Axis resistance in Tunisia had ended. The Middle East and North Africa had cost the Axis 300,000 casualties, killed, wounded and missing, four times the Allied total.

The Allied forces were now poised to invade Sicily and Italy. They reached the mainland of Europe four years after the declaration of war in 1939.

The German forces were well equipped and used the 88mm gun to advantage.

Invasion of the Soviet Union 1942–1945 (Operation 'Barbarossa')

In November 1940 Germany recruited Hungary, Rumania and Slovakia into the Axis and Bulgaria in March 1941. In April, Germany over-ran both Yugoslavia and Greece. German forces were thus poised to invade the Soviet Union on 22 June 1941, irrespective of any treaty. Britain had picked up German Intelligence reports of the impending invasion through Ankara and tried to alert Stalin. He did not listen.

Some Intelligence sources gave the Red Army six weeks[1] – the German army would 'cut like a knife through butter'. The Russians, trading space for time, retreated to strong points, so that by mid-winter for which the Germans were not prepared (they had been issued only with light clothing), the Wehrmacht found itself still besieging Moscow and Leningrad. The latter had been reached in August. In September the Germans had occupied Kiev, capital of the Ukraine.

In this campaign two thirds of the German Army would be committed, over one hundred and sixty divisions. A third of the Soviet Union would be devastated and twenty million killed.

A year after the invasion, the German Army, pinned down in the North, mounted a second wave into the Caucasas. In November 1942 the Germans needed to take Stalingrad to control traffic on the River Volga. Artillery reduced the place to rubble but the river was never reached. On 19 November 1942 two Russian Armies cut the two railway lines on which German supplies depended. A third Russian Army completed the encirclement of the German 6th Army. Starved of petrol for transport, the Germans were unable to break out, and the 6th Army under Von Paulus surrendered on 2 February 1943, with a loss of 330,000 men, killed, wounded or taken prisoner. (They were victims of Hitler's personal taking over command after failure to take Moscow earlier on. Hitler sacked Generals who advised retreat to regroup and conserve.)

[1] Certain German High Command documents speak of a twenty week war, i.e. their troops would be safely *inside* Moscow by Christmas. Even so, the highly professional German Command for a twenty week campaign would have issued winter clothing. They must have believed in an earlier end. Instead German troops shivered in minus 30° in the open, held up at Smolensk, using poor maps, on poor roads with deficient Intelligence.

Stalingrad proved the turning point. The military loss had a traumatic effect on the German army, not only on the Eastern front. From Stalingrad onwards the Soviet armies swept westwards under Marshal Zhukhov through Poland and Central Europe to meet their Western Allies on the River Elbe in Germany in April 1945 and take Berlin.

Most of the German casualties in World War Two were inflicted by the Soviet armies. Without this the British and American armies may not have prevailed. Britain played its part operating a supply route by sea to Murmansk – at great cost in men and ships.

The Italian Campaign 1943–1945

Sicily was captured in July 1943. On 25 July King Victor Emmanuele III ordered the arrest of Mussolini and directed Marshal Badoglio to form a government. When the joint American-British forces landed at Salerno, Italy surrendered on 8 September. The Allies aimed to use the airfields of southern Italy to bomb Roumanian oil supplies at Ploesti. The Germans, after first deciding to withdraw north, changed their minds and so ensued an exhausting campaign from Calabria to the Po Valley and the Alps, where the American 5th Army on the western side of the Appenines, and the British 8th Army to the east, had to fight from one wide river crossing to the next in a two-year campaign, in mountainous terrain and cold wet winters, that matched the attrition of the Western Front in the First War.

The Allied forces included Polish, New Zealand, French and Indian troops. (The 7th Armoured Div, 50th and 51st Divs and the Army Commander General Montgomery were detached early on for the Normandy landings.) The major battle centred on Cassino, where the Germans blocked the Allied advance through the Liri valley. To bypass Cassino, British infantry landed at Anzio to the north-west on 22 January 1944, but having lost their original impetus, the troops had to hold onto a strip of coast until May. On 18 May the Polish Corps of the 8th Army finally stormed the mountainside and took Cassino, enabling the Allies to drive through to Rome, which was liberated on 5 June 1944, the day before the Normandy landings.

The war in Italy ended on 2 May 1945. Over twenty German divisions had been tied down. (Tito's Partisans in Yugoslavia also tied down over twenty divisions.) Nearly 53,000 troops of the British 8th Army were killed, wounded or missing in Italy.

On 28 April Italian Partisans caught up with Mussolini near Como and hanged him, along with his mistress Clara Petacci.

The United States and Pearl Harbor: War in the Pacific and South-East Asia. 1. 1941–43

On December 7 1941 over one hundred Japanese planes and several midget submarines attacked the US Pacific Fleet anchored at Pearl Harbor, Hawaii. Five battleships were severely damaged or lost, three destroyers, one target ship and a minelayer. Japan lost 28 planes to the Navy and 20 to the Army and three submarines.

US casualties totalled over four thousand, killed, wounded or missing.

The next day, the USA, already involved in supplies to Britain through Lend-Lease, declared war on Japan, Germany and Italy, leading to the United States naval and land forces participating in North Africa (1942), Sicily and Italy (1943–45) and in the advance from Normandy to Germany (1944–45). The United States would also provide the Supreme Allied Commander in the West, General Dwight Eisenhower and a large part of the equipment and supplies of the Allied forces. [See 'Normandy to Germany – "D Day"']

In the war in the Pacific, three days after Pearl Harbor, Japanese aircraft sank two Royal Navy ships, *Prince of Wales* and *Repulse* off the Malayan coast. Japanese land forces took Hong Kong on 25 December and then swept through Malaya to Singapore, which surrendered on 15 February 1942, so committing tens of thousands of British and Commonwealth troops to three years in primitive POW camps, forced to work under inhumane conditions, on railways in Burma, Siam and Sumatra.

Japan's advance threatened Australia. Both Australian and New Zealand troops were sent to New Guinea and neighbouring Pacific islands. Japan took Manila on 2 January 1942, and then the Philippines. By May 1942 Japanese infantry, having invaded Burma from Siam, had driven British and Indian troops across the Indian frontier. The Americans at last turned the tide in a first defeat for Japanese forces at Guadalcanal in January 1943 in a four-month action. (Part 2, p. 347.)

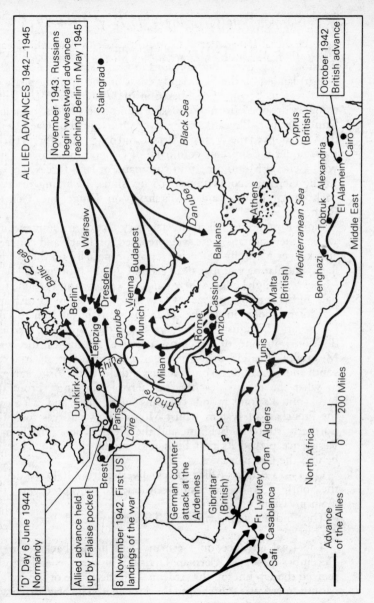

ALLIED ADVANCES 1942–1945

November 1943. Russians begin westward advance reaching Berlin in May 1945

October 1942 British advance

'D' Day 6 June 1944 Normandy

Allied advance held up by Falaise pocket

8 November 1942. First US landings of the war

German counter-attack at the Ardennes

Advance of the Allies

0   200 Miles

Stalingrad
Black Sea
Warsaw
Danube
Berlin
Dresden
Leipzig
Vienna Budapest
Munich
Balkans
Athens
Cyprus (British)
Alexandria
Cairo
El Alamein
Tobruk
Middle East
Mediterranean Sea
Malta (British)
Benghazi
Rome Cassino
Anzio
Milan
Rhine
Danube
Rhône
Loire
Paris
Dunkirk
Brest
Baltic Sea
Tunis
Algiers
Oran
Ft Lyautey
Gibraltar (British)
Casablanca
Safi
North Africa

Normandy to Germany – 'D Day' 1944–1945

On 6 June 1944, 'D Day', 20 US divisions and 12 Britis
divisions, plus five other divisions (3 Canadian, 1 French and
Polish) landed on the Normandy coast, in the opening phase c
what was to become the liberation of Western Europe. Para
troopers dropped from a thousand planes and gliders, on a lin
from Carentan-Bayeaux to the river Orne north of Caen, wit
the US troops to the West and British and other allied forces to th
East, under the supreme command of General Eisenhower, an
with General Montgomery in command of land forces.

The Germans could muster 65 divisions, including reserve
back in Germany, under Marshal Von Kluge and Genera
Rommel.

Notwithstanding Allied diversionary tactics in the precedin
weeks, the Germans were well prepared for attack and counter
attack over naturally defensive terrain, especially on the Britis
flank: undulating country, dead ground and the Normandy *bocag*
– lanes with high hedges where tanks nosed down and ground to
halt. In fierce fighting, Caen was eventually taken by British an
Canadian troops on 9 July. Then divisions pushed on to tak
Falaise on 17 August, where they closed the gap on 12 Germa
divisions, in one of the most decisive actions of the wa
Meanwhile the US 3rd Army under General Patton attacke
south and west of St Lo on 1 August and closed the Argentan ga
in what the record described as 'terrible fighting'. From th
break-out, Patton's mobile columns swept south and east alon
the French road system whilst Montgomery's forces took th
northerly route to Belgium and the Netherlands. The Frenc
Resistance played its part both with intelligence and sabotag
behind the German lines.

On 14–15 August Allied forces, diverted from Italy, landed i
the South of France, east of the Rhone, to join forces with th
main invasion.

The 2nd French Armoured Division entered Paris on 2
August.

The final advance on Germany had its set-backs. On 1
December 1944, 15 German Divisions under General Mode
pierced the US lines in the Ardennes, in the Battle of the Bulg
Montgomery was switched to the Ardennes. The Nazi drive wa

stopped on 25 December and the bulge closed a month later. US losses were estimated at 40,000. German at 220,000 dead and prisoners.

Three months earlier, in September, Allied forces had tried to secure a crossing of the Rhine at Arnhem. If they had succeeded, it could have brought the war to an earlier end. The landings by the British 1st Airborne Division were to follow the US 101st Airborne at Eindhoven and the US 82nd at Nijmegen, from where British troops secured the road and railway bridges. Aircraft were first committed to the American forces. The British were then to be carried in two sections. The first party landed at Arnhem on 17 September and the second group next day, delayed by cloud and fog over British airfields. While the Guards Armoured Division could make no headway on the road to Arnhem, an elevated causeway swept by artillery fire, the British airborne troops in Arnhem fought a ten-day battle. On 27–28 September those who remained were withdrawn in boats across the Rhine. Out of the 10,095 who went in, 7,605 were lost, killed, wounded or missing.

On 9 March 1945 the US 9th Armoured Division found the Ludendorff Bridge at Remagen intact. Eisenhower ordered five divisions across. On the fifth day, the army switched to the Teadway floating bridge built in 10 hours 11 minutes. The Remagen bridge later collapsed. On 25 April Russian and US forces met up at Torgau on the Elbe. Up to the last minute, with Russian forces over-running Germany from the East, the Germans resisted, even after Hitler's suicide on 30 April in his bunker in Berlin. But on 4 May they began surrendering, signing an unconditional surrender on 7 May. (8 May, VE Day).

War in Pacific and South-East Asia. 2. 1944–45

The war continued though in the Far East. While the British 14th Army under General William Slim conducted an arduous campaign in the jungles of Burma, American forces began their island-hopping, costly actions that would take them to Okinawa, the principal Japanese base in the Tyuku group on 1 April 1945, in the final land action of the war.

En-route, McArthur had returned to the Philippines on 20

October 1944 and Iwo Jima in February 1945. The Pacific saw the major naval engagements of World War Two.[1]

Leyte Gulf in the Pacific provided the setting for the biggest naval action ever fought. Between 23 and 27 October 1944 three engagements virtually destroyed Japanese naval power.

In the action 166 US ships and 1,280 US aircraft encountered 65 Japanese ships and 716 planes.

Earlier naval actions in the Coral Sea, May 1942, and at Midway a month later, led to heavy losses on both sides.

In South East Asia, the British and Commonwealth forces gradually turned the tide against the Japanese. Orde Wingate's Chindits operated behind enemy lines and Mountbatten secured increased supplies for the so-called 'forgotten army'. The Burmese capital, Rangoon, was liberated on 20 May 1945. Even then, however, more than 50,000 Japanese in the jungle refused to give themselves up. The last acts of World War Two came on 6 August and 9 August 1945.

A US plane dropped the first atomic bomb on Hiroshima on August 6.

A second atomic bomb was dropped on Nagasaki three days later.

On 14 August 1945 Japan surrendered.

---

[1] In the Atlantic the Royal Navy dealt chiefly with lone German raiders. It sank the Bismark in May 1941 and the pocket battleship Scharnhorst in February 1941. Its main task was to provide vital escort protection to the merchant and troopships sailing from the USA to the UK and to the Middle and Far East.

Pacific and S.E. Asia 1942–5

→ Allied advances   * Sea battles   ★ Atom bomb raids on Japan

USSR

MONGOLIA

AUG 1945

SAKHALIN

Aleutian Islands

MAY 1943

CHINA

Vladivostok

HOKKAIDO

KOREA

JAPAN

Peking

MAR 1945

Hiroshima

Nagasaki

HONSHU

Osaka

Pacific Ocean

Shanghai

Okinawa MAR 1945

Mandalay

Hong Kong

Iwo Jima

Wake Island

INDIA

BURMA

TAIWAN

JAN 1945

APR 1945

LUZON

Marianas Islands

Philippine Sea

Saipan

JUL 1944

Guam

Manila

Leyte Gulf

PHILIPPINES

FRENCH INDO-CHINA

Rangoon MAY 1945

Palau

SEP 1944

Caroline Islands

FEB 1944

Bangkok

South China Sea

JUN 1945

MAR 1945

Gilbert Islands

MALAYA

Singapore

BORNEO

SEP 1942

FEB 1944

SUMATRA

NEW GUINEA

CELEBES

Solomon Islands

JAVA

TIMOR

Port Moresby

AUG 1942

Guadalcanal

Darwin

SEP 1942

New Hebrides

New Caledonia

Indian Ocean

AUSTRALIA

Conclusion

The Yalta Conference of 1945 – Churchill, Roosevelt and Stalin – the link-up between the American and Russian forces on the Elbe and the Russians taking Berlin, all these served to shape post-war Europe. Germany was divided, the Prussian military relegated to history.

The German Federal Republic became the most successful manufacturing and commercial state of Western Europe. East Germany became the most viable state in the Soviet bloc, where new masters replaced the old.

War in the West became unthinkable.

In the rest of the world, however, local wars and larger scale wars have continued for forty years with more casualties than World War Two.

Out of the triumph and exhaustion of the Second World War, two super-powers emerged, the United States and the Soviet Union.

Britain lost its predominant position in world affairs, having paid a heavy economic cost and, as an aftermath, the dollar came to replace the pound sterling in international deals. Ironically, the dollar would later look to the yen for support.

The Cost of War

Soviet Union	7,500,000–10,000,000 military deaths plus 10–12 million estimated civilians
	14,000,000 wounded
Germany	2,850,000 killed
	7,300,000 wounded
Japan	1,510,000 killed
	500,000 wounded
China	650,000 killed
	1,800,000 wounded
Britain	326,000 killed plus 62,000 civilians
	480,000 wounded
USA	293,000 killed
	590,000 wounded

France	211,000 killed
	400,000 wounded
Italy	78,000 killed
	120,000 wounded

Commonwealth

Australia	29,437 killed
	23,214 wounded
India	24,338 killed
	64,354 wounded
New Zealand	11,625 killed
	15,749 wounded
South Africa	12,080 killed
	14,363 wounded

The following are estimates:

Yugoslavia	305,000 killed
	425,000 wounded
Poland (military)	320,000 killed
	530,000 wounded

Poland also suffered 6,028,000 civilians killed. This figure includes 3,200,000 Jews (most of whom are incorporated in the figure of 6,000,000 Nazi concentration camp Jewish victims).

May they Rest in Peace.

The Editors and Dr Christoph Seidelmann

Acknowledgements

Once again we acknowledge the generous response to the appeals from Field Marshal Lord Carver and General Sir John Hackett in the media for poetry mss from World War Two. Over a two and a half year period hundreds of letters arrived each month with poems or books or advice – sound advice from people we have never met and expected no reward – on where to locate the poetry we sought. Help came not only from Britain but from Australia (Ian Gollings, Returned Services League), New Zealand (William E. Morris) and South Africa (Dr Denis Saunders and Professor G. Hutchings[1]). We have been overwhelmed. The *Oasis* series would not have been possible without this voluntary support of those who served in World War Two, their families or friends or just those interested in helping us.

In this, as before, the media have played their part. (Without the media there would have been no *Oasis* in the Middle East in 1942/3.) We say thank you to the Press Association (story picked up by so many provincials and local BBC radio), *The Times*, *Independent*, *Guardian* and *Daily Telegraph*. The BBC have played a vital role. Aside from appeals on radio and TV (London and South East), the Open Space programme '*War Poets of '39*' (producer, Peter Lee-Wright) which went out on BBC 2 and was repeated on BBC 1, Remembrance Sunday 1987 drew a record mail-bag for a poetry programme – over 4,000 letters. Aside from thanking the producer, the cast[2] and staff, we are indebted to the programme researcher, Simon Purcell, for his handling of correspondence before passing on the relevant mss and queries to the Trust.

We thank also Charlie Chester for his request for poetry on his programme on BBC Radio 2, and Edward P. Thompson for mss of his late brother Frank.

As always Hamish Henderson has advised on Gaelic poetry. This time Dr John MacInnes has directed us on the Macleod poem, which is of literary significance to Gaelic specialists.

The Imperial War Museum have again helped in biographical information. Roderick Suddaby, Keeper of Records at the

---

[1] University of Zululand.
[2] Paul McGann, Irene Richard, Neil Dudgeon and Paul Jesson. Contributions also from Spike Milligan and General Sir John Hackett.

Museum, has promptly answered our requests for information, help and mss. Mss sent to us, used or not in the anthologies, are lodged in the Museum archives. The London Law Agency – Sally Hopgood – have played a valiant role in handling the flood of correspondence and mss – to be tackled by our right-hand – Tamara Soom.

The work of the Trust and hence the production of the anthology would not have been possible without the enthusiastic services of our honorary legal adviser, Christopher Frere-Smith and we must thank again our honorary advisers, Field Marshal Lord Carver and General Sir John Hackett who not only have contributed to the anthology but advised on poems and structure and corrected copy. Whilst Gavin Ewart and John Brookes have been most prompt in their forewords to two sections of the book.

One name we must add. A young Cambridge graduate in English, Sarah Costelloe, came in to help in the tedious work of sorting mss – counting lines, getting the biographies to tie up with the poems and then performed a necessary task, reading each poem carefully to tell the editors points she could not follow – as this anthology will be read, we hope, by generations to come with no experience of World War Two. Hence explanatory footnotes under certain poems.

Before thanking contributors we must apologise to a few who sent mss – RAF and Australians chiefly. On 16 October 1987 the most severe storm in two hundred years hit the south of England. Some mss were detached from senders' letters and some destroyed. We have advertised in the press in Britain and Australia for senders to get in touch. We fear though that we have not traced all the missing mss.

Fortunately we must have had a presentiment for we had transferred most of the Trust's documents and mss to safe storage a week before. We must still apologise to disappointed poets, though we did spend a great deal and made every effort to contact senders. Here we thank Sheila O'Connor, Australia House, London, Yvonne Preston of the *Sydney Morning Herald*, the Returned Services League, Australia, and The Australian for carrying our appeal, as did the RAF News in Britain.

For poems from the RAF we must thank Group Capt. (Rtd) Palmer for the use of his anthology. Thanks for help from Air Commodore Harry Probert. The Head Master of Winchester

College, Mr Sabben-Clare, sent us Frank Thompson's poem 'Polliciti Meloria' and biography, greatly appreciated. We are grateful for the loan of 'Wartime in the Middle East' from Eric Smart. We thank also the following:

General Gow for poem by R. G. A. Gow.
Isabel Beard for poem by Harry Beard
Mrs E.A. Waters for poem by Bernard Charles Paterson Robinson
Gladys A. Smith for poem by Trevor M.L. Smith
Irene Horn for poems by Frederick Horn
Robert Cole for poems by Bert Cole
Mrs McBride for poems by D.W. McBride
Mrs M. Oates for poems by W.G.R. Oates
Anna McIlwraith for poems by Richard Spender
Colin McIntyre for poem by Andrew Todd
Gervase Belfield for poem by Eversley Belfield
H.G. Easton for poem by James Coldwell
Gay Wills for poems by Molly Repard
John Marsh for poems by Frederick Rackstraw
John Atkins for poems by Brian Allwood
J.A. Edwards for 'The Romantic Charter' – Anon
Mr. E. Hobday for 'The Fortress of the East' – Anon
H.G. May for 'The Last Posting' and 'Cotton Wool Bombs' – Anon

The Trust gratefully acknowledges permission by Secker & Warburg to publish the poems by Roy Fuller; permission from Penry M. Rees for his poem on the Sumatra Railway (Hell's Railway) and permission to reprint Gavin Ewart's 'Oxford Leave'. The Trust also acknowledges E.M.I. permission in respect of Lili Marlene in U.K. and Commonwealth.

Biographies

The editors have compiled basic biographies of the poets in this collection, where the information was available.

Drummond ALLISON: Born 1921, Caterham, Surrey Bishop's Stortford and Queen's College, Oxford Sandhurst, 1942. East Surrey Regiment. North Africa and Italy. Killed in action on the Garigliano, Italy, 2 December 1943.

Brian ALLWOOD: Born 1920. Mass observation pre-war. Joined RAF 1941, North Africa & Italy. Mentioned in despatches. Killed 30 June 1944. Bridge collapse. Buried at Caserta, Italy.

'ALMENDRO': Denis Saunders, South African Air Force, poet and joint founder of *Oasis* in Cairo, 1942. Served later in Italy. Today homeopathic doctor, Ferndale, Johannesburg, South Africa.

Alleyne ANDERSON: Born Oswestry, Salop 4 May 1917. Stone University, Grenoble, Tulane. Flying officer RAF. 100% disabled 1943. Special interest, languages. British Consulate, New Orleans, Louisiana, USA. Lives Putney, London.

John ANDERTON: Born 8 August 1923 Lancashire. Worksop College. Royal Navy, North Atlantic Arctic, Normandy Landings, Far East. Retired Lieutenant Commander. Real Estate and Textiles. Contributed to Countryside Magazines. Director, British Association Shooting and Conservation. Lives at Worthenbury, Clwyd.

Michael ARMSTRONG: Born Newcastle-upon-Tyne, 12 December 1923. Educated, Sedbergh. Served in Army 1942–47. With the KSLI in Italy 44–45. Sergeant, Education Corps, Palestine and Egypt 46–47. Librarian, Newcastle and London. Hotel proprietor Jersey, Channel Islands 1957–60. Tended the gorillas and orang-utans at Gerald Durrell's zoo. Poems published in Britain and USA. Three sets of poems set to music by William Alwyn, broadcast on Radio 3.

A. Henry BAILEY: Born 1908. Served in Middle East and Italy: contributed to Army publications. Has published two small volumes of poetry. Lives at Hilsea, Portsmouth.

Geoffrey Vernon BALL: Born 28 December 1924 Moseley, Birmingham. King Edward's Grammar School, Aston. Ordinary Seaman April 1943–February 1944 (HMS *Duncan*, North Atlantic convoys). Sub-Lieutenant June 1944. ML's Normandy; West Africa; Nigeria and Gold Coast 1944–45. Reserve Lieutenant Commander RNR. Professor Emeritus, University of Aston, 1981. Lives at Sutton Coldfield, West Midlands.

S.C. BATEMAN: Born 1924 Coleraine, Northern Ireland. Coleraine Academical Institution 1936–41. Queen's University, Belfast 1946–52. University Air Squadron/RAFVR 1941. Trained Navigator/W.T. Canada 1942–43. Tour of Operations 140 Sqn. PRU Mosquitoes 2nd TAF. No. 1 Ferry Squadron 1944–45. No. 2 Group Control Centre UK & Germany. MB, BCh, BAO 1952. Senior Medical Officer, British Airways 1957–82. MO Manchester International Airport. Consultant Aviation Medicine 1982–86. Member Faculty Occupational Medicine 1981. R.AeS. 1981. Chrono-biology Papers published on effect of rapid time zone changes on circadian rhythms. Lives at Bramhall, Cheshire.

Stephanie BATSTONE: Born Croydon 1922. St Peter's School, Coulsdon & Southampton University. Visual Signaller in Oban 1943–45; Larne 1945; 1945–54 Medical Social Worker, 1957–75 at University College Hospital, Guy's Hospital, St Helier Hospital, Carshalton. Written 'Wren's Eye View' (privately published). Lives in Carshalton, Surrey.

Roy BAUME: Born 1921 Halifax, Yorkshire. Local technical college. Clerk before joining RAF in 1941, Bomber Command, sergeant air-gunner, stationed in England, until 'demob' in 1945. Operations over the 'roaring Ruhr' – came through 'fairly unscathed'. After the war trained as a male nurse, medical career, senior hospital post to 1984. Published poetry post-war.

Harry BEARD: Born 1912 Hale, Cheshire. Clifton College,

Worcester College, Oxford. Trained in Rome as a singer. Recitals in UK on Radio Luxemburg. Commissioned 1941, Egypt and 8th Army in Italy. Fluent Italian, interrogation of prisoners of war; Intelligence. Post-war *The Times* overseas operatic critic. Died 1970.

E.G.C. BECKWITH (Ted): Captain, Sherwood Foresters, taken prisoner in Norway. Edited *The Quill* in POW camps. Post-war, Hon. Colonel of the Regiment.

Eversley BELFIELD: Born 1918. Ampleforth College and Pembroke College, Oxford. Commissioned Royal Artillery until May 1942, transferred to RAF September 1943–October 1945 pilot with 661 Air Observation Post Squadron flying Auster aircraft. North-west Europe campaign with Canadian Army and flew 120 operational sorties. Mentioned in Despatches. Staff officer Control Commission in Germany. Senior Lecturer Adult Education Department, Southampton University, specialising in Military History. Died 12 February 1986, Sark.

Sven BERLIN: Born 14 September 1911 Sydenham. Educated Art Colleges, Beckenham and Redruth. Tutored in Humanities; Royal Artillery, Normandy. Caen to Arnhem. Hospitalised. Biography Alfred Wallis. Primitive Painter, 1949; I am Lazarus, Dent 1961; Lives Wimbourne, Dorset.

Jack BEVAN: Born 1920. Read English at Cambridge. Royal Artillery-Commissioned, 1943. Action in Italy. Post-war teacher, poet and translator of Quasimodo. Poem first published in own collection 'My Sad Pharaohs', (Routledge and Kegan Paul).

Allen D. BIRKS: Born 9 October 1912 Crewe, Cheshire. Enlisted Regular Army 1926. King's Shropshire Light Infantry. BEF, Dunkirk. Musician and sportsman. Runs private car hire company. Lives at Mablethorpe, Lincs.

Ted BIRT: Enlisted TA 1938, aged 18. Hvy. AA, Battle of Britain, Thames Estuary, Tyne & Tees, Clydeside, Bath, Bristol etc. Mil. Intell. 'Far Eastern Warfare'; Instr. 211 HAA Mobile Trg. Regiment RA: Tp. Commander 1st Hong Kong & Singapore HAA Regiment RA Captain. After war Production Officer, British Military Printing Press, HQ, Allied Land Forces, SEAC. Lives at Katikati, Bay of Plenty, New Zealand.

Angela BOLTON (née Noblet): Born Preston 1918. Winckley Square Convent School. Nursed Burma retreat casualties in Calcutta and from Imphal and Kolima and on hospital steamer, patients from 14th Army and Wingate's Second Campaign. Post-war, brought up four children and worked as nursing sister to Balliol College, Oxford. Husband, Captain James D. P. Bolton, classics don at Queen's College, Cambridge. Wrote 'The Maturing Sun'. (Imperial War Museum). Lives at Storrington, Sussex.

John Cromer BRAUN: see **John CROMER**

John BROOKES: Private with 2/5 Bn Australian Infantry Force (AIF). Served 1940–45. Worked his passage from Liverpool to Australia pre-war landing with 2/6. On outbreak of war walked from Broken Hill to Melbourne to enlist. Today living at Castle Cary, Somerset.

William George BURRELL: Born Wellington, New South Wales, 5 March 1907. Royal Australian Air Force, Pilot Officer/Flt. Engineer, served with Catalina Squadrons. Began writing poetry at early age: contributed to *Sydney Bulletin*, *Smiths Weekly*, *The Spinner*. Farmer and grazier, station owner. Lives at Orange, New South Wales.

John BUXTON: Born 1912 in Cheshire. Malvern and New College, Oxford. No. 1 Independent Company. A pre-war poet, taken prisoner in Norway 1940, interned in Oflag VII.

Angus CAMPBELL (nickname Am Puilean): Born 1903 Isle of Lewis, Outer Hebrides. Educated Ness. After short spell as merchant seaman joined Regular Army 1924. 1929 campaign against the Pathans. Rejoined regiment 4 September 1939, 51st Division. Captured at St Valery. POW Camp Stalag XXA, Thorn, Poland on River Vistula. 1972 collection of poetry 'Mowl is Cruithnehd' (Chaff and Wheat). Autobiography 1973. Died 1982.

Michael CARVER: Field Marshal, Lord. Middle East GSO 1,

7th Armoured Division at El Alamein. Commanded 4th Armoured Brigade 1944–7. Author of *El Alamein, Tobruk, Second to None, Seven Ages of the British Army. Out of Step* (autobiography) 1989.

Bruce CASTLE: Born Wandsworth, London. Educated Grammar School. Royal Artillery. North Africa, Sicily, Italy. Post-war, local government (Town Planning).

Louis CHALLONER: Born Blackpool 1911. Grammar School, Preston Univeristy College, Southampton. Teacher West Ham 1931–39. 'Knightsbridge', Alamein (twice) Tobruk to Tunis. Returned to OCTU, UK. Post-war head teacher, Newham Primary School, 1947–76.

William CLARKE: Born Walworth Common 1908. Secondary School, Barnes, London. Regular soldier. RAMC. Army Special Certificate, English. Dunkirk. Discharged medical 5 November 1943. Clerk RAMC AND Territorial Army post-war. Poetry published *Shades of Khaki* (Popular Poets) and biography *The Branfers were here* (E. F. Morten); poems included in *Anthology from X* (OUP).

Les CLEVELAND: 2 New Zealand Expeditionary Force, 25th Battalion, Pacific, then Egypt and Italian campaign, where wounded. Published poet, *The Iron Hands*. Reader in Political Science at Victoria University, Wellington, New Zealand.

Ken CLIFT: Born Waverley, Sydney, Australia 7 January 1916, Crown and Cleveland Street High Schools: 2nd AIF, Middle East; Corporal 16th Brigade Palestine, Egypt, Libya, Greece, Syria and Ceylon. Distinguished Conduct Medal. Lieutenant 1st Australian Parachute Battalion. Post-war Holiday Camp proprietor, Hotel and Club equipment sales and service; written 8 books including *War Dance* (story of 2/3 Australian Infantry Battalion) and *This Magic Land*. Lives at Bondi.

Peter CLISSOLD: Born Leamington 7 February 1904. St George's School, Windsor Castle. The Nautical College, Pangbourne. Royal Navy, Armed Merchant Cruiser; Commodore Coastal Convoys. Assistant King's Harbour Master. Benghazi, HMS *Centurion* (D-Day). Lieutenant Commander RNR Lecturer. School of Nangahoh, Warsash,

Southampton. Written *Basic Seamanship*, *Radar in Small Craft*. Lives in Southampton.

George E. COCKER: Born Liverpool 1921. Flight Lieutenant Air Gunnery Officer. 31 operations with 218 Squadron. 1000 bomber raids 1942. Post-war Head of Adult Education Centre. Lives in Kenninghall, Norfolk.

Jack COCKS: Born Gunnedah, NSW, Australia 1923. Gunnedah Intermediate High School. RAF navigational courses, Commonwealth Bureau of Meteorology Training School for forecasters. Navigator RAF Mediterranean theatre. Post-war Commonwealth Bureau of Meteorology as a forecaster. 15 years at RAAF Base, Richmond. Lives at S Windsor, NSW, Australia.

James COLDWELL: Born 1920. Cadet RN College, Dartmouth. Won boxing championship on Mediterranean fleet at Malta. At Dunkirk 1940 HMS *Scimitar*. Western approaches HMS *Rockingham*. Lieutenant Commander of visiting frigate. Killed in road accident South Africa 1953.

Bert COLE: Born Fulham 1915. Private 8th Army. Wounded at Alamein. Post-war, Fleet Street printer. Died 1986, Southend-on-Sea.

Lyn COOPER: Born Sheffield 1920. Commercial College, Fighter Operations plotter in WAAF 1942–45. 1987 Yorkshire Arts Writer's award.

Herbert CORBY: Born 1911 London. RAF Armourer in a bomber squadron. Foreign Sevice post-war.

Joy CORFIELD: Born 1925 Manchester. Joined ATS 1944 at Guildford. Special Wireless Operator, then driver in Germany. Married 1947. Disabled by polio 1950.

John CROMER, OBE: Major, served Middle East. Intelligence. Co-founder of the Salamander Society with Keith Bullen. Post-war, legal profession, magistrate, City Councillor, Portsmouth. Secretary Advertising Standards Authority and head of Consumer Protection EEC.

D.E. CURTIS: Born 1923. Archbishop Temple School for

Boys. Royal Armoured Corps. Insurance executive. Lives at Sidcup, Kent.

Lisbeth DAVID: Born 1923 Wales. WRNS 1942, W/T Operator – commissioned Third Officer WRNS 1943, Cypher Office on staff of NCSO Belfast, C-in-C Portsmouth (Fort Southwick) and C-in-C East Indies (Colombo). St Hugh's College, Oxford, MA (Theology); in industry and government service until retirement 1983.

Erik de MAUNY: Born 1920 London. French and English parents. Educated New Zealand Victoria University College, Wellington; School of Slavonic and East European Studies, University of London. Pre-war journalist in New Zealand. 1940–45 served with NZ Expeditionary Force in Pacific, Middle East and Italy. BBC Foreign Correspondent for seventeen years. Novelist. Lives in Lancaster.

Brian DOOLEY: Born 23 July 1916. Sale, Cheshire Secondary School. Army Electrician Signaller posted to Nairobi and from there to Diego Suarez, Madagascar, seconded to Intelligence Corps to start the Army Broadcasting Station, Radio Diego Suarez as Station Manager and announcer, Sergeant. 1946 returned to England, Instructor of radio announcers with the Army Broadcasting Depot company, Sloane Square. Later, bank official and radio and television actor.

Frank DOSSETOR: Born 9 June 1914 London. Bishop Cotton's School, Bangalore, Western Australia; Guildford Grammar School, Taunton School and St Peter's, Oxford. Served two curacies in South London. Attached Third Mountain Regiment, RA, Chaplain 1st Battalion, The Duke of Wellington's Regiment, Baghdad. 25 Indian General Hospital. After war parish of Black Torrington, Devon, had the livings of St John's, Stone, (near Aylesbury), chaplain to the County Mental Hospital and St Andrew's, Lower Streatham, London. Teaching posts: one at the Windsor School, Hamm (1953 to 54), an Army Residential Comprehensive, and The City of London Freeman School, Ashtead. Publications include *Introducing Psychology*, a Penguin handbook with Dr Henderson (1963), *Shakespeare the Comprehensive Soul*, contributor. Lives in Salisbury.

Keith DOUGLAS: Born 1920. Captain, Royal Armoured Corps. Professional soldier and poet. Independent-minded, he disobeyed orders to take tank into action at El Alamein, wounded. Made final revision of his poems and arranged for the revenues to go to his mother before leaving for Normandy, June 1944, where he was killed 9 June 1944. The poems were handed by him to Tambimuttu, Editions Poetry London, from whom the Trust has taken the poet's version in contrast to others who have revised the poetry years later.

Norman Maxwell DUNN: Born Sydney, Australia 1916. Associate of the Australian Society of Accountants and Chartered Institute of Secretaries and Administrators. First officer commissioned under Empire Air Training Scheme, Australia; 258 Hurricane Fighter Squadron, Isle of Man and Kenley. POW Germany, four years. Flight Lieutenant. Chairman Council, Australian Telecommunications Development Association. Lives at St Ives, New South Wales.

S.J.H. DURNFORD (John): Born Edinburgh 9 March 1920. Sherborne School; Trinity Hall, Cambridge. Commissioned Royal Artillery; India, North Malaya, POW 1942–45 in Siam. Post-war Regular Commission, Royal Artillery. Holder Army Flying Brevet. Sales representative industry and wine company. Bath Abbey Choir, Wells and Bath Choral Societies. Author (1988) *Branch Line to Burma*. Lives at Bath.

Gavin EWART: Born 1916. Wellington and Christ's College, Cambridge. In advertising and literary work before the war. Officer RA, North Africa, Italy. Today poet and critic, living in Putney, London.

Olivia FITZROY: Born 1921. Daughter of Viscount Daventry. Educated by governess. From early childhood wrote prolifically. Worked in library of London store at beginning of war. First book *Orders to Peach* published by Collins 1942. WRNS fighter direction officer Yeovilton later Ceylon, 1944. Her pilot boyfriend killed near Singapore early 1945. A WRNS girlfriend killed car smash. These two events affected her deeply. Travelled with Chipperfield's Circus, to write a book *Wagons And Horses*, Collins 1955. Rented croft in Highlands of

Scotland in 1951 and lived there for 5 years. Died 24 December 1969.

Frank FLETCHER: Born 29 June 1918 Preston, Lancs. Preston Grammar School, St Chad's College, Durham University. Commissioned, Manchester Regiment. Normandy Landing. Captain Military Legal Adviser for the Defence, War Crimes Trial. Post-war, headship of J.M. & I. School in Essex. Contributed to *Poetry One*, *Poetry Two* and *Assegai* (Essex Publications). Lives at Dartford, Kent.

Ian FLETCHER: Born 1920 London. Served in Middle East, including Sudan. Poetry includes: *Orisons*, *Picaresque & Metaphysical Motets* and *Twenty One Poems*. Formerly Professor of English, Reading University. Specialist in twentieth-century poetry. Died 2 December 1988 Queen Elizabeth Hospital, Birmingham, (Liver Unit), having completed his work for this anthology a few days before. In his hospital bed, knowing time was short, he read through and selected the poems from his friend from the Middle East, Frank Thompson – poems that had just been sent by Frank Thompson's brother, the historian, E.D. Thompson, who had held them safely for 45 years. Ian Fletcher's *W.B. Yeats and his Contemporaries* (1985) is the definitive work on the subject. He left school at fifteen, gained his PhD without ever taking a first degree at university.

Ivor George FLETCHER: Born 8 July 1920, Stafford. Grammar School. Lieutenant in North Staffordshire Regiment. North Africa (Tunisia) – severely wounded 29 April 1943. Subsequently invalided. Post-war teaching, after obtaining a degree at Keele University. Lives at Cheam, Surrey.

G.S. FRASER: Born 1915. MA, St Andrews, trainee journalist *Aberdeen Press & Journal*. Warrant Officer Class 2, Army Middle East, Ministry of Information. Post-war lectured in Japan and Leicester University. Helped found The Salamander Oasis Trust. Died 1980.

Roy FULLER, CBE: St Paul's School. Ordinary Seaman 1941. 'Service discipline made my verse more precise'. 1942 East Africa. 1943 Fleet Air Arm. Left Navy 1946. Professor of

Poetry 1968–73 at Oxford University. Governor of BBC 1972/3–80. In 1970 awarded Queen's Gold Medal for poetry. Lives in Blackheath, London.

David GASCOYNE: Born 10 October 1916 Harrow, Middlesex. Educated Salisbury Cathedral Choir School, Regent Street Polytechnic. Pre-war and post-war in France. *Poems 1937–42* (P.L. Editions); 1965 OUP *Collected Poems*. Lives at Cowes, Isle of Wight.

D.S. GOODBRAND: Born Manchester, 1921. Elementary School. Leading Telegraphist, Royal Navy, Home Fleet destroyers, LST, Far East, 1944–45. Post-war, British Rail clerical, Post Office eighteen years. Radio operator RAF 1957–76. Student Merchant Navy radio college. Published poetry in various magazines, including *Poetry Australia*. Radio BBC Midland region and Scottish Oversea Service. Lives in Manchester.

R.G.A. GOW: Born 1920. Scholar of Winchester College 1933–38 and kept wicket for the school XI. Christchurch, Oxford 1938–39. Commissioned Royal Artillery. Served UK and North Africa. Forward Observation Officer in 1st Airborne Division. Killed in action Arnhem 18 September 1944. Buried Oosterbeck Commonwealth War Cemetery.

Bernard GUTTERIDGE: Born 1916, Southampton. Cranleigh School. Hampshire Regiment. Served in Combined Ops and with 36 Div. in Burma (with Alun Lewis), reaching rank of Major. Died 1985.

John HACKETT: General, Sir. GSO1 Raiding Forces, Middle East. Commander-in-Chief British Army of the Rhine 1966–8. Visiting Professor in Classics, King's College, London. Publications include *I was a Stranger* and (jtly) *The Third World War*.

J. P. HALDANE-STEVENSON (Patric): Born Llandaff 1910. King Edward's School, Birmingham; St Catherine's College, Oxford. Army Chaplain, Flanders, 1940. Italy, 2nd Lancashire Fusiliers. Post-war Australian Church – Anglican. Author, *Religion and Leadership*, 1948; *Collected Poems*, 1948; *Beyond the Bridge*, 1943. Lives at Canberra, Australia.

Mary E. HARRISON: Born Smalley, Derbyshire 21 August 1921. WAAF as Special Duties Clerk Operations Room HQ 12 Group Fighter Command. Watnall, Notts. 2½ years later remustered and trained as Model Maker RAF Nuneham Courteney, Oxon. Posted to Allied Central Interpretation Unit (Photographic Intelligence) RAF Medmenham, Bucks with team making models for Dam raids, Ploesti oil fields. Peenemude flying bomb sites and Cologne which inspired the poem. Also models for Normandy landings. Lives at Radcliffe-on-Trent, Notts.

Norman J. HIGGERTY: Born South Norwood 12 July 1919. REME Advanced Gunshops in the Desert. Sicily and Italy. Stores Manager – telephone manufacturing company. Musician/Entertainer at night. Articles published in *Magic* and *Showbiz* journals under stage name of Norman Lee. Lives at Croydon, Surrey.

John Buxton HILTON: Born 1921, Buxton. Cambridge University. Beds & Herts and Royal Norfolk 1941–42. Royal Artillery 1943 (Gunner). I Corps 1943–46 (Sergeant, in despatches). Language teacher, then headmaster, Chorley Grammar School. HM Inspector of Schools. Crime novelist. Died 1986.

Geoffrey HOLLOWAY: Born Birmingham 1918. Educated Alsop High School, Liverpool. Royal Army Medical Corps, 225 Parachute Field Ambulance, 6 Airborne Division, NW Europe. Post-war social work in Cumbria. Now retired.

Peter HOPKINSON: Born Catford 1925. Grammar School, Teachers' Training College. RAF 1941–42. Army 1943–46. Post-war teacher, electronic engineer. Published poetry.

Frederick HORN: Born 1906, Bradford. Bradford College of Art. Advertising Art Director. Royal Army Ordnance Corps. Organised Publicity Department at Chilwell. Typography specialist. Wrote *Lettering and Work*. Died 1975.

In HOVELL: Born North London 1922. Highgate School. Air Ministry for two years before joining 61st Training Regiment, Royal Armoured Corps in March, 1942. Commissioned 155 RAC and Yorkshire Hussars, North-west Europe 1944,

Liaison Officer with HQ33 Independent Armoured Brigade
Post-war advertising and public relations, retirement in 198
Lives Ruislip, Middlesex.

John S. INGRAM: Born Willesden 1915. The Perse Schoo
Cambridge. TA 1938; Searchlights. Commissioned 194
Gibraltar. Contributed *The Rock Magazine*. Joint writer
one-Act Play 'Nothing Ever Happens' and other plays. Po
war, rejoined family business of Jewellers and Antique Deale
Founded Harrow Theatre Group.

Robin IVY: Born 1919. Served in Italian campaign. Re
English at Cambridge. Schoolmaster. Retired early to wr
poetry. Lives in Cambridge.

Robin C. JACKSON: Born Liverpool 1914. St Francis Xav
College, Liverpool; Liverpool School of Navigation a
Marine Wireless. Fleet Chief (Communications) Royal Nav
Destroyers and Intelligence work with Naval Special Servic
Blown up in HMS *Grenville* by magnetic mine January 194
Post-war Ministry of Civil Aviation (Heathrow Rad
approach control). Teacher home-counties and West Countr
organist and choirmaster at Clovelly, Hartland Male Voi
Choir.

John JARMAIN: Captain 51st Highland Division, anti-ta
unit. Chiefly Western Desert, but killed in Normandy, 26 Ju
1944. The night before he worked through the records of I
unit, assessing each man. Like Keith Douglas, he foresaw I
own end. Against advice he went on a recce into St Honorine
Chardonnerette, to be killed by a German mortar bomb.

Norman G. JONES: Born Ebbw Vale, Gwent 8 March 192
Ebbw Vale County School. RAF Halton Apprentices Scho
Cpl. Airframe/Engine Fitter, Pilot's Training, Canada. Wi
less operator. Post-war HQ Air Command, Singapore. Brit
Steel, safety officer.

Eric Douglas JORDAN: Born 1913. King Edward VI Scho
Birmingham and Wadham College, Oxford. Teacher
Classics. Commissioned Royal Artillery, mobile Light An
Aircraft Battery, Middle East. Seconded as a Staff Officer

HQ Paiforce (Persia and Iraq Command) at Teheran, Kermanshah, Basra and Baghdad.

Denis KNIGHT: Born Volvos, Greece, 1921 at the British Consulate; St Edmund's College, Ware; Christ's College, Cambridge. Royal Tank Regiment, served with same crew Sicily, Italy, Normandy, to the Rhine crossing. Teacher and farmer. Written *Cobbett in Ireland: A Warning to England* (Lawrence & Wishart, 1984). Contributor *Tribune*; *Peace News*, *Catholic Herald*. Lives in Enfield, Middlesex.

Uys KRIGE: Born 1910 Bonteboksfiof, Swellendam. University of Stellenbosch. Joined Rand *Daily Mail* 1930; war correspondent in Egypt at outbreak of war. POW in Camp 78 Italy. South Africa's leading poet of World War Two. Died 1987.

Ted LANE: Born London 1924. RAF, ground crew and flying duties UK, Middle East, Far East. Post-war, advertising; acting, stage and television. Broadcast own script for BBC about Christmas day in Singapore, 1945. Lives Orpington, Kent.

Kenneth LANG: Born Newcastle-upon-Tyne 1916. Studied music at Matthey School (Liverpool) and Trinity College of Music, London. Royal Engineers, blew up bridges on retreat in Greece. Laid minefields between Bir Hakim and Bir Harmet. Later joined ENSA, theatre manager in Germany. Music teacher, concert artiste. Short-story writer. Lives London NW1.

Jack LAVERS: Born Binstead, Isle of Wight 1920. Sandown Secondary School. Corporal Wireless-op RAF. With 3 Wing South African Air Force in Western Desert and Italy and with Army Air Support Unit in Italy. Solicitor. Compiled *Dictionary of Isle of Wight Dialect* (1988). Lives at Sandown, Isle of Wight.

Louis LAWLER: Born Preston, Lancs. 7 December 1918. Cotton College, North Staffs. Army 1939–45, mainly Palestine. BBC Executive Monitoring Service. Poems in *Country Life* and *Spectator*. Lives at Henley-on-Thames.

Audrey LEE: Born Liverpool 8 March 1924. Wallasey High

School for Girls, Cheshire. WAAF 1941–44. Flt. Mechanic & Fitter II E. Post-war Mrs A. Pilsworth. Lives at Byfleet, Surrey.

Pauline LENDON (now Ralph): Born Hampstead 1924. Camden School for Girls. Added year to age in 1941 to volunteer for the WAAF. Assisted in teaching adults with reading and writing difficulties. Lives at Barnes, London.

Sorley MACLEAN: Born 1911, Isle of Raasay. Edinburgh University. School treacher at Portree, Skye. Signals Corps in the Desert, wounded at Alamein. Post-war taught at Borough-muir, Edinburgh, then Plockton, Western Ross as headmaster (1956). Now living in Braes, Skye.

Malcolm MACLEOD: (Nickname Calum Cuddy) from the village of Callaraish, Isle-of-Lewis. Brought up in a croft house near the standing stones of Callanish. Served with The Seaforth Highlanders, 51st Highland Division in North Africa.

John MANIFOLD: Born 1915, Australia. Geelong Grammar School and Jesus College, Cambridge. British Army in West Africa and Europe. In 1949 returned to Queensland, Australia.

Derek MARTIN: Born 1920 Cheam, Surrey. Started pilot training at age 18. Flew Sunderland flying boats over the Bay of Biscay and Atlantic. March 1941 crashed in bad weather at night off west coast of Scotland and became a founder-member of the Guinea Pig Club. (Crash survivors – so-called as they became guinea pigs for surgeons – in this case McIndoe at East Grinstead Hospital Burns Unit, pioneer of plastic surgery.) After a year in hospital commanded flying boat unit at Pembroke Dock. 1944 India Chief of Staff joint-service force Cocos Islands off Java. After Japanese surrender, Far East Air Force Headquarters in Singapore, staff officer i/c Maritime Operations. Commanded early jet fighter airfields. Badly injured serving with NATO in Norway. Invalided 1973. Chairman of Chiltern Society and various committees. Wing Commander OBE. Lives in Medmenham, Buckinghamshire.

Geoffrey MATTHEWS: Born 1920. Kingswood School, Bath and Corpus Christi College, Oxford. Royal Signals, Middle

East. Lectured at Finald and Leeds University. Reader at Reading University. Died 1984.

Derek W. McBRIDE: Born Eccles, Manchester, April 1917. De La Salle College, Pendleton. Studied to be a cotton dyer. RASC: North Africa, First Army, Italy. Post-war ran village general stores in Kent. Lives in Cockham Hill, Edenbridge.

Charles McCAUSLAND: Born Glen Innes, New South Wales 1910. Glen Innes High School, Sydney University. AIF (Australian Infantry Force), Egypt, Lebanon and Libya; New Guinea campaign, Australian Army Education Service. Teacher, New South Wales. Visiting Associate Professor, University of Calgary, Alberta. Vice-Principal, Bathurst Teacher's College, NSW. Lives Woollahra, NSW.

John McINNES: Born 1932, Lewis. Ph.D on 'Gaelic poetry'. Senior lecturer University of Edinburgh, School of Scottish Studies.

L.A. McINTOSH: Born Hull, East Yorkshire 1918. Sidmouth St Elementary School, Hull. Enlisted 1938. Scots Guards, North Africa & Italy. Taken prisoner at Anzio February 1944; liberated by Russians April 1945. Trained as teacher, 20 years headmaster; retired 1982. Lives at Maidstone, Kent.

Colin McINTYRE: Born Argentina 1927. Commissioned Black Watch, Company Commander Lovat Scouts, Greece GSO III (Ops) 6th Airborne, Palestine. AB (Hons) Harvard University and BA (Hons) the Open University. BBC journalist 30 years, last eight as Editor, CEEFAX.

Alexander McKEE: Born Ipswich, 25 July 1918. St Helens College, Southsea. Learned to fly aged 15, Portsmouth Aero Club; but failed RAF medical (eyesight). 2 London Scottish and 2 Gordon Highlanders; attached HQ First Canadian Army, Normandy 1946, the Rhine 1945. 303 Town Major, Siegen; with 2 Division Newspaper 'Keynotes', in Ruhr. Four years writer-producer British Forces Network, Hamburg. Awarded Best British radio features script 1969 (BBC). Author of some 25 Books of war history – underwater subjects. Initiated project (1965) to locate, excavate and recover Mary Rose. Lives at Hayling Island.

William E. MORRIS: NZEF in Western Desert and Italy. NCO on railway lines to run military stock in Desert Construction Unit, June 1940 (12th Railway Survey Company). Member of International Poetry organisation. Tagore Institute and New Zealand and Poetry Society. Poems translated into Hindi and Russian.

Martin MOYNIHAN: Born 1916. Birkenhead School and Magdalene College, Oxford. Indian Army 1940, North West Frontier and Burma. Liberation under Slim and Mountbatten. Post-war Diplomatic Service, High Commissioner Lesotho, Kennedy Memorial Trust (British graduate scholarships to USA). Lives in Wimbledon. Wrote book *South of Fort Herz*.

Charles Edward NAYLOR: Born 21 November 1920 Birkenhead. Birkenhead Grammar School. RAF Radar in Burma. Post-war teacher. Died 1964.

Arthur Ernest NEWALL: Born Heaton Park, Manchester 27 October 1921. Blackpool Grammar School, City Grammar School, Chester. RAF Bomber Command, Methwold. First operational tour; Second tour, flew Hurricanes and Thunderbolts in Burma. Baled out May 1942 returning from St Nazaire. Post-war teacher. British Families Education Service. BAOR Headmaster Verdun Army School and Bruggon RAF School; St Swithun's School, Oxford, retired 1981. Prize winner National Poetry Foundation, 1982.

William Geoffrey Ronald OATES: Born London 1909. Died Farnham, Surrey 1976. Westminster and Corpus Christi College, Oxford and the Law Society. Qualified as Solicitor 1936 with Honours. Territorials, August 1939. CO in Royal Welsh Fusiliers for two years. Staff of 1st, 5th and 8th armies and Allied Commission, North Africa and Italy. Secretary and Registrar of the Royal College of Veterinary Surgeons from 1946–1965. Director of University Education and Examination Institution 1965–1976.

Eric A. OXLEY: Born Sydney, Australia 1914. Sydney High School and Sydney University. Commissioned 1st Australian Armoured Regiment, Royal NSW Lancers; Community Pharmacist. Lives at Springwood, NSW Australia.

eoff PEARSE: Born 19 May 1921 Wandsworth, London. Whitgift, Croydon and Imperial College of Science & Technology, London. Navigator/bomb aimer Desert Air Force, Flight Lieutenant. Imperial Chemical Industries, manager. Gold medal for professional paper 1975. Joined publishing company in 1975, journalist/editor. Lives at Welwyn Garden City.

illiam Harry PROCTOR: Born Sheffield 1913. Sheffield Central School (later High Storrs Grammar school) and Freckleton Teacher Training College. RAFVR 1940–46. Teaching staff Sheffield Education Committee. Various posts 1948–1976. Retired 1976. Poetry published during War by BBC. Lives at Rochdale, Lancs.

ederick RACKSTRAW: Born Aylesbury 1908. Son of Sergeant killed at the Dardanelles. Royal Corps of Signals attached to Malaya Command in 1941–42. Prisoner of war Singapore, Thailand/Burma Railway 1943–45. Entertainer/siffleur in POW camps. Assistant Divisional Manager Pearl Assurance Co. Ltd. Died January 1980.

nry M. REES: Born 1908, Chelsea, London. Univesity College of South Wales and Monmouthshire. Linguist. Gunner: POW in Sumatra, organised camp education with Colonel Laurens van der Post. Senior French master, Cathays High School, Cardiff; Head Master, Bassaleg Grammar School. Enthusiastic golfer. Lives at Newport.

olly REPARD: Born 16 June 1911 Cornwall. Educated London. Radar Operator WAAF. Ran guest house in Tunbridge Wells. Continued to write poetry. Died Odstock Hospital, Salisbury of burns from fire at her home February 1982.

orge Sydney RICHARDSON: Born 29 April 1914 Ponteand, Northumberland. Educated Berwick Grammar School and Durham Univeristy (B.A. Hons.). Joined Royal Air Force 1937. Posted to 36 (Torpedo Bomber) Squadron at RAF Station, Seletar, Singapore in 1938. Shot down and killed by Japanese Zero fighters while the squadron's elderly Wildebeest' torpedo bombers were attacking Japanese troop

372 **BIOGRAPHIES**

transports off Endau, Johore, Malaya on 26 January 194{
Buried in Kranki War Cemetery, Singapore. Mentioned
despatches.

Peter ROBERTS: Born November 1919 Hove, Sussex. We:
minster School. Navigator, 10 Squadron. Bomber Comman
Leeming. April 1942 shot down at Trondeheim during atta
on *Tirpitz*. 1942–45 Stalag Luft 3, Silesin. 1945–46 /
Ministry; Advertising Manager. *Take off at Dusk* (Fr(
Muller). Lives at Shepperton, Middlesex.

Richard M. ROBERTS: Born 1909 Burnley, Lancs. Elemen
ary School. Western Desert and Italy. Managing Direct(
furniture business, now retired. Lives at Burnley, Lancs.

William C. ROBERTS: Born 21 July 1921 Frodsha.
Cheshire. Chester City & County School for Boys. Diploma
Public Administration (London University). RAF. Chesh
County Council, Public Assistance and Welfare Departmen
Assistant Director of Social Services. Founder member Abb(
field Gloucester Society – provides sheltered accommodati
for elderly people. Lives at Westbury-on-Severn, Glos.

Bernard C.P. ROBINSON: Born Liverpool 15 Septeml
1916. Wade Deacon Grammar School, Widnes. Artic
solicitor. Royal Army Pay Corps. Transferred to (
Lancashire Fusiliers. Killed at Monte Cassino, 17 May 19.
Was a keen cricketer and played in local teams.

Alan ROOK: Born 1909. Uppingham and Oxford. Ro
Artillery, Dunkirk. Major with 6th AA Division. La
invalided out. Editor of the Oxford Magazine *Kingdom Co*
with Henry Treece.

Peter RUSSELL: Born Brisol 1921. Army in Europe. Ind
Army in Burma and Malaya. Edited *Literary Review* (Ni)
1976–77; poet in residence Dundee University and Univers
of Victoria, British Columbia. Written *Elemental Discou*
(1982). Lives in Venice.

Russell Harrison SAGE: Born 1911 Ipswich, Suffolk. Nor
gate School, Ipswich. Queen Mary College, London; fir
class honours in French. Intelligence Corps. Algiers 19

Eighth Army in Italy. Head of Modern Languages Sir William Borlase's School, Marlow and deputy Head. Retired 1976. President, Marlow Players. Lives at Bourne End, Bucks.

Victor SELWYN: Journalist and researcher, wrote *Handbook on Map Reading & Navigation, Middle East,* now updated 'Plan Your Route' (David & Charles). With David Burk (pre-war *Daily Mirror,* post-war *Daily Express, National Enquirer* and *Bild,* Hamburg), met Denis Saunders at the 'Music for All' Services Club, Cairo, 1942, from where Oasis was launched. Manages Salamander Oasis Trust. Lives in Brighton.

Malcolm N. SHARLAND: Born Bournemouth 17 December 1917. West Hayes (Winchester) and Dean Close (Cheltenham). Articled in Survey Dept. Winchester. Commissioned Royal Engineers N. Africa, Italy. Wounded bridge constructing over Rapido River, Cassino. Died 19 July 1946.

Colin SHEARD: Born 6 December 1912. Education, Nil – Tuberculosis; Served with BEF: Back to France via Caen, Falaise, into Antwerp. Corporal PTI, RE units. Post-war Health Club instructor. For 18 years written for Physical Culture Magazine.

George SHEPPERSON: Born Peterborough, 1922. King's School, Peterborough, St John's College, Cambridge. Commissioned Northamptonshire Regiment, seconded to the King's African Rifles; served in East Africa, Ceylon, India and Burma with Nyasaland battalions of the KAR. Kabaw Valley campaign 1944, Burma. University teacher Scotland, United States, Canada and Africa: Professor of Commonwealth and American History, Edinburgh Univesity; Visiting Scholar, WEB Du Bois Institute, Harvard University. 1973–89 Chairman of the Scottish Committee of the Commonwealth Institute. Author of *Independent African: John Chilembwe* (with T. Price), *David Livingstone and the Rovuma,* etc. Lives at Edinburgh.

Charles SMITH: 2nd NZ Division, HQ Defence Platoon, Egypt, then G 'runner' in Greece and Crete. Evacuated by destroyer *Napier* to Western Desert, then Italy and Trieste. Died January 1987.

Trevor M.L. SMITH: Born Romford Essex 25 October 1920. Secondary School, Hornchurch, Essex. Corporal fitter (RAF) Hornchurch 1940–41, East Africa 1942–46; post-war Raw Sugar Supervisor, Sugar Association of London. Poems published in Eastleigh, Views, E. Africa.

Martin SOUTHALL: Born 18 May 1924 Aston, Birmingham. Elementary School. Royal Warwickshire Regiment; Commissioned Infantry platoon commander, Queen's Royal Regiment, Italy. RWAFF Gold Coast. 34 years with engineering firm. Contributed the Moorlands Review, the PEN and other publications. Poems published under title *Behold a Pale Horse*, 1987 (Envoi Poets Publications). Lives in Daventry, Northants.

Richard SPENDER: Born 1921 Hereford. King Edward VI School, Stratford-on-Avon. Won scholarship to Oxford in 1940 but enlisted London Irish Regiment. Officer, the Parachute Regiment. Killed 28 March 1943 leading troops against German machine-gun positions near Bizerta, Tunisia.

Patrick STEWART (Tom): Born 25 January 1921, Hernani via Arridale, NSW. St Johns College, Lismore, NSW. Royal Australian Air Force. Wireless operator/air gunner, attached RAF. 22nd Squadron. Twenty-two operational raids. Europe, Arnhem. Flight Lieutenant. Associate Australian Accountants; supervisor Australian Bureau Statistics. Lives at Penshurst, NSW Australia.

Douglas Arthur Manatanus STREET: Born 1915, mother, Belgian artist, father, member Air Council. Scholar Hertford College, Oxford. French Foreign Legion, extricated by Foreign Office, 1938. Commissioned 1/7 Middlesex, MMG (Medium Machine Gun) TA British Expeditionary Force, 3rd Division Dunkirk. Chief instructor Intelligence Staff Course., Liaison with General Leclerc, Free French. GSO 1 Intelligence 8th Army. SOE Yugoslavia and Greece, liaison in Trieste. Commanded Allied Information Services under the then General Sir John Harding, Foreign Office post-war.

John STREET: Born Slough 1917. Windsor Secondary School. Imperial Services College. Commissioned Queen's Royal

Regiment TA 1936. Mons OCTU Instructor, SE Command Weapon Training School Instructor. Ran family nursery business. Freelance journalist and author. Published works on gardening, specialist books on Rhododendrons and Azaleas – one volume of autobiography – *Fool's Mistress*. Lives at Woking, Surrey.

Barry SUTTON: Born Whitney, Oxford, 1919. Northampton School, Northampton. Chronicle and Echo 1939. 56 Squadron RAF Fighter Command. Wounded in one foot during Fall of France. Flew Hurricanes July/August over Channel. Shot down August 26. RAF Hospital, Halton. 135 Hurricane Squadron, Mingaladon, Burma. DFC. 1962 joined British Defence Liaison staff Australian Command RAF Bassingborne, wrote *Way of a Pilot*, 1942. Died 1988.

Leslie E. SYMES: Born Southampton 1924. Educated Springhill Roman Catholic School, Southampton. Coldstream Guards, severely wounded near Castiglione, Italy October 1944. Invalided 1945. Field Surveyor Ordnance Survey 1946–54. Laboratory Technician Exxon Chemical Company 1955–88.

W.D. THOMAS: Born 1909 Westminster, London. Westminster City School, London School of Economics. Intelligence (Sig/Int) Staff Sergeant. India, Burma, Singapore. Postwar insurance official. Lives at Mitcham, Surrey.

William Frank THOMPSON: Born 17 August 1920, son of Edward Thompson poet and Indian historian. Winchester College 1933–38. Won English Verse and Latin Verse Medal Tasks and Hawkins English Literature Prize. Began to learn Russian and Slav languages which led to special services in the war. British School Athens, modern Greek. From New College, Oxford, volunteered although under-age. Commissioned Royal Artillery 1940. GHQ liaison regiment, Libya, Persia, Iran and Sicilian landings. Dropped in Yugoslavia; ambushed in May 1944 with a group of Bulgarian partisans near Sofia. Notwithstanding wearing the King's uniform, treated as a rebel. 'Tried' at Litakovo defending himself in fluent Bulgarian condemning Fascism. Shot 31 May 1944. Had working knowledge of nine European languages. Poetry compares with the best of the First War.

Michael Rayner THWAITES: Born 30 May 1915 Brisbane, Australia. Geelong Grammar School; Trinity College, Melbourne University; New College, Oxford. Rhodes Scholar for Victoria 1937. BA (Hons) Melbourne, B. Litt, MA Oxon. Royal Naval Volunteer Reserve 1939–45. Trawlers and corvettes. Atlantic and North Sea. Commanded corvette. 1947–49 Lecturer English Department, Melbourne University. 1950–70 Australian Security Intelligence Organisation. 1971–76 Parliamentary Library, Canberra (21/C). Published Poetry: *Milton Blind* – Newdigate Prize Poem 1938. (King's Medal for Poetry 1941) (Blackwell, Oxford). *The Jervis Bay and Other Poems* (Putnam, New York & London 1943). *Poems of War and Peace* (Cheshire Melbourne 1968, Grosvenor, London 1970). Prose: *Truth Will Out – ASIO and the Petrovs* (Collins, Australia 1980).

Andrew TODD: Born Dundee, Angus 1919. Glebeland School and Morgan Academy. Commissioned Seaforth Highlanders, 1940, 51st Highland Division, Alamein to the Rhine; twice wounded, and mentioned in despatches. BBC External Services, sub-editor Central News Room 1947. Retired 1979, having served as editor BBC TV News; Deputy Director News and Current Affairs; Controller, Scotland. Lives at Potters Bar, Herts.

Joy TRINDLES: Born London 1922. Fulham High School for Girls. Hammersmith Hospital – Nurse Training. Institute of Education, Reading University. Easthampstead College – Teacher training. 1943–46 Nursing Sister QAIMN. S/R. France, Belgium and Germany. With invasion forces 1944. Nine weeks in Belsen with 29th Br. General Hospital. Nursing until 1959. Then, teaching and lecturing Biology and History. Lives at Chandlers Ford.

R.W. TUCK: Born Apsley, Hertfordshire 1925. King Edward VII Grammar School, King's Lyn. Sapper – Royal Engineers; Guards Armoured Division, North-West Europe; 3rd Infantry Division Egypt, Palestine. Post-war Cambridge School of Art. Reading University. Retired teacher. Lives at King's Lynn, Norfolk.

Dennis UTTLEY: Born Manchester 1915. Stockport School. Manchester University, Dept. Education of the Deaf. 1947–48

(Emergency Teacher Training Scheme). Sorbonne & Lille Universities (French Institute) 1956–58. HMS *Collingwood* (Training Visual Signals) Fareham, Hants. June 1941. Convoy Escorts (West Africa – Londonderry). Normandy Invasion (Ammunition Supply Vessel). Signals Camp, Rochester. Teacher of the Deaf 1946–70. Founder 'Friends for the Young Deaf' Trust, 1964. Co-Founder, 'Breakthrough' Trust (Deaf and Hearing Families Integration). Lives in W. Bradley, near Glastonbury.

Roger VENABLES: Born 4 March 1911, British Consulate Varna, Bulgaria. Educated Beaumont College, Christchurch College Oxford. RAOC and Intelligence Corps, 38 Security Section Bari, 1942–5. Lecturer Army College and Further College of Education. Member Lancs Authors. Published *Combe Valley* 1941, *The Night Comes* 1961, *Leaves & Seasons* 1961, *Forebodings* 1961. Bard of Cornish Gorsedd. Lives in Penzance, Cornwall.

Edward VENN: Born Gilfach Goch, South Wales 1915. Ogmore Grammar School, Aberystwyth University College of Wales (B.Sc), Bristol University, (Dip Ed). Captain Som. LI. Senior lecturer, Education, Swansea. Poetry published post-war. Lives at Colchester, Essex.

Donald Eric VINCENT: Born 20 January 1923 Penarth, S. Glam. Penarth County School. Served with 142 and 104 Squadrons CMF September 1944 until March 1945. Flight-Sergeant Bomb-aimer, on Wellingtons. Post-war, civil servant in Inland Revenue for eight years but could not stand being closed in. Produced pigs and poultry for six years until the advent of mass-produced breeding and fattening. Sales representative, enjoyed every year until retirement in 1985. Lives in Glamorgan.

John WARRY: Born 7 May 1916, Ilford, Essex. Haileybury and Queen's College, Cambridge. Intelligence Corps; Army Educational Corps. Post-war lecturer in English Language and Literature, Alexandria University Educational officer. Cyprus, Lecturer at University of Lybia. Senior Lecturer RMA Sandhurst. Published *Greek Aesthetic Theory* (Methuen 1962); *Warfare in the Classical World* (Salamander Books 1980), *The*

Coming of the Prince (St Michael's Abbey Press 1983). English translation of Plautus' *Rudens* with Gwyn Williams. Lives a Camberley, Surrey.

Victor WEST: Born Clapham, London, 1919. Simon Langton School, Canterbury. Lance Corporal 1st Rangers KRRC Greece and Crete 1941. POW 4 years, escaped off-line march 17 April 1945; in debacle of 3rd Reich took control of German village, Brunn, Bavaria. Post-war taught junior school Treasurer London Poets Workshop 1973–76. Actor, chora speaker, muralist and painter. *The Horses of Falaise* (Salamande Imprint, 1975). Lives at Bedfont, Middlesex.

Jo WESTREN: (now Francesca Josephine Grace Wreford). Bor Essex 1914. Boarding school. RAMC nursing member attached anti-aircraft command; Colchester Military Hospital Post-war; published own poems in Harvest 1978. Also contri buted *Anthology of Suffolk Poetry*. Lives at Felixstowe.

Phillip WHITFIELD: Born Bromley, Kent 18 March 1918 Tettenhall College (Staffs), University College, London University College Hospital. Captain RAMC, concerned with ex-prisoners of Belsen. Specialist, Community Medicine and paediatrician, Hampshire County Council. Retired 1984 Council member, Amnesty International. Governor of Treloa College for Physically Handicapped; contributed to medica press; poems in Critical Quarterly Outposts. *A Dram of Tim* (selected poems) 1987. Lives at Dorchester.

Lyall WILKES: Middlesex Regiment, commissioned 1941 afte machine gun officer Corps Training Unit Princess Louis (Kensington) Regiment. Overseas 1942. Military Liaison (Greece). Attached to Force 133 for reconnaissance in Occupie Greece 1944 (despatches). Member of Parliament 1945–51 Circuit Judge until 1982. Three books on the art and archi tecture of the North East.

Donald Creighton WILLIAMSON: Born 2 January 192(Rochdale. T & L Regiment, BEF, Norway, wounded in Sicily August 1943. Greek Islands: GSO3 HQ 50 Division 1944. Sta College Haifa. Interpreter in French. Lieutenant Colonel Gree Howards 1962. Senior British Liaison Officer C-in-C French

Forces in Germany. Associate Member British Institute of Management; Associate Member Institute of Linguists; Author *The York and Lancaster Regiment – Famous Regiments* series. Associate of the Royal Historical Society.

Kenneth WILSON: Born Hull 1916. Joined Royal Navy as a boy, 1932. (HMS *Ganges*), Petty Officer Telegraphist, Malta and Atlantic convoys in destroyers. Dunkirk, Narvik, Salerno and Far East. Teacher post-war. Published works include *The Abbeys of Yorkshire*; two books of poetry; eight times winner of Prix d'Honneur for poetry annual Guernsey Eisteddfod. Lives in Alderney.

Peter YOUNG: Born Portsmouth 1920. Portsmouth Municipal College. 1941–46 trooper Westminster Dragoons, RAC Sergeant Army Education Corps; teacher Hampshire, senior inspector schools Leicester and tutor Cambridge Institute of Education; member Warnock Committee Enquiry on Children with Special Needs. Has written over thirty books for schools, joint author *Dyslexia or Illiteracy* and *Teach Your Child to Read*; Joint Editor of Open University Children with Special Needs Series; poetry and verse for children anthologised UK, Europe and USA. Lives at Lyme Regis.

Index of Poets

Everyman
A selection of titles

*indicates volumes available in paperback

Complete lists of Everyman's Library and Everyman Paperbacks
are available from the Sales Department, J.M. Dent and Sons
Ltd, 91 Clapham High Street, London SW4 7TA

BIOGRAPHY

ESSAYS AND CRITICISM

*Milton, John. *Prose Writings*
Montaigne, Michael Eyquem de. *Essays* (3 vols)
Spencer, Herbert. *Essays on Education and Kindred Subjects*
*Swift, Jonathan. *Tale of a Tub and other satires*

FICTION

---

*Alcott, Louisa May. *Little Women*
American Short Stories of the Nineteenth Century
Austen, Jane
    Emma
    Mansfield Park
    Northanger Abbey
    Persuasion
    Pride and Prejudice
    Sense and Sensibility
Australian Short Stories
*Barbusse, Henri. *Under Fire*
Bennett, Arnold
    The Card
    The Old Wives' Tale
Boccaccio, Giovanni. *The Decameron*
Brontë, Anne
    Agnes Grey
    The Tenant of Wildfell Hall
Brontë, Charlotte
    Jane Eyre
    The Professor and *Emma* (a fragment)
    Shirley
    Villette
*Brontë, Emily. *Wuthering Heights* and *Poems*
Bunyan, John
    Pilgrim's Progress
    Grace Abounding and *Mr Badman*
*Carroll, Lewis. *Alice in Wonderland*
Collins, Wilkie
    The Moonstone
    The Woman in White
*Conrad, Joseph. *Lord Jim*

*Locke, John. *An Essay Concerning Human Understanding*
     (abridgement)
*More, Thomas. *Utopia*
 Pascal, Blaise. *Pensées*
 Plato. *The Trial and Death of Socrates*
The Ramayana and Mahábhárata
*Spinoza, Benedictus de. *Ethics*

SCIENCES: POLITICAL AND GENERAL

Coleridge, Samuel Taylor. *On the Constitution of the Church
     and State*
Derry, John. *English Politics and the American Revolution*
Harvey, William. *The Circulation of the Blood and other
     writings*
*Locke, John. *Two Treatises of Government*
*Machiavelli, Niccolò. *The Prince and other political writings*
*Malthus, Thomas. *An Essay on the Principle of Population*
*Mill, J.S. *Utilitarianism; On Liberty: Representative
     Government*
*Plato. *The Republic*
*Ricardo, David. *Principles of Political Economy and
     Taxation*
Rousseau, J.-J.
     Emile
     The Social Contract and *Discourses*
*Wollstonecraft, Mary. *A Vindication of the Rights of Woman*

TRAVEL AND TOPOGRAPHY

Boswell, James. *The Journal of a Tour to the Hebrides*
Darwin, Charles. *The Voyage of the 'Beagle'*
*Hudson, W.H. *Idle Days in Patagonia*
*Kingsley, Mary. *Travels in West Africa*
*Stevenson, R.L. *An Inland Voyage; Travels with a Donkey;
     The Silverado Squatters*
*Thomas, Edward. *The South Country*
Travels of Marco Polo
*White, Gilbert. *The Natural History of Selborne*

Scott, Walter
  *Rob Roy
  *The Talisman
*Shelley, Mary Wollstonecraft. *Frankenstein*
*Smollett, Tobias. *Roderick Random*
*Somerville and Ross. *Some Experiences of an Irish R.M.*
        and *Further Experiences of an Irish R.M.*
*Sterne, Lawrence. *Tristram Shandy*
Stevenson, R.L.
    *Kidnapped
    The Master of Ballantrae and *Weir of Hermiston*
*Swift, Jonathan. *Gulliver's Travels*
*Thackeray, W.M. *Vanity Fair*
  Thirteen Famous Ghost Stories
*Thomas, Dylan. *The Collected Stories*
*Tolstoy, Leo. *Master and Man and other parables and tales*
Trollope, Anthony
    Dr Thorne
    Last Chronicle of Barset
    *The Warden
*Twain, Mark. *Tom Sawyer* and *Huckleberry Finn*
*Victorian Short Stories
*Voltaire. *Candide and other tales*
Wells, H.G.
    *The Time Machine
    *The Wheels of Chance
*Wilde Oscar. *The Picture of Dorian Gray*
*Wood, Mrs Henry. *East Lynne*
Woolf, Virginia. *To the Lighthouse*

HISTORY

---

*The Anglo-Saxon Chronicle
*Burnet, Gilbert. *History of His Own Time*
  Gibbon, Edward. *The Decline and Fall of the Roman Empire*
        (6 vols)
*Hollingshead, John. *Ragged London in 1861*
*Stow, John. *The Survey of London*
*Woodhouse, A.S.P. *Puritanism and Liberty*

LEGENDS AND SAGAS

* *Beowulf and Its Analogues*
* Chrétien de Troyes. *Arthurian Romances*
* *Egils saga*
* *Kudrun*
* *The Mabinogion*
* *The Saga of Gisli*
* *The Saga of Grettir the Strong*
* Snorri Sturluson. *Edda*
* Wace and Layamon. *Arthurian Chronicles*

POETRY AND DRAMA

* *Anglo-Saxon Poetry*
* Arnold, Matthew. *Selected Poems and Prose*
* Blake, William. *Selected Poems*
* Brontës, The. *Selected Poems*
* Browning, Robert. *Men and Women and other poems*
* Burns, Robert. *The Kilmarnock Poems*
* Chaucer, Geoffrey, *Canterbury Tales*
* Clare, John. *Selected Poems*
* Coleridge, Samuel Taylor. *Poems*
* Donne, John. *The Complete English Poems*
* *Elizabethan Sonnets*
* *English Moral Interludes*
* *Everyman and Medieval Miracle Plays*
* *Everyman's Book of Evergreen Verse*
* *Everyman's Book of Victorian Verse*
* Gay, John. *The Beggar's Opera and other eighteenth-century plays*
* *The Golden Treasury of Longer Poems*
* Hardy, Thomas. *Selected Poems*
* Herbert, George. *The English Poems*
* Hopkins, Gerard Manley. *The Major Poems*
  Ibsen, Henrik
     * *A Doll's House; The Wild Duck; The Lady from the Sea*
     * *Hedda Gabler; The Master Builder; John Gabriel Borkman*

* Keats, John. *Poems*
* Langland, William. *The Vision of Piers Plowman*
* Marlowe, Christopher. *Complete Plays and Poems*
* Marvell, Andrew. *Complete Poetry*
* Middleton, Thomas. *Three Plays*
* Milton, John. *Complete Poems*
* *Palgrave's Golden Treasury*
* *Pearl, Cleanness, Patience* and *Sir Gawain and the Green Knight*
* *Poems of the Second World War*
* Pope, Alexander. *Collected Poems*
* *Restoration Plays*
* *The Rubáiyát of Omar Khayyám and other Persian poems*
* Shelley, Percy Bysshe. *Selected Poems*
* *Six Middle English Romances*
* Spenser, Edmund. *The Faerie Queene: Books I to III*
* *The Stuffed Owl*
* Synge, J.M. *Plays, Poems and Prose*
* Tennyson, Alfred. *In Memoriam, Maud and other poems*
  Thomas, Dylan
    * *Collected Poems, 1934–1952*
    * *The Poems*
    * *Under Milk Wood*
* Webster and Ford. *Selected Plays*
* Wilde, Oscar. *Plays, Prose Writings and Poems*
* Wordsworth, William. *Selected Poems*

RELIGION AND PHILOSOPHY

* Bacon, Francis. *The Advancement of Learning*
* Berkeley, George. *Philosophical Works*
* *The Buddha's Philosophy of Man*
* Carlyle, Thomas. *Sartor Resartus*
* *Chinese Philosophy in Classical Times*
* Descartes, René. *A Discourse on Method*
* *Hindu Scriptures*
* Hobbes, Thomas. *Leviathan*
* Kant, Immanuel. *A Critique of Pure Reason*
* *The Koran*
* Leibniz, Gottfried Wilhelm. *Philosophical Writings*